100 YEARS OF FOOTBALL
THE FIFA CENTENNIAL BOOK

100 YEARS OF FOOTBALL
THE FIFA CENTENNIAL BOOK

FÉDÉRATION INTERNATIONALE DE FOOTBALL ASSOCIATION

FIFA

100 Years

1904–2004

WEIDENFELD & NICOLSON

First published in the United Kingdom in 2004 by Weidenfeld & Nicolson,
a division of the Orion Publishing Group

Designer: Nicolas Trautmann / Paris ntrautmann@noos.fr
Editorial: Nic Cheetham, Sue Harper
Printed and bound in Italy by Printers Trento.

A CIP catalogue record for this book is available from the British Library.

ISBN 0 297 843869

Weidenfeld & Nicolson
The Orion Publishing Group
Wellington House
125 Strand
London WC2R 0BB

CONTENTS

Player Portraits:
BECKENBAUER, CHA BUM, CHARLTON, CRUYFF, DI STEFANO, EUSEBIO,
MANDELA, MARADONA, MASPOLI, MILLA, PELÉ, PLATINI, RIMET, WEAH.

100 YEARS OF FIFA

Foreword from the FIFA President

Individuals, organisations, companies and states all have one thing in common – from the day they are born, they not only start to write history, but also become part of history themselves. Depending on how much influence, importance and power they have, their actions, whether on a small or major scale, can have a temporary or permanent effect and change the lives of a few or even the whole of humanity.

Founded by seven national football associations in Paris on 21 May 1904 with limited means at its disposal, FIFA can now look back upon its first 100 years, a time in which it has had a lasting effect on the lives of the whole of humanity by transcending all borders and cultures.

So what conclusions can be drawn from our first 100 years? How great has FIFA's influence been? To what extent do the actions of FIFA's leaders and those on any of its many committees, having been faced by the vicissitudes of world history, economic challenges and humanitarian imperatives, stand up to a critical evaluation? Has FIFA been a true guardian of football's ideals? If so, does it still play this role?

These are just some of the questions that four renowned international historians have been trying to answer for the last four years. With meticulous precision, the inquisitiveness of detectives and a methodology encompassing a whole range of disciplines, these historians have trawled FIFA's archives. Over the course of the last four years, they have also analysed countless publications, minutes of meetings and correspondence with associations, companies and private persons, as well as a stack of memos and notes. Their painstaking research was not restricted to FIFA's files, as they have also spent many an hour sifting through the archives of associations and the confederations in order to uncover more information for the book you are now holding.

This book documents the history of FIFA so far and it is the end result of their research. It details the development and growth of an organisation that has survived two World Wars and countless regional conflicts, mainly because it has successfully used football as a means to promote greater understanding between peoples without interfering in the world of politics. But it is also a chronicle of the visionaries and unsung heroes, of the winners and losers, and of the stadiums in which football has been played and history written. It is also the story of a sport that has astutely used the advances in civil aviation and television technology to boost its development worldwide. In essence, it is the story of how the most beautiful pastime in the world became one of the world's greatest obsessions, and it is an insight into how the game of football touches people like no other pastime by continually arousing new emotions.

The following pages provide a critical assessment of the game's story and of its main protagonists and their actions. Countless photographs, illustrations and graphics – the likes of which have never before been published in such a manner – supplement the extensive source material and the resulting conclusions. Words and images come together not only to form a chronicle of FIFA and football, but also to allow you, the reader, to take a look at the last 100 years of world history from an entirely new – but fascinating – perspective.

I am immeasurably proud to lead FIFA into its momentous Centennial year and to be able to present to you the story of the first 100 years of our organisation. I hope you enjoy following FIFA's development and finding the answers to the questions posed above. But I also hope that you will continue to show interest in and support for FIFA's work – for the good of the game.

Joseph S. Blatter

INTRODUCTION

One hundred years ago, in meetings held over three days in May 1904, the Fédération Internationale de Football Association (FIFA) was founded in Rue Saint Honoré, Paris. The history of this international organisation from its insignificant origins with no headquarters or administrators forms the subject of this book.

The aim is to give a detailed account of the foundation of FIFA, its growth and activities. Today, FIFA is powerful, controlling world football, and is at the point of becoming, as Jules Rimet said in 1950, an empire over which the sun never sets. At the same time this project clearly involves a presentation of the history of football around the world. Through a study of FIFA over the past century, we will examine previously unpublished aspects of the history of football as a whole.

In 1954 the Executive Committee of had tried to produce what it called a 'Golden Book' to mark the 50th birthday of the organisation. It found the task very difficult. As late as November, 26 member football associations had failed to send in summaries of their histories and 13 had not returned questionnaires. The statistics of world football were incomplete and several promised articles had not been delivered. Even some of those that had were unfinished. Furthermore, it proved to be very difficult, and in certain cases impossible, to find the necessary photographs to illustrate the book. They doubted whether it could come out in 1954. In fact, it never appeared. This time, FIFA adopted a more professional approach.

FIFA brought together a small group of academic historians, in the knowledge that they had all written extensively on the economic, social and political history of football. Joseph Blatter, the President of FIFA, suggested the anniversary study. Jérôme Champagne, FIFA Deputy General Secretary, has chaired the committee of management. The international composition of the group necessitated the support of the Centre International d'Étude du Sport (CIES) – The International Center for Sport Studies - linked to the University of Neuchâtel. Jean-Philippe Dubey from the CIES managed this link between FIFA and the academic world.

FIFA allowed us unrestricted access to its archive collection. Heidrun Homburg and Paul Deitschy, two experienced researchers, ensured the comprehensive examination and presentation of the records. Their richness inspired a certain frustration among the authors. It would have been possible to write many books on different aspects of this history, but for editorial reasons it was crucial to present only the key features. Ultimately, the authors are aware that due to the size of the task they were not able to do everything they would have liked.

Another problem was that there was no blueprint. The structure of the book had to be created and the different themes decided. The authors did not wish to approach the subject from a solely European perspective.

Working in the archives produced many questions, which fell into three general areas:

Firstly, that there should be a consideration of the people who inspired the creation of FIFA and also the many individuals who took part both in football and FIFA: players, directors, referees, journalists and business partners and the motives that guided them.

Second, it was important to confront the question of chronology. How far does the history of FIFA have key moments when things changed? How far does its history follow that of the history of the twentieth century as a whole?

The third main area concerns the work and achievements of FIFA with regard to the game of football itself. How did FIFA come to govern football the world over? In the spread of football around the world how far did FIFA act proactively, how far was it content simply to work alongside a spontaneous process of development? In the extraordinary spread of football during the twentieth century, what were the roles of the growth in travel and improvements in transport, the migration of players, and the passion of supporters? What were the effects of the World Cup and the arrival of television?

Finally, the authors would like to thank FIFA for their continued support and for the total freedom which they have enjoyed during the writing of this book.

Christiane Eisenberg
Pierre Lanfranchi
Tony Mason
Alfred Wahl

2

THE INVENTION OF FOOTBALL IN BRITAIN

Football has been found in many different cultures but the modern game was a nineteenth-century innovation of the British. It used to be thought that its origins were to be found in the public schools but recent research suggests that it also has a more popular history. Public schools played their own idiosyncratic games of football in part dependent on the space and conditions available for play.

< 1

Previous pages

1 'English Football'. A depiction of the ball games played by Greenlanders in 1741, by the Danish missionary Hans P. Egede.

2 Mayan tlachtli player. Pottery, from the late classic period 650–1000 AD (Mexico).

3

3 In Greece and Rome ball games were an educational and healthy exercise for everyone, both male and female. Sculpted marble, 5th century BC, from the National Archaeological Museum of Athens.

4 The oldest balls in existence are Egyptian from the year 2000 BC. They were made of wood, leather and even papyrus.

5 Tlachtli players sketched in 1529 by the painter Christophe Weiditz, a travelling companion of Herman Cortez. Artist's description: 'The Indians play the game with an inflated ball. The ball is played off their behinds without their hands leaving the floor. They wear leather gloves and a leather guard on the part of the back which plays the ball.'

4

Football in the early nineteenth century

At Charterhouse, in the City of London the 'field' was a cloister seventy metres long and only four wide. Buttresses protruded from one side with doors at either end as the goals. When the school moved to rural Surrey in 1872 and playing fields replaced cloisters the old game was discontinued, much to the regret of some Old Carthusians.

Compulsory games were probably first introduced at Harrow school and were encouraged in other schools mainly to bring some discipline to the spare time activities of the boys. Because they were popular they were also used to establish better staff-pupil relations and gradually, between about 1840 and 1870, to foster the virtues of loyalty and self-sacrifice of the individual to the institution, an important part of that culture of con-

formity for which the public schools became notorious. Hard exercise became a craze among the educated classes from about the middle of the nineteenth century and sport in general, and cricket and football in particular, became a cult, not only at the public schools but also at the universities of Oxford and Cambridge.

Public school football tended to be similar in form to the traditional Shrove Tuesday games. The number of players was unlimited, scrums or mêlées were a common feature with both handling and kicking allowed. Such rules as there were tended to be passed on orally. It was not until 1846, for example, that the rules of the game at Rugby School were first written down. Two years later, in 1848, ex-public schoolboys at Cambridge tried to establish a common code and wrote the Cambridge Rules. But

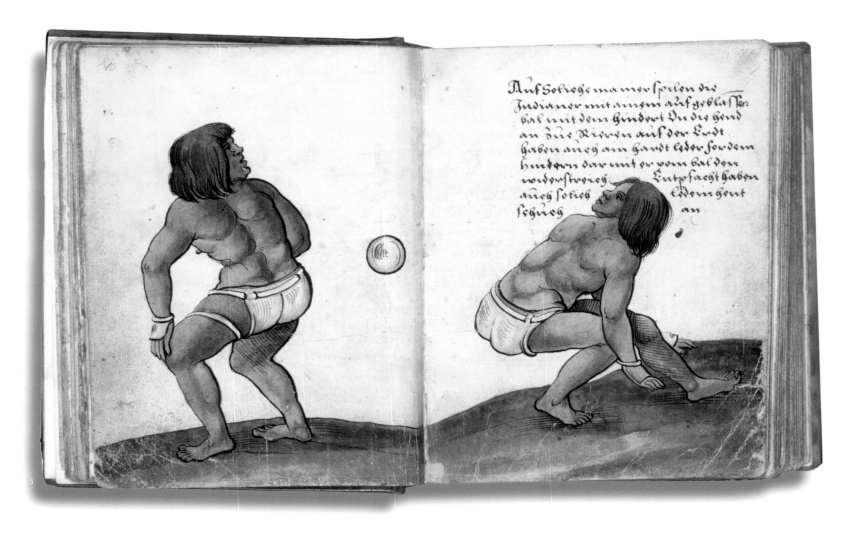

Aufsolche manier spilen die
Judianer mit ainem aufgeblasen
bal mit dem hindert Vn die hend
an die Rieren auf der Erdt
haben auch ain handt leder for dem
hindern dar mit er vom bal dem
widerstreich   Entpfacht haben
auch solich   leder hent
schuch   an

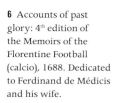

6 Accounts of past glory: 4th edition of the Memoirs of the Florentine Football (calcio), 1688. Dedicated to Ferdinand de Médicis and his wife.

7 Calcio was not only 'fiorentino'. A match played in Padova in approximately 1595. Engraving by Pietro Bertelli.

8 Kemari players photographed in Japan, 1940. A tradition which survived into the Meiji era.

6

7

8

these had little chance of being widely accepted as former public school men were reluctant to give up the form of football they had learned at school.

We now know that there was much more organised football activity going on in the wider world away from that of the privileged public schools. Advertisements in contemporary, sporting and local newspapers report many challenge matches, often for money stakes, taking place all over Britain. At Leicester in the East Midlands in 1838:

A match at football will be played at the cricket ground, Leicester, on Good Friday next, between eleven (principally printers) from Derby and the same number of Leicester. The winners to challenge an equal number from any town in England, for a purse not exceeding £25.

Moreover, between 1830 and 1860 the existence of over seventy football teams has been identified, based on clubs, public houses, particular occupations and the army, even some villages. Little detail is known about the activities of these teams, many of which probably did not last long. But, their existence demonstrates that time and energy and places to play, however rough, were more available in a rapidly industrialising and urban

9

10/11

9 The game of Pallone, a sporting and licentious metaphor from 1614. Engraving after the German artist Mattaeus Merian the Older. 'The lilies of the valley are often wet – which can also be seen on the green fields'.

10/11 In Brittany, Soule was played between Bachelors and Fathers or parish against parish, sometimes even between women. Drawings by Olivier Perrin, from the first third of the nineteenth century.

12 The ball used at Harrow was not very round!

12

Britain than was once thought. We also know that spectators were often attracted to these games, betting on the result was common and referees or umpires might officiate to see that the rules agreed for particular challenges were kept. Well before the foundation of the Football Association or the Rugby Football Union, a number of clubs were playing various forms of football in Britain and informal and low-profile games with varying degrees of organisation and rules were common occurrences. In the manufacturing town of Sheffield in south Yorkshire a football subculture was about to devel-

op that would make an important contribution to the modernisation of the sport.

The Sheffield Football Club was founded in 1857 by young middle-class friends who had already set up a cricket club. At first they played among themselves and wrote down a few basic rules in 1858. Their activities being noticed, other groups of local young men began to play and the Sheffield Club had their rules printed in 1862. By 1863 they were playing eleven-a-side matches although other local teams might play fourteen-a-side or more. Before the FA in London was formed, up to

FOOT BALL, KINGSTON-UPON-THAMES,
SHROVE TUESDAY, FEB. 24TH, 1846.

13

seventeen clubs in the Sheffield district were already playing football to a code of rules locally agreed.

Interest in football was also growing in the London area. This was partly due to former public schoolboys, some of whom formed the Forest Club in 1859. By the early 1860s at least twenty-five teams, mostly middle-class and ex-public school in membership were playing some variety of football. The lack of an accepted set of rules meant that half a game might be played under rules favoured by one club, half under those supported by the other. Or, if two fixtures had been arranged, each match would be played to a different set of regulations. In 1862 the Dingley Dell team were thought by *The Field* not only to have the best team but a good code of rules. It would be surprising if, with all this growing activity, footballers were not talking about the efficacy of putting together a uniform code of laws. In fact we know they were, because some of their letters began to appear in papers like *The Times*, *The Field* and *Bell's Life*

Foot Ball Played at Market Place Barnet

14

13 Football and Fête: One of the last town matches played on Shrove Tuesday, 1846 in Kingston-upon-Thames.

14 Despite royal and town bans, football has been played in the streets of English towns since the Middle Ages. This example is football in Barnet, an engraving from 1750.

15 Footer at Harrow, one of the early versions of public school football. Etching from a drawing by Walter Cox (1887).

15

suggesting exactly that: that if football was to develop further, a comprehensive code that could be universally applied was needed to remove all the complications and arguments provoked by the current variety.

In the autumn of 1863 John Cartwright wrote a letter to the sporting paper *Bell's Life* suggesting a meeting between representatives of different schools and colleges in order to see if a uniform code of rules for football could be agreed. Representatives from six schools met in Cambridge and most present favoured a dribbling version of the game rather than a rugby version, deciding to ban parts of the latter, including hacking, tripping and running with the ball. Not surprisingly the representative of Rugby School withdrew. There was a further meeting between representatives of eleven London clubs and schools at the Freemasons' Tavern, Great Queen Street on 26 October 1863 and it was at this one that the Football Association was set up. The aim was still to forge a uniform football code, one set of rules for one game and the discussion ranged over the most basic

issues such as the dimensions of the pitch, width and height of the goals, when a goal should be considered to have been scored, to offside, hacking and tripping and running with the ball. A further meeting on 1 December seems to have pushed through the adoption of the rules drawn up at Cambridge. Effectively this meant no running with the ball and no hacking but neither the Cambridge rules, nor the new FA rules forbade touching the ball with the hands — only running with it. Both the FA and the Sheffield rules also allowed players to make a fair catch but both disallowed hacking, holding, pushing and tripping. Looking back it seems clear that a compromise was not out of the question.

It never came, although it would be eight years before the followers of rugby set up their own national organisation, the Rugby Football Union, in 1871. Nor did the Football Association, it did not sweep all before it in the first decade of its existence. For one thing only eighteen clubs joined. Most others continued as before adapting the rules under which they played according to the opposition, playing a version of the rugby rules. The exception was Sheffield where fourteen clubs had a thousand members and Sheffield FC was an active and encouraging member of the FA. They had begun to play matches outside the city against clubs in other towns and in February 1866 challenged the FA to a game agreeing to adjust their own rules so it could take place. They also persuaded the FA to adopt a more liberal offside rule by allowing the forward pass. Sheffield formed its own football association in 1867. At least eight rules of the Sheffield code of 1870 were eventually adopted by the FA but it was not until 1877 that the

Sheffield FA finally accepted the FA rules that their own initiatives had done so much to bring about.

The Football Association was not a very powerful organisation in the 1860s and 1870s. The young men who had set it up were not sure what they wanted or what the eventual outcome would be. Football was growing in popularity but the FA's rules had not been accepted by many clubs. More clubs played rugby rules but many games were governed by a mixed bag of local and traditional regulations. Even Sheffield FC, when it played Leeds twice in 1864, played the away match under rugby rules because Leeds played a rugby game. The same thing

THE GRAPHIC, January 8, 1870

16

Freemasons Tavern Great Queen Street. Lincolns Inn Fields.

happened in 1868 when Sheffield played home and away games with Manchester. Moreover, the first representative match under rugby rules between Yorkshire and Lancashire in 1870 included some Sheffield footballers because the organisers wanted a team as representative of all parts of Yorkshire as possible. But the Sheffielders had little idea of how to play rugby rules, which must have convinced many who were there that two separate codes of football were emerging.

This process began to gather momentum in the 1870s when association football, as it came to be known, gradually established itself as a national sport. There were three major factors in this development. First, the Football Association, under secretary Charles Alcock, became

16 Football at Rugby. Illustration by W. Thomas in *The Graphic*, 8ᵗʰ January 1870.

17 The Freemasons' Tavern, a place of debate and invention. This is where the Football Association and the rules of the game were founded on the 26 October 1863.

DEFINITION OF TERMS.

A Place Kick—Is a Kick at the Ball while it is on the ground, in any position which the Kicker may choose to place it.

A Free Kick—Is the privilege of Kicking the Ball, without obstruction, in such manner as the Kicker may think fit.

A Fair Catch—Is when the Ball is Caught, after it has touched the person of an Adversary or has been kicked, knocked on, or thrown by an Adversary, and before it has touched the ground or one of the Side catching it; but if the Ball is kicked from out of touch, or from behind goal line, a fair Catch cannot be made.

Hacking—Is kicking an Adversary on the front of the leg, below the knee.

Tripping—Is throwing an Adversary by the use of the legs without the hands, and without hacking or charging.

Charging—Is attacking an Adversary with the shoulder, chest, or body, without using the hands or legs.

Knocking on—Is when a Player strikes or propels the Ball with his hands, arms or body, without kicking or throwing it.

Holding—Includes the obstruction of a Player by the hand or any part of the arm below the elbow.

Touch—Is that part of the field, on either side of the ground, which is beyond the line of flags.

The Secretary also called the attention of the Meeting to an announcement which had appeared in the newspapers of the preceding Saturday that rules for the Same kind been drawn up to be

I.
The maximum **length of the ground** shall be 200 yards, the maximum **breadth** shall be 100 yards, the length and breadth shall be marked off with flags, and the **goal** shall be defined by two upright posts, 8 yards apart, without any tape or bar across them.

II.
The Game shall be commenced by a **place kick** from the centre of the ground by the side winning the toss, the other side shall not approach within 10 yards of the ball until it is kicked off. After a goal is won the losing side shall be entitled to kick off.

III.
The two sides shall change goals after each goal is won.

IV.
A goal shall be won when the ball passes over the space between the goal posts (at whatever height), not being thrown, knocked on, or carried.

V.
When the ball is in **touch** the first player who touches it shall kick or throw it from the point on the boundary line where it left the ground, in a direction at right angles with the boundary line.

VI.
A player shall be **out of play** immediately he is in front of the ball, and must return behind the ball as soon as possible. If the ball is kicked past a player by his own side, he shall not touch or kick it or advance until one of the other side has first kicked it or one of his own side on a level with or in front of him has been able to kick it.

VII.
In case the ball goes behind the goal line, if a player on the side to whom the goal belongs first touches the ball, one of his side shall be entitled to a free kick from the goal line at the point opposite the place where the ball shall be touched. If a player of the opposite side first touches the ball, one of his side shall be entitled to a free kick from a point 15 yards outside the goal line, opposite the place where the ball is touched.

VIII.
If a player makes a **fair catch** he shall be entitled to a **free kick**, provided he claims it by making a mark with his heel at once; and in order to take such kick he may go as far back as he pleases, and no player on the opposite side shall advance beyond his mark until he has kicked.

IX.
A player shall be entitled to run with the ball towards his adversaries' goal if he makes a fair catch, or catches the ball on the first bound; but in the case of a fair catch, if he makes his mark, he shall not then run.

X.
If any player shall run with the ball towards his adversaries' goal, any player on the opposite side shall be at liberty to charge, hold, trip, or hack him, or to wrest the ball from him; but no player shall be held and hacked at the same time.

XI.
Neither tripping or hacking shall be allowed, and no player shall use his hands or elbows to hold or push his adversary, except in the case provided for by Law X.

XII.
Any player shall be allowed to charge another, provided they are both in active play. A player shall be allowed to charge if even he is out of play.

XIII.
A player shall be allowed to throw the ball or pass it to another if he make a fair catch, or catches the ball on the first bound.

XIV.
No player shall be allowed to wear projecting nails, iron plates, or gutta percha the soles or heels of his boots.

19

20

18 Definitions of the first Association Football terms before they became a universal language.

19 Table of the Law: facsimile of the fourteen laws of the game established in 1863.

more proactive, ironing out inconsistencies in the rules, sending circulars to the leading clubs and even organising a demonstration match to show how the revised laws would work. His work as a sporting journalist writing for three different newspapers also helped promote a game that he was still playing. Other clubs began to form themselves into regional football associations, Birmingham in 1875, Surrey 1877, Lancashire 1878 and Northumberland and Durham 1879. The Scottish FA was founded in 1873 and that of Wales in 1876.

A second factor that helped the spread of association football and particularly contributed to it winning the battle with rugby for the hearts and minds of fooballers was the idea that it was just as manly but less rough than the rugby game. This was important to many young men who had to work for a living and could not afford to lose time due to injuries at football. When Lancashire met Yorkshire under rugby rules in 1870, their captain had asked his Yorkshire counterpart if they could play without hacking because it would

be serious if members of his team were hurt and unable to go to work on Monday. He agreed but the Lancashire players do not seem to have received the message and hacked with enthusiasm from the start!

But it was the invention of competitive cup football which changed the nature of the game. This was another idea of Alcock's, who claimed he took it from the inter-house competition of his old school, Harrow. But it is worth noting that a similar competition had been started for local clubs in Sheffield in 1867. It was sponsored by a local theatrical impresario and it is most unlikely that Alcock did not know about it. The first Football Association Challenge Cup Competition was held in the 1871-72 season. Only fifteen out of fifty members of the association competed and Queen's Park of Glasgow reached the semi-final by only playing one match. It was drawn and the Scotsmen could not afford another trip south for a replay. It seems unsurprising, if hardly fair, that Alcock's team, the Wanderers, won the first final by 1-0 against the Royal Engineers.

20

The popularisation of football

The FA Cup was a national competition and the number of clubs entering gradually increased, reaching 43 in 1878-79 and 100 by 1883-84. Over the same period the associations of Scotland, Wales and Ireland and the many county associations of England established similar competitions of their own. Such tournaments not only advertised the association game but helped it to succeed over what had become its rugby rival. Most of the Rugby Football Unions turned their back on cup football, which almost certainly lost them much popular support. In Yorkshire, where the local rugby authorities did run a knock-out competition, rugby remained the number one winter sport until at least 1914.

County and national cups not only advertised football but built on existing local community rivalries and provided opportunities for excitement, gambling and competition. Newspapers began both to reflect and promote the new sport and the urge to defeat local rivals led to teams trying to secure the best players, if

necessary by poaching them from other clubs with offers of jobs and eventually money. The importance attached to the English FA Cup was seen as early as 1879 when Darwen, a team of working-class cotton operatives from Lancashire, went to London for three symbolic matches with the Old Etonians. Their travelling costs were met largely from money collected in mills and workshops. The plebeians lost to the patricians on this occasion but in 1883 another team of Lancashire working men, the five-year-old Blackburn Olympic, beat the Old Etonians in the Cup Final. No team of southern amateurs would win it again. More crucially the Olympic had spent a week before both the semi-final and the final undergoing special training at Blackpool paid for by a local manufacturer, leading a southern-based football magazine to characterise them as mature and accomplished professionals.

It was the spread of football to the provinces that began to change its social class base. The young men who set up the FA were from the well-established middle class but the activists in the county FAs and even more in the individual football clubs were leavened by large num-

bers of lower middle class and even working-class males.
They had been attracted by the excitement and sociability of this modern sport if not always convinced by the
values of *esprit de corps*, fair play and physical fitness
with which its elite inventors liked to invest it. Football
clubs began to spring up in London, Birmingham,
Glasgow, Sheffield, Nottingham and Lancashire and
from these centres the virus spread to infect most
districts by 1914.

Many of the clubs that became leaders in the British
game, like Blackburn Rovers, for example, were started
by ex-public school and grammar school boys but many
others were grafted on to existing institutions, cricket
clubs, churches, public houses and workplaces. Even
streets and neighbourhoods might have their clubs,
although many did not have very long lives and were
never formally affiliated to local or national football associations. These short-lived clubs were run for
working men by working men. And it was working men
who would make up most of the players and the
spectators especially in the Midlands and the North and
in Scotland.

Commercialisation

Football was supposed to be recreation rather than a job
or a business. The young men who had established the
FA had neither expected nor wanted to see their creation
disfigured by the growth of professionalism. But it was
clear by the 1880s that this reformed, modern sport had
become a craze, especially in the industrial and urban
centres of the Midlands and North of England and in
Glasgow and its hinterland. Big crowds of working men
were prepared to pay to see the top teams play cup football and local businessmen willingly gave up their time
and resources to run the leading clubs. Scotsmen were
leaving homes and jobs to play football for English clubs
– fifty-five were with eleven Lancashire clubs in 1884.
The Saturday afternoon holiday and relatively high and
regular wages meant that playing and/or watching
football was well within the financial compass of many
young skilled or semi-skilled working men and lower
middle-class clerks.

The FA tried to outlaw the paid player by suspensions
and disqualifications. The turning point came in 1884-85.

21

At the beginning of 1884 Preston North End played host to Upton Park in the fourth round of the FA Cup. After the match had been drawn, the visitors from London, a team of gentleman amateurs, accused Preston of including professionals. There was an FA inquiry and the charge could not be proved but Preston were found guilty of illegally importing players from other districts and finding them jobs. They were disqualified from the Cup. This led to a group of largely Lancashire clubs meeting in order to explore the possibility of breaking away from the London-based FA. Representatives of forty clubs met in Manchester threatening to set up a rival British Football Association. The arguments were social, regional and emotional. North-South rivalry and anti-London feelings were important elements in the struggle but it was clear to some FA leaders, secretary Charles Alcock in particular, that if the FA wished to remain in control of all football, an accommodation would have to be achieved with the professionals and in 1885 a compromise was reached whereby professionalism was legalised under the control of the FA.

The next major step by twelve of the leading English professional clubs from the Midlands and the North was to arrange a regular schedule of home and away matches with each other at the end of which the club with the best record was declared the champion. This was the Football League, which began operations in 1888-89. Regular training and practice for the best players and the more intense competition that the League stimulated further guaranteed quality and promoted interest. In Scotland, where professionalism was resisted until 1893, a Scottish League was formed in 1890-91. Soon there would be second divisions in both England and Scotland and football leagues everywhere from the professional Southern League in 1894 to the hundreds of semi-professional junior and amateur leagues, church leagues and works leagues which could be found throughout the British Isles by 1904.

22 A stroll in the countryside for the West Bromwich Albion players in 1900.

23 Preston North End, the unbeaten champions of the first Football League 1888.

22

23

Schoolboy football

That football was firmly embedded in working-class culture can be shown by its crucial place in the schools. We have already seen how the modern reformed game emerged partly out of the public schools and many grammar schools also began to play it from the 1880s. But most British children went to neither of these but to the elementary schools where drill was the only kind of physical education allowed in the curriculum. However, football was introduced by young male teachers outside the formal hours of schooling. Many teachers would have played either at their school, college or university and football was a simple and pleasant means of physical activity which did not disadvantage the smaller sons of working-class parents. Birmingham seems to have been a pioneer in the field of schoolboy football, the Chairman of the School Board donating £100 of his own money to provide equipment in 1881. By 1882 twenty-

three schools had football clubs involving over a thousand boys. Pupil teachers in Swindon were playing football with the boys after school in 1886 and using the names of famous professional players in arithmetic lessons in 1888. Preston North End had offered a challenge shield to be competed for by local schools in 1884 and by the 1890s schoolboy football was becoming systematically organised. Key moments were in 1885, with the formation of the South London Schools Football Association, soon to be imitated in many towns and cities and 1890 when Sheffield played South London in a schools representative match. The English Schools Football Association was formed in 1904 and a national knock-out competition begun in the following year. The Department of Education agreed in 1906 that games could be formally added to the curriculum of the state elementary schools. By the time of FIFA's formation most British boys were introduced to the football at school.

24

Home internationals

Football in Britain also had its own international dimension from the start of the reformed modern game. The United Kingdom was made up of four countries all with a clear sense of cultural distinctiveness. Charles Alcock, Secretary of the FA, wrote to a sporting newspaper in February 1870 saying that there would be a match between leading Scots and English players at the Oval in a couple of weeks time and giving the names and addresses of people to be contacted by interested players. Frost caused this game to be cancelled but it was played on 5 March 1870. Four other games were arranged between November 1870 and February 1872 and took place between teams of well-off Englishmen and Scots living and working in the London area. The Queen's Park club of Glasgow, formed by lower middle class young men in 1867, proposed that one of the matches for 1872-73 should be played in Scotland (Glasgow in fact) and on 30 November 1872 the first official football international between England and Scotland was played. The Scottish team was chosen by the captain of the Queen's Park club and he did the same for the match in London in March 1873. One week later the Scottish Football Association was formed. The FA of Wales was set up in 1876 and of Ireland in 1882. These four associations

formed the International Football Association Board (IFAB) in the same year to deal with changes in the laws of the game and the British championship became a regular feature of the season from 1883-84. Indeed the England-Scotland match became for the Scots not simply an opportunity to defeat their more powerful neighbour but to celebrate Scottish identity. It was in the first decade of the twentieth century, especially in those alternate years when the match was played in England and large numbers of Scots travelled south to support their team, that a national tradition was born: a sturdy subculture of symbols, slogans, heroes and myths which combined a strong sense of being Scottish and therefore different from the English, with diluted nationalist politics.

24 Clocking off from the Stadium. Supporters leaving the stadium at Nottingham County in 1901.

25 'Pa' Jackson with his team The Corinthians.

26 The troops prepare for battle. Newcastle schoolboys play pupils from London in May 1914.

25

The export of football

The first official tour abroad took place in November 1899 when the FA sent a mixed team of amateurs and professionals to Germany, comfortably winning three times against a team labelled Germany and once against a combined Germany-Austria eleven. In September 1901 Germany became the first Europeans to visit England, playing one match against a team of English amateurs and one against eleven English professionals. England played amateur internationals against teams from France and Holland in 1906-07 and in June 1908 the first professional England team visited Austria, Hungary and Bohemia and repeated the visits to Vienna and Budapest in 1909. After that, only English amateurs played internationals against Europeans until after the First World War.

The English FA were not football proselytisers. They did not energetically seek to carry football either to Europe or the British Empire. Nonetheless, individual Britons did take the game with them as they took jobs abroad and young men in British communities played

26

27

27 (previous pages)
First media coverage.
The first international
between England and
Scotland (London,
February 1872) as
reported in *The
Graphic*.

28 The Scotland team,
1896.

29 Humorous cartoon
and match report.
Illustrated reportage
of the Scotland v.
England match played
in Glasgow on 30
November 1872
(*The Graphic*,
December 1872).

30 *The Boys' Own
Paper* (1908)
and *The Champion*
(1947 and 1952)

29

the game in Europe, Africa and South America. They
often formed the first clubs and established the first
competitions but other foreign nationals – French,
Germans, Italians and Swiss – played important roles
in the development of football in many parts of the
world. The British were flattered to see foreigners
taking up what they considered to be a British game –
copies of the Sheffield rules had been sent to Germany,
Switzerland, America and China as early as 1876 – and
many amateur and professional clubs undertook summer tours of the continent and British professional
players obtained coaching jobs there, but there was no
wish to become more closely involved. When FIFA was
set up in 1904 the FA's response was that 'it could not
see the advantages of such a Federation but on all such
matters on which joint action was desirable they would
be prepared to confer ...'

Meanings

By the time of FIFA's formation, football in Britain was not simply another form of urban circus forced on the masses by a sociologically alert and politically conscious middle class. The professional game was a northern invention that flourished in pre-existing local urban rivalries which cut across class lines. It was part of a commercial leisure world which also included trips to the seaside, the music hall and the cinema but it was not merely another aspect of petty consumerism. Its strength was its ability to reflect and construct local loyalties and identities. Out of a myriad of local struggles the strongest team had emerged to represent each city and town and it did not matter that the players themselves were drawn from all over Britain. Any one of them could become a local hero. Football was an exciting and dramatic setting for acting out inter-urban rivalries, even inter-village ones. Few towns with pop-

ulations of more than 20,000 were without a professional or semi-professional team by 1914.

These clubs were commercial operations but not capitalist ones. The businessmen who ran professional football clubs did not do it for profit but for a complex of motives including pleasure, prestige and their own assertion of identity. Directors were not paid fees and the maximum wage for players, introduced in 1901, and the retain and transfer system which went with it, all served to prevent a small number of clubs from dominating the competition. Most football organisations were in the hands of middle-class men. There were working-class shareholders of clubs in both England and Scotland but they held few shares. Shareholding for them was an extension of being fans. The FA Cup Final at the Crystal Palace became a national day out for which some northern workers put

31 An important British and European occasion. The FA Cup Final in April 1923, the inauguration of Wembley Stadium, 'home' of football.

32 An era of enormous crowds. Crystal Palace stadium, during the FA Cup Final between Tottenham Hotspur and Sheffield United in April 1901.

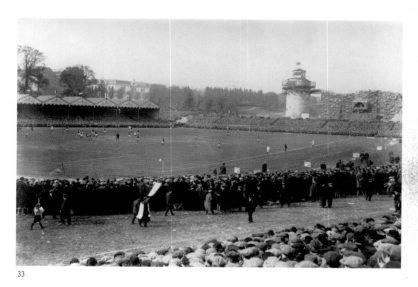

34

33 More than 100,000 spectators, including King George V, watched the FA Cup Final between Burnley and Liverpool at Crystal Palace stadium in April 1914.

34 William Julian, footballer. Captain of Woolwich Arsenal in 1891 he is an example of the new profession.

small amounts of money into saving clubs all the year round. Only royal occasions provided an opportunity for the gathering of bigger crowds. Iin 1914 it was accorded the ultimate accolade of respectability when the King attended for the first time. By the 1920s it would be watched by 90,000 ticketed fans in the new Empire Stadium Wembley with the crowd standing bare-headed before the kick-off to sing *Abide with Me*. It was one of a small number of English sporting occasions that were celebrated by press and radio as national —

although this left out the Scots who had their own cup final in Glasgow.

Nor was football merely a sport that many watched. It was extensively played too although shortages of urban space limited the numbers who could play the organised game. But boys and youths could be regularly found, well into the twentieth-century, playing on waste ground or in the street. Football was embedded in many of the formative institutions of the country, not only schools, as we have seen, but attached to chapels and churches, youth organisations of all kinds, workplaces, and as important in the Army as the coffee shop or the canteen. It was, of course, largely a male world, the players and spectators being mainly boys, youths and men from the working and lower-middle classes, aged between fourteen and fifty. Football was an opportunity to get away from the family, to spend time away from home with your mates, to talk and be sociable.

Some contemporaries on both the left and right of politics thought that the commercialised leisure world in general and football in particular distracted the workers from the more serious concerns of politics and trade unionism. Labour activists especially felt it made

35

35 The new opium of the people. Postcard from 1914.

36 Apprenticeship for a virile and sporting life: *The Boy's Own Paper*, 10th September 1904.

their task of recruiting workers to the cause that much harder. But it is difficult to demonstrate that football actually performed the role of keeping workers quiet. For one thing, while not denying its popularity, many working men were untouched by it. When news-papers gave it wide coverage it was in part because they recognised that there was a significant public interest but they were also promoting that interest. Many employers enjoyed football for the same reasons as their workers did. It might also provide positive publicity that was good for business and industrial relations. There are plenty of examples of workers combining an interest in their local football team and the Labour Party. It is also likely that football would not have been as popular as it was if more recreation-al choices had been available to working-class males. Football may not have been the game for all of the British people all of the time: it may not even have been the game for some of the people all of the time but it could probably be fairly concluded that it was the game for some of the people for most of the time. And this was the powerful national football culture with which the fledgling FIFA had to cope!

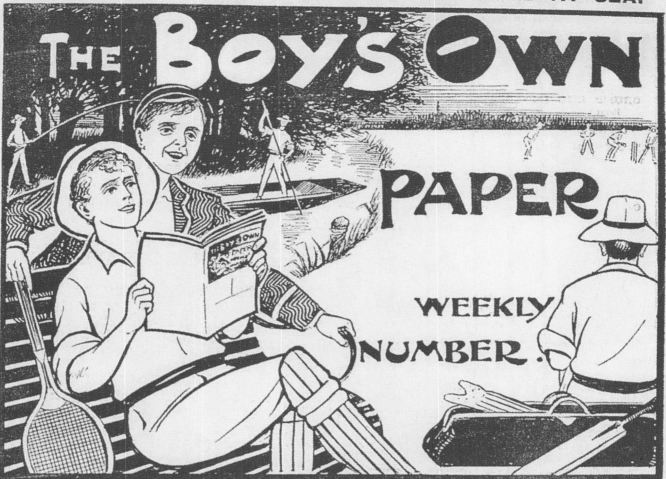

THE BOY'S OWN PAPER

WEEKLY NUMBER.

JOHN PIGGOTT (LTD.)

COMPLETE FOOTBALL OUTFITTERS.

SEND FOR OUR NEW FOOTBALL LIST.

SENT POST FREE ON RECEIPT OF CARD.

FOOTBALLS.

The (J.P.) Cup Tie.

A better ball than this cannot be produced. Each one is stamped with our Trade Mark, and is manufactured from the finest quality extra Stout Cowhide.
No. 5, each, 9/9. Case only, 8/-.
Postage, 4d.

Brass Football Inflators, 9d., 1/5, 1/11, and 2/6 each. Postage, 1d.

OTHER FOOTBALLS.
THE CROWN, 5/-.
THE CLUB, 5/9.
THE GOAL, 6/9.
THE BRITON, 7/6.
THE BOYS OWN, small size, 3/9. Postage, 4d.

SHIN GUARDS.
White Canvas, 9d. per pair.
Cane Bars, covered leather, 11½d. per pair.
Cane Bars, gold cape, well padded, 1/4 per pair.
John Piggott's Special Cork Barred Guards, unequalled for protection and lightness.
Covered Chamois, 1/8 per pair.
Covered Smooth Hide, 2/3 per pair.
Ditto, with Ankle Guards, 3/3 per pair.
Postage, 3d.

ORDERS BY POST SENT PER RETURN.

The "LEAGUE" REFEREE WHISTLE, 6½d. each. Postage 1d.

SHIRTS.

2/- allowed on Orders for 1 dozen.

BOYS' FLANNELETTE, 2in. stripes as sketch, 1/8 and 2/4 each.
Ditto, Harlequin, 1/8 and 2/4 each.
Plain Flannelette, with sash, 2/6 each.
Plain, with Coloured Collar and Cuffs, 1/8 and 2/4.
MEN'S, 2d. EACH EXTRA.
MEN'S, with sash, 3d. EXTRA.
Any Special Design to Order.

BOYS' FLANNEL SHIRTS, 5/-.

KNICKERS.

2/- allowed on all orders for 1 dozen KNICKERS.

Strong Navy Serge, Boys' Size, 2/2 per pair.

Our Special Beltless Knicker.
No dangerous Buckle. No belt required.
Boys' Strong Navy Serge, 2/2. 24/- doz.
Ordinary make, 1/8, 2/3, 3/6, and 4/8.
White Swansdown, 1/4, 2/-.
Best Lambskin, 3/1.
Men's size, 2d. per pair extra.
Postage 3d.
Boys' size up to 3 inches leg, 28 inches waist.
Men's sizes, 2d. per pair extra.

BOOTS.

FOOTBALL STUDS.
4d. a Set. Postage 1d.

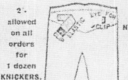

BOYS' & YOUTHS' FOOTBALL BOOTS.
Russet Hide, with Corrugated Toe Cap and Back Counter.
Size 2 to 5, 5/11.   Pad, 5/6.
„ 12 to 1, 4/9.   „ 5/11.
Postage, 6d.

SPECIAL FOOTBALL BELT.
3 in. wide, 9d. each. Postage, 2d.

BAGS.

THE FOOTBALL BAG.
13 in. 14 in. 16 in. 18 in.
3/4   4/1   4/9   5/4
Postage, 6d.

FOOTBALL HOSE.
Special Lines Heather.
1/11, 2/6, 3/6, 4/11 per pair.
Postage, 3d.
Navy or black, with coloured striped tops, 1/11 per pair; 21/6 per doz.

(Dept. L) 117 & 118 Cheapside, and Milk St., LONDON, E.C.

AN EAST COAST CRUISE IN A CANOE-YACHT.   [Price One Penny.

"JOHN BULL" FUSSBALLSTIEFEL

Man erfrage die nächste Bezugsquelle durch die alleinigen Fabrikanten Rollmann und Mayer Schuhfabriken · Köln – Nippes

Lith. u. Druck: Kölner Verlags-Anstalt & Druckerei A·G.

1870–1910

THE SPREAD OF FOOTBALL FROM GREAT BRITAIN

The spread of association football from Great Britain across continental Europe and America followed the standardisation of rules in 1863. The expansion of football resulted largely from Britain's economic and industrial strength in the latter half of the nineteenth century.

2

The agents of expansion

The British agents of this expansion, the tradesmen, technical managers, businessmen etc, were not motivated by the idea of exporting association football. In fact, football took advantage of the fertile ground left by the demise of traditional rural games in a increasingly urbanised world.

It is known that British seamen played football when putting in at European and American ports such as Rio, Savona, Marseille, and Callao, but there is no real evidence to show they took the opportunity to teach the game to the indigenous population, or indeed if the natives had time to learn the game adequately enough to play it among themselves. Football was ini-

tially played by groups of British colonists such as bank employees, trade or transport companies, engineers and managers of mines and factories, or teachers and students in the many British schools, and last but by no means least, the ambassadors and consular staff. These groups of people played exclusively amongst themselves before they accepted playing against the indigenous population. The British kept a tight control over the rules and insisted their language was used for all aspects of the game.

It is difficult to be sure of the exact chronology of the introduction of association football around the world. Because the spread started slowly it did not leave any traces until after it had developed significantly. In addition, when examining the source material it is not clear if the football in question is association football or rugby football, which were both commonly referred to as 'football'. The term football could also mean a mix of rules or different rules altogether. These problems were more prevalent in the period before 1880, when the British, especially those who had been abroad for a long time, did not completely appreciate the radical separation of the two games which happened in 1863, and then again in 1871.

The football appeared first in Belgium in the 1860s in British schools in Brussels, Bruges and Antwerp. At the same time, Morrogh of Killarney joined a boarding school in Ghent with a ball, but it is not known if it was round or oval. Morrogh was a close friend of Emile Seeldrayers, the father of the future FIFA President, successor of Jules Rimet, in 1954. In 1880 British students established the first football club in

1 'Modern' feet and legs to advertise 'John Bull' football boots (before 1911).

2 One of the first depictions of 'football - national winter sport' published in Europe. *Le Monde Illustré* 1867.

3 Relaxation and Camaraderie in 1897. The Brussels Sporting Club playing a match against an English club from Tunbridge Wells. Emile Seeldrayers, one of the founders of Belgian football, in the centre, his son Rodolphe William, a future President of FIFA, on the front row.

3 >

4 Footballers from Thessaloníki take part in the Athens Olympics, 1906.

5 The team of WAC (Wiener Athletik Sportclub, Austria) next to a giant advertising ball, taken in 1904.

6 An improvised setting for the match between Berlin and Dresden clubs in April 1892. The match is being played in Berlin.

Antwerp. Echoing events in Belgium, in 1876 the British were also playing football in Copenhagen and in the Netherlands.

The long history of football in Switzerland is explained by the fact that there were many British pupils in private schools. In 1855 at the Institut du Château de Lancy, near Geneva, a ball game with imprecise rules was played many years before the English FA was set up. An unknown ball game was also played in the Institut de la Châtelaine in Geneva in 1869 and it was the English who founded the Lausanne Football and Cricket Club in 1880. The FC Saint-Gall (1879) and FC Grasshoppers of Zurich (1886) were both specialised football clubs and both established by the British.

Germany had many enclaves of British residents in Hamburg, Bremen, Frankfurt and Hanover. They followed various careers: tradesmen, businessmen or specialist gas, water and drainage engineers. There were also the employees of English textile mills and salesmen of luxury products and many were accompanied by their families. In the larger towns the communities had an Anglican clergyman, who organised sporting activities such as boating or football. There were also tourists and those who came to spend longer periods of time taking a cure at the spa towns of Baden-Baden or Wiesbaden. Towards the end of the nineteenth century, there were also sports' equipment salesmen and newspaper editors – all sport and especially football enthusiasts. One such person was Andrew Pitcairn-Knowles who launched an illustrated sports periodical in 1895. At the same time British students arrived to study at the Technischen Hochschulen and brought football with them. Clubs created by the British were mainly in Bremen and Berlin. In 1893 stu-

Fußball-Wettspiele zwischen dem Berliner und dem Dresdener Fußballclub auf dem Exercierplatz „Einsame Pappel" bei Berlin. Nach einer Skizze von E. Hosang. (S. 499.)

6

dents from Manchester studying at the Mulhouse School of Chemistry, then part of Germany, formed the FCM 93 football club whose members included friends who were living locally.

In Vienna, two British Clubs were formed after 1890. The First Vienna club of Baron de Rothschild involved engineers, businessmen, and bureaucrats, and the Vienna Cricket and Football Club was made up of landscape gardeners from Britain.

Penetration of the game into France was totally different. Association football played to the FA's rules was definitely played in Le Havre from 1872 by the British employees of the South Western Railway, which at that time ran a connection from Le Havre to Southampton, and their college-age children. This is only certain for a few years that followed, but without doubt, by the end of the 1880s, Le Havre Athletic Club played football to FA rules again. Soon after this, football was also being played in Paris where two British teams were established: the White Rovers in 1891 and the Standard Athletic Club in 1892. The latter was made up of workers who had travelled to Paris to work on the

Exposition Universelle in 1889. The French themselves influenced the spread of association football with the game's adoption by the Parisian lycées.

In Russia, football was first played in St Petersburg in 1890 between teams of Englishmen: factory owners, trading companies, or members of the diplomatic corps. The British maintained their hegemony over Russian football until the start of the twentieth century.

Due to established commercial ties with South American countries there were many British emigrants on the continent, particularly in Argentina where football was established from very early on. Most notably the British in Argentina started boarding schools where sports were played. The first association football club was Buenos Aires FC, a subsidiary of the Buenos Aires Cricket Club, which probably dates from 1867. In 1883 another Briton, Alexander Watson Hutton, the founder of the Buenos Aires English School, was president of an association football league. The committee of this league was exclusively British and all proceedings were carried out in English. This leads us to believe that the

7 Military footballers. A team of Argentinian conscript soldiers in the town of Paraná in 1912.

8 Sporting conversion via literature. Book by Josep Elias y Juncosa published in Barcelona, 1914.

9 The Anglo-American Club from Berlin in 1889. The team were pioneers of football in Europe and America. The Scotsman Andrew Pitcairn-Knowles in the centre of the team, accompanied by Fred Manning (on the left) and Ivo Schricker (standing, 2nd in from the left).

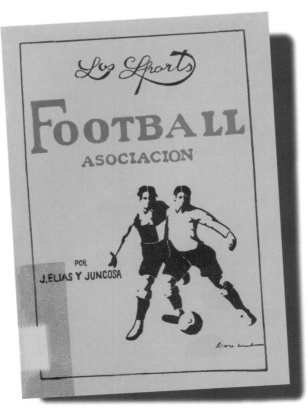

9

clubs were almost exclusively British. Between 1893 and 1898 the old boys' team from a boarding school at Lomas de Zamora dominated all competitions. From 1900 to 1911, at a time when the British had lost their monopoly over the game of football around the rest of the world, the Argentinian Championship was won by the Buenos Aires School's Alumni team. At the start of the twentieth century it was the second generation British emigrants who played football. Tours by the teams of Southampton, Tottenham Hotspurs and Chelsea show the continuing influence of the British game. Britain left a strong and long lasting mark on Argentinian football.

The influence of Britain on football in Brazil started later and was less durable. Charles W. Miller, a diplomat's son in São Paulo, introduced football to Brazil, playing alongside employees and managers from the gas company, the Bank of London and the São Paulo Railway. The British were also founder members of the Montevideo Rowing Club in Uraguay in 1891.

The next region to discover football was southern Europe. In Portugal the game was played by employees of a telegraph company established in Lisbon and the employees of wine merchants in Porto. Italian ports became a key source for the spread of football, due to the presence of British inhabitants. At Genoa this was mainly merchants and the long-term consulate employees. But in Italy, as in Spain and Greece (which also had teams formed by expatriate businessman and engineers), the British were not the sole football influence. The presence of the Swiss, German and Austrian enthusiasts was also already noticeable.

The start of twentieth century saw an increase in football participation in Central and Latin America that involved fewer British players than before. In Honduras in 1900, the majority of players were still British, but in Salvador a match was played where only seven of the 22 players were British. In 1910 the Argentinian team had nine British players and Chile had eight. These numbers were an improvement on earlier ratios: a game played in Lima, on a pitch reserved for English players, managed only one native footballer. The game of football was introduced to Peru by English seamen who put in at Callao.

In British colonies, some of which were already independent, football participation increased but did not set down such deep roots as elsewhere. This was the case in the United States at the end of the 1860s where association football faced stiff competition from baseball and American football. Both association and rugby football had been established in Canada before 1870, at which time the separation had only just become official in Great Britain. In Toronto in 1876, a match was played to FA rules and in 1885 British teams toured Canada and played matches.

Strong links between Great Britain and Australia and New Zealand explain the presence of football in this part of the world from 1870 onwards. At this time most football was played to rugby rules although association football was played in the environs of Sydney by 1880.

It was in the 1850s that students in Indian schools first played football. Eton rules seemed to have been known in 1868. The number of clubs for colonists grew

10

during the 1880s under the influence of teachers who had arrived from Great Britain. In Calcutta in the late 1880s and early 1890s matches took place between the military and the indigenous population.

The British established football in locations where they had a strong commercial presence, in Europe and in Latin America. However, despite British efforts on the Gold Coast and in Egypt, in 1914 Africa and Asia were still not football-playing regions. The British had achieved a type of world domination over football by establishing standard association football rules wherever the game was played. The foundation of FIFA in 1904 assured additional support for the development of association football around the world.

11

10 Burmese locals playing football. British engraving (circa 1901).

11 Reality or wishful thinking? The multicultural British Empire team, 1903.

12 Football rolls into Africa. An unofficial match in English Sudan, 1915.

12

13 A game of the Parisian social elite. Pupils from the Ecole alsacienne playing football in the Bois de Boulogne, 1888.

14 Vittorio Pozzo, nationalist, polyglot and coach of the *squadra azzurra* between 1912 and 1948.

13

14

Other pioneers

While the British were exporting football around the world, Europeans who had spent time in Britain returned home with a football and enough knowledge of the game to teach close friends and acquaintances. Some of these people were English teachers who had completed training courses in Britain. For example, in 1898 both Mr Beltette, a teacher at the French lycée in Tourcoing, and Mr Desagnes from the Lycée of Amiens founded football clubs. In 1898 there were football pioneers like the students from the Ecole Monge in Paris, who had spent time at Eton College with the specific aim of learning to play association football. Some students had been in Britain for many months, such as Eugène Frayasse and Charles Bernat, the latter having stayed in Dumfries in Scotland. Raymond Dubly, who had studied in Uckfield in Sussex, played for a team from Roubaix on his return to France.

This process was repeated in Italy where Eduardo Bosio from Turin worked in Nottingham for a merchant. On his return to Italy he founded Internazionale FC in Turin. It is likely that football had been introduced to Germany in a similar way. Konrad Koch of Brunswick received a genuine English football from his friend August Hermann, who almost certainly brought it back from a trip across the channel. Koch translated the rules of the game and introduced it into German schools. Walter Bensemann is the most emblematic example of the spread of football sponsored by the indigenous population. Born in 1873, his father was a doctor from a family of bankers. He studied in Switzerland, Germany and Great Britain. Between 1887 and 1892 Bensemann founded clubs in Montreux, Strasbourg and Karlsruhe. There is evidence of many other pioneers: Wim Mulier founded the Haarlem club in the Netherlands following his time studying in Britain; the Hungarian Karoly Lowenrosen formed a team with his friends from a singing society on his return from Britain in 1896; in 1902 Delfino Sanchez Latour, who became a diplomat on his return from a Surrey college, established the first football club in Guatemala.

A later phase of development happened when young people who had learned the game abroad, not in Great Britain, but in another country that already played football, encouraged their fellow citizens to play. , Two Frenchmen, Julien and Falgueirettes, learned to play football in Switzerland. The former established FC Cette (Sète) in 1894 on his return from studying in Geneva. Henry Monnier, a keen anglophile who chose to spell his first name the English way, set up a club in Nimes in 1898 on his return from Geneva. Switzerland well deserves to be called 'little England on the continent' considering the role the country played in the spread of football from its renowned business schools. Vittorio Pozzo, who eventually became coach of the Italian national team, studied international business and languages at Winterthur and Zurich before promoting the game in his home country. In Guatemala, young people like Arturo Aguirre Matheu who returned from France and others who had been in Belgium and Germany, brought the game back to their country.

An original variation on this route occurred in Bolivia after an entrepreneur watched a game played by the English in Chile. In May 1896, on his return to Bolivia he founded the Oruro Royal Football Club.

15 Joan (Hans) Gamper, Swiss football missionary. The founder and later President of FC Barcelona (circa 1910).

16 FC Barcelona in 1903. The team were Swiss and Catalan. From left to right: standing: llobet, Terradas, Reig, Vidal; sitting: Ossó, Stemberg, Meyer, Witty, Gamper, Witty, Lasaleta

15

European promoters of football

European countries that had adopted football emulated the British and in turn exported the game to countries that were still to discover it. The presence of many Swiss citizens in the western Mediterranean basin, managers and traders, was fundamental to this. Hans Gamper, a student from the Institut technique of Winterthur, travelled to Barcelona in 1899 and soon established a football club. Also in Catalonia, Hispano-Suiza, the car manufacturer, encouraged his employees to play the game. Swiss nationals assisted by some Britons introduced the game to Naples. Internazionale de Milan owes its existence and name to its Swiss founders, in fact there was a majority of Swiss members in the club in 1908. Among the French and German founders of Bari FC there was also the Swiss grain and flour trader Gustav Kuhn. Swiss residents in Marseille created the Swiss Cercle to play football for the Stade Helvétique, which at that time was a general sports club. The Union Sportive Suisse in Paris was created in the same way.

Germans imported football to Prague and then Belgrade. Ferdinand Hueppe, who was to become the founder President of the Deutscher Fussballbund (DFB) in 1900, joined Deutscher FC in Prague in 1899. In 1902 in Montevideo there was a Deutscher Fussball Club, and in Mexico a German club won the national championship in 1919. In Paraguay, in approximately 1900, Mr William Paats, a Dutch PE teacher, introduced football to his students. The French also helped spread the game both in Athens prior to 1900, and in Smyrna where they formed a team with the British to take part in the Athens Olympics in 1906.

16

THE SPREAD OF FOOTBALL FROM GREAT BRITAIN

Match de football
La lampe Osram invulnérable

17 Will Dunbar Attrill, pioneer of Association Football in France as Captain and defender for Standard A.C. of Paris (circa 1885).

18 Football tests the power of electric light. Postcard, circa 1914.

19 The business of sport, birth of an industry, 1914.

20 The Kronprinz watching a match between the English and German Civil Services in Berlin. 'Like many young people of his generation, the German Prince shows a keen interest in all sports.' *L'Illustration,* 13 May 1905.

20

The social origins
of the first footballers

British colonists did not make any special effort to spread the game of football to other countries. Indeed, they did not wish the game to be played by the indigenous populations of the countries where they lived. The players of the two Parisian clubs, White Rovers and Standard Athletic, only allowed non-Britons to join on the understanding that English was used when playing the game. This was one way of underlining the fact that football was exclusively British.

This strictness regarding the nationality or language of players could not hold off interest from anglophiles who were fascinated by all things British. In Germany, the social elite showed enthusiasm for a game that symbolised modernity and many sent their children to study in Britain. The same was true in other countries that were undergoing industrialisation, such as Latin America. But football was not the only athletics initiative of this era. Gymnastics were promoted as an activity for the masses, an activity that promoted rigid discipline in contrast to football, a game that encouraged principles of liberty and freedom of spirit.

One can characterise this movement as open to modernity but suspicious of Englishness. Football was not yet a game for the people; it was was mainly played in schools or colleges, places where only young people from affluent families came together. In addition it was played at business schools, universities and other technical colleges or polytechnics in France, Germany and Switzerland. Football was almost exclusively a pursuit of the urban elite.

The earliest football players were businessman, commercial agents, lawyers and representatives of other liberal professions. Anglophilia was the catalyst. The aristocracy also took up football, notably diplomats and people employed in modern jobs. For all these groups of people, there was an importance attached to social interaction. Also among the pioneers were the Jewish and Protestant communities. Possibly, the aim of the Jewish players was to integrate into society at a time when anti-Semitism was particularly rife. For both groups, football was an indicator of their receptiveness to new things, in particular to economic modernity.

For these social groups the ability to play football was helped by their affluence and leisure time, at a time when the working classes were still disadvantaged. The newly urbanised workforce started playing because, via football, an activity without roots or tradition, they could integrate into their new community with no reference to their recent arrival in town.

Football was played by affluent or new social groups who sought to achieve distinction. This led to the exclusion of manual workers from both the pitch and the touchline as they were considered incapable of understanding the game played before them. For a long time the elite held onto the notion of amateurism, meaning the refusal of all expense payments. The upper classes suspected that the less well off players would seek to follow the British example, where the popularity of the game had to led to professionalism as the directors accepted that it was necessary to pay the working men a 'loss of earnings' payment, which then became a salary.

THE SPREAD OF FOOTBALL FROM GREAT BRITAIN

21 Sporting friendship or another siege in Paris? The first match between France and Germany (0-7) December 1898 in the suburbs of Paris. On the third row (standing) on the right, is the 'Strasbourgeois' Ivo Schricker.

22 The players and directors of Fluminense from Rio, 1906.

The desire for recognition and an enthusiasm for all things English, led to the use of English names for the clubs. There were many 'Britannia' and 'Racing clubs' across Europe and Latin American.

The interval between the time when only the English played football and when the indigenous people of other countries started to play was actually very short. Before the end of the nineteenth century football was played in many French secondary schools (in Paris, Roubaix, Tourcoing, Amiens and Le Havre). Tournaments were played between colleges in Cherbourg, Bayeux, Dreux and Coutances. There were also competitions in Germany: in Brunswick, Hamburg, Hanover and Duisburg, and also in Peru where in 1895 two schools in Lima played football.

The majority of the teams that had been established were at the modern business schools attended by progressive young men. In France and Germany football developed in all towns where business schools or higher technical colleges existed. In Mulhouse, students from Manchester played alongside the sons of the city's textile industrialists. They played a match against the Zurich Polytechnic school in 1894. The welcome at the train station followed by a tour of the town and then a banquet and toast to the visitors illustrated that standard bourgeois social ceremony was observed. This type of ritual before and after the match also occurred in Berlin and Hamburg. We may well ask if these festivities dominated the games. Football matches and the accompanying formalities clearly show the influence of the elite.

Footballers from the schools soon entered university and formed 'civil' teams that were mainly made up of law students, such as AS Strasbourg founded in 1892, medical students in St Petersburg and arts students in Peru. The German Bensemann and his friend Ivo Schricker were among the first student footballers. Schricker played for AS Strasbourg, then Karlsruhe and subsequently was called up to play for the German national team in 1896. Later Schricker became Vice President and then General Secretary of FIFA over the period 1932 to 1950.

When these young people became managers or owners of their own businesses after leaving university, they carried on playing football and formed new clubs. The Petit brothers, young textile businessmen from Amiens, followed this path, as did others in Catalonia and in Germany.

Football also interested the aristocracy. In Belgium Baron de Laveleye, who was an industrialist, was President and an active player within a club. The old Brazilian families who founded the Fluminense club were another example of aristocracy showing an active interest in the game. During this early period of football, founders, directors and players were from the same generation and performed all roles within the clubs.

23

Popularisation and 'Nationalism'

By the start of the twentieth century workers were gradually joining football teams, and in some rare cases they formed their own. Before the introduction of workers' football by the socialist movement, the catalysts for growth in football participation were frequently employers motivated by specific aims: to motivate employees to serve their company by encouraging them to identify with their workplace. The owners and office workers of the Hispano-Suiza factories in Catalonia were quick to accept manual workers into their teams. In Russia in 1894, Harry Scharnock, the son of the owner of a Lancastrian textile factory, encouraged his employees to play football in an attempt to stop them drinking vodka on a Sunday. Genuine workers' clubs started at the Putilov factory in St Petersburg and played in the regional league.

There was a similar story soon afterwards in Brazil. A textile factory in the suburbs of Rio created Bangu AC, which was initially open only to office clerks. Manual workers were later allowed to join and soon were the majority. The workers who were members of the company team experienced privileged treatment in the workplace to help them prepare for matches. Those in charge of rival clubs condemned this early form of professionalism. The expansion of participation to include manual workers progressed further when coloured players were accepted by Bangu AC.

24

23 A Scotsman in Russia. Sir Hamilton Bruce Lockhart (on the right), with the players of the Morozov textile factory, a few hundred kilometres from Moscow (1912).

24 Coloured footballers take their place in a Brazilian team for the first time. The team of Ponte Preta (Campinas), 1912.

25

Shortly before the Great War, social pluralism became standard in countries where there was mass immigration, such as Australia and Argentina. A flood of workers from countries such as Great Britain arrived in Australia and brought with them a more democratic game. In Argentina the best teams were composed of Italian and Spanish immigrants. When Racing Club Buenos Aires, a team formed by recent immigrants that did not have any British or gaucho players, won the championship in 1913, it was deemed a 'Creole success'.

Football retained certain elitist characteristics well up to 1914 or even 1920. In reaction, the manual workers of Germany and Russia, conscious of the class struggle, initially refused to participate in an activity of their class enemy, and few workers played in South America. In Germany the Arbeiter-Turner-Bund (Workers' Gymnastic Association) was founded in 1893 and considered footballers to be class enemies.

Over time, football evolved national characteristics. The first signs of this were seen in Argentina where the style of play changed. The long ball game, a direct and physical approach which had been the style of the British

pioneers of the game, gave way to a more creative game based on shorter and slower passes. Almost every country developed their own unique style that was the subject of never-ending journalistic commentary and the source of many clichés.

The development of national styles went beyond playing the game. Countries around the world keenly followed the rules of the International Board, but were not so accepting of other British requests, particularly regarding the vocabulary of the game. Italians used the word 'calcio' instead of football. The Brazilians used 'futebol', and the Argentinians started to use 'futbol' in 1934. Despite this, English remained the official language of FIFA. In Germany some people reacted against the anglophilia (*Engländerei*) of the 1890s. The founders of the DFB in 1900 were followers of the Jungdeutschlandbund that fought against the 'corruption of youth' and the DFB developed in a nationalist and anti-British atmosphere. In collaboration with the Deutscher Sprachverein (Society of German Language) the DFB translated the English terminology used for the positions of players, the various rules and types of play,

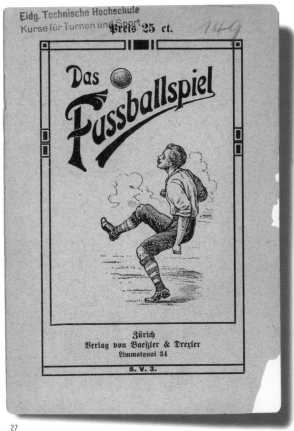

25 The imperial eagle. The German national team at the Olympics of 1912.

26 Sportsmen were faced with a wide choice of pursuits. Cover of *La Vie au Grand Air*, April 1898.

27 Football language is nationalised. A technical teaching guide published in Zurich, 1910.

In the United States, resistance to the imperialism of the FA took a more radical turn and the game failed to set down roots. The main cause for this was the reluctance of Americans to imitate their ex-coloniser. Baseball was already popular in America and in a rare example football, known as soccer in the United States, failed to establish itself, and the development of association football was restricted.

Rugby football was not entirely successful either. Initially dominant in France its popularity gave way to that of association football around 1905. The upper classes were attached to playing more than one sport and football had to fit in with the omni-sport tradition; athletics was preferred in summer and football was played only in winter.

In 1914 the influence of British players was still felt as they were playing all over the world. Teams fought over English coaches. In Germany William Townley coached Karlsruhe and then Fürth prior to 1914. Reynolds even became the coach of the German national team, and in France FC Cette (Sète) employed a coach called Gibson.

The number of participants continued to grow in the countries that had been conquered by football. In 1895 there were 10 teams in St Petersburg, which grew to 23 in 1914. In 1905 the DFB had 14,000 affiliated players, 82,000 in 1914 and more than 400,000 in 1920. In 1905 France had slightly fewer footballers than other countries, with only approximately 4000 members of the various French football associations. The growth of the number of people playing football was due in part to the establishment of one or more football associations in each country.

fouls etc. into German. The first thing to change was the name of the game itself, which became '*fussball*', a penalty was '*Strafstoss*' and a corner '*Eckball*'.

In Russia football survived a rebellion in 1903. The dispute came about due to the lack of Russian involvement in the running of the game. In 1912 nationalisation was clearly the goal when a limit of three British players per team was imposed.

28

29

28 Galt Football Club. The Canadians have just won the Olympic Games football tournament in Saint-Louis (United States) 23 November 1904.

29 Georgy A. Duperron, secretary of the All-Russian Football Federation which joined FIFA in 1912.

30 The Russian team take to the international stage during the Olympic Games of 1912.

Football associations and federalisation

In almost all countries where football had taken hold, the desire to imitate the British extended to the establishment of football associations. This was by no means an easy process. More than twenty associations had been established by 1903 and a few more were created before 1913. In 1880 in Toronto, Canada, 19 clubs including FC Galt, the 1904 Olympic Champions, founded the Canadian Western Football Association, and in 1912 in Toronto it became the Dominion of Canada FA. The Indian Football Association, initially controlled by the British and whose name reflects English involvement, dates from 1893. In 1912 FIFA enforced their rule to ensure that only one association should be established under the name of the US Football Association.

The older European football associations suffered least from internal tensions. The Dutch and Danish football associations date from 1889. The Swiss football association followed in 1895, as did Belgium's. The Union Belge des Sociétés de Sports Athlétiques (UBSSA) was a multi-sport association at first. The federalisation of football in Belgium happened in 1912 with the foundation of the l'Union Royale Belge des Sociétés de Football Association (URBSFA).

The creation of a French football association went through a much more complicated and conflict ridden process. The Union des Sociétés de Sports Athlétiques (USFSA), a multi-sport organisation, reluctantly added a football department in 1893. Other associations such as the FCAF and the Fédération des Patronages catholiques (FGSPF, The Association of Catholic Youth Clubs) existed at the same time and also organised football competitions. A founder member of FIFA, the USFSA gave way to the CFI as the French member in 1908. The CFI eventually

30

brought together all the other French football associations, but French football was not united under one association until 1919. The French experience shows the importance of FIFA as a unifying force. Italian footballers founded the Federazione Italiana de Football in 1898, although initial moves to establish a football association went back to 1886. Germany did not establish the DFB until 1900. The length of time taken to set up the DFB was mainly due to the federal structure of the country. Thanks in great part to the efforts of FIFA, the DFB was able to maintain its monopoly when it was challenged by the Turnvereine (Gymnastic Association). FIFA also insisted that the Russian football clubs formed an association following their membership application in 1912.

Attempts to organise national competitions happened before federalisation took place. In some countries it was impossible to organise a truly national competition mainly due to the distances between teams in countries such as Canada, France and Germany. In these countries there was a system of regional competitions with the winners going on to play in the final knockout stages.

International matches took place before the foundation of FIFA, often between countries that shared a border. At the end of the nineteenth century British teams travelled to play teams in Berlin, Brussels and Paris among others. The outcome of all the matches was the same: a severe defeat for the home side.

FIFA soon set up matches between representative teams. Belgium played France in 1904, and Switzerland travelled to play a match against France the following year. In 1906 a French team was annihilated 15-0 by a Great Britain amateur team. France was beaten again by Denmark in 1908 during the London Olympics, and twice by Belgium. However, before 1914 France

was able to beat the Italian team twice. These results illustrate the hierarchy of the time: dominance by the far superior British team and the first teams to imitate them. Elsewhere, Russia played a match against Finland and Central European football had already reached an excellent level. Matches between European and South American countries had yet to take place.

Federalisation had barely started in football-playing countries when some people started to put forward the idea of an international organisation. It was hoped that this international structure could resolve the difficulties in setting up national associations.

31 Learning British values and fair-play during a match between teams from Paris and London, November 1905.

32 The Scandinavians make life difficult for British players. Middleboe, a Danish player, dribbles past two adversaries during the Olympic Games Final which was won 4-2 by Great Britain. 4 July 1912.

33 An extraordinary game. The Dutch score a goal during the match for third place between the Netherlands and Finland (result 9-0), 4 July 1912 in Stockholm.

RAPPROCHER LES NATIONS LES UNES DES AUTRES

1904-1945

THE
BIRTH
OF FIFA

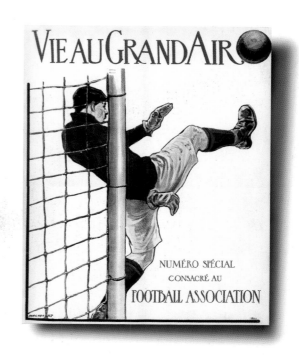

Initiated by Robert Guérin, the treasurer of the USFSA – a French general sports federation – FIFA was founded in rue Saint-Honoré in Paris during three days in May 1904. In fact, the idea could have germinated at the same time within the Nederlandsche Voetbal Bund, and to a lesser extent the URBSSA in Belgium.

1 C. W. Hirschman. The Dutch representative at FIFA's founding Congress. Hirschman was FIFA Vice-President and subsequently Secretary and Honorary Treasurer until October 1931.

2 Robert Guérin. Journalist for *Le Matin* newspaper, and Secretary General of the Union des Sociétés Françaises de Sports Athlétiques (Union of French Athletic Sports Societies). The first FIFA President from 1904 to 1906.

3 Henri de Laveleye. Belgian sportsman and industrialist. FIFA Vice-President from 1909 to 1921, and also member of the IOC and the International Board.

(1902-1906)
Prehistory

At the start of the twentieth century, the few football associations that already existed decided to create an international body where they could meet. This was partly in response to a widespread enthusiasm within Europe for international matches, and partly in the hope that an international organisation could oversee a unification of the laws of the game. At the same time, European footballers were mesmerised by British football and wanted to be recognised there. An international organisation seemed to be a way to convince the FA to end its condescending attitude and to join together with other national football associations. In order to defend their own associations, the promoters also wanted to recognise only one football association per country. The USFSA sought to marginalise the rival French associations. In general, the existing football associations thought that an international organisation would encourage the other countries that played the game to establish an FA that could then join up.

It was Heckenberg, the secretary of the Dutch football association (NVB), who seems to have had the first conversations with the English FA. Subsequently, C.A.W Hirschmann wrote to Frederick Wall, the secretary of the FA, on 8 May 1902, to ask their opinion. It is possible that before this he may have first spoken to Baron de Laveleye of the URBSSA. One year passed by as Hirschmann's letter was sent to the Council of the FA, then to the International Board and then on to the other British associations. Eventually, the FA deigned to reply and stated that they would invite the European football associations to a meeting in England, but did not indicate when this would take place.

1

2

3

The Dutch seemed happy to leave the next step to the USFSA who had commenced a similar initiative under the auspices of Robert Guérin. He went to London twice at the start of 1903 first to meet with Wall, then to meet Lord Kinnaird, the then president of the FA. His efforts were in vain. It was like 'slicing water with a knife', wrote Guérin, who was upset at the ignorance of continental football that the British showed.

Having learnt his lesson, Guérin invited the European football associations to a meeting in Paris planned for August 1903. His attempt failed and the European championship planned for the occasion did not take place.

The USFSA did not declare itself beaten, even though a negative response was finally received from the British on 14 November 1903. Wall cast doubt on the organisation of European football. The British opinion seemed logical: why create an international federation when the creation of national associations had barely began on the continent?

Guérin chose to persevere and proceeded without the British. In consultation with Dr Karding of the DFB and Mülinghaus the secretary of the UBSSA, Guérin outlined plans for an international organisation. On 13 January 1904, the USFSA noted the progress they were making towards a treaty following regular contact with other western European associations. They suggested a meeting should be held in Brussels or Paris on 3 and 4 of August with the aim of signing an agreement.

The proposed treaty would bring rationalisation and standardisation to the rules governing international matches. The first article underlined the wishes of the football associations concerned to mutually recognise each other 'as being the only associations governing the sport of Association Football in their respective countries'. This arrangement sought to establish the authority of each national association in its own country and in turn address British doubts. One association per country was the preoccupation of the USFSA and also interested Sweden where there was fierce rivalry between existing football associations. Guérin suggested the name 'International League or International Union' for the new organisation. In addition, he again raised the idea of a 'European Championship', which would be run under the control of this new authority.

Urged on by Guérin, a meeting finally took place. On 12 April he reviewed the suggestions that had reached Paris and passed them on to the associations who had expressed an interest. Soon afterwards he called a meeting in Paris for 21–23 May 1904. Hirschmann (Netherlands), Schneider (Switzerland), Sylow (Denmark), Mülinghaus and Kahn (Belgium) along with Guérin and Espir (France) attended. Sylow also represented Sweden and Espir FC Madrid – i.e. Spain. Germany wired their intention to sign up to a future agreement.

These meetings led to the creation of a committee consisting of Guérin, the young twenty-eight-year-old President, Schneider and Hirschmann as first and second Vice-Presidents, Mülinghaus as Secretary, and Sylow as Assistant Secretary. The statutes were agreed and consisted of ten articles. The associations that joined were now part of the Fédération Internationale de Football Association (FIFA) and as such recognised each other as the only associations governing association football in their respective countries. These associations would be the only ones to have the power to resolve problems between themselves, especially concerning international matches. The rules of the game would be those of the FA, meaning the

1re Année — No 2.   1er Septembre 1905.

BULLETIN OFFICIEL

DE LA

FÉDÉRATION INTERNATIONALE DE FOOTBALL (ASSOCIATION)

Offizielles Centralblatt des

Internationalen Fussball (Association) Verbandes.

Administration et Rédaction : Victor-E. SCHNEIDER, à GENÈVE (Suisse)

La Fédération Italienne de Football Association
membre de la F. I. F. A.

Je viens de recevoir le communiqué officiel adressé au délégué suisse de la F. I. F. A. :

Fédération Internationale de Football Association

Paris, le 19 août 1905.

Monsieur Victor-E. Schneider, à Genève.

Cher Monsieur,

J'ai l'honneur de vous informer que la *Fédération italienne de football* vien d'adresser son adhésion à la Fédération internationale.

Les clubs de votre association pourront dès lors conclure des matches avec les clubs de la Fédération italienne.

Veuillez agréer, cher Monsieur, l'assurance de mes meilleurs sentiments.

Robert GUÉRIN
Président de la F. I. F. A.

Je suis très heureux d'apprendre cette bonne nouvelle et j'espère que les associations ne faisant pas encore partie de notre fédération ne tarderont pas à en faire autant. En tous cas, dans l'intérêt même de notre sport favori, je le souhaite vivement.

V.-E. SCHNEIDER.

* * *

Comme la saison de football va bientôt recommencer, je vous soumets encore une fois le règlement de la F. I. F. A.

Je vous prie d'en prendre bonne note.

STATUTS DE LA F. I. F. A.

ARTICLE PREMIER. — Il est créé à Paris, le 21 mai 1904, une union internationale sous le nom de Fédération Internationale de Football Association.

International Fussball-Association Verband.
International Football-Association Fédération.
International Association Vœtball Unie.
Internationalt Association Foudhold Ferbund.
Internacional Football Associacion Federacion.

par les fédérations ci-après : U. S. F. S. A., France ; U. B. S. S. A., Belgique ; A. S. F., Suisse ; N. V. B., Hollande ; Dansk Boldspil Union, Danemark ; Swenska Bollspels Forbundet, Suède ; Madrid Fooball-Club, Espagne.

Ces fédérations se reconnaissent réciproquement comme les seules fédérations régissant le sport du football association dans leurs pays respectifs et comme les seules compétentes pour traiter des relations internationales.

ART. 2. — Elle a pour but de régler et de développer le football international et de prendre à cœur les intérêts de ses fédérations affiliées.

ART. 3. — Le sport international peut seulement être traité entre ces fédérations ainsi reconnues.

ART. 4. — La fédération de chaque pays fixe son calendrier comme elle l'entend.

Il est défendu aussi bien aux joueurs individuels qu'aux clubs et associations locales de jouer, dans la même saison et simultanément, pour différentes fédérations nationales.

ART. 5. — Toute société, tout membre radié de l'une des fédérations contractantes, l'est de fait dans les autres.

ART. 6. — Aucun match international ne peut être conclu entre des sociétés appartenant aux fédérations contractantes sans l'autorisation de leur fédération respective.

Toute notification de forfait doit être faite par lettre recommandée avant les dix jours précédant le match sous peine d'indemnité équivalente aux frais occasionnés par le match et indépendamment d'une amende de cinquante francs au bénéfice de la Fédération internationale.

ART. 7. — En cas de litige survenant à l'occasion de matches internationaux organisés sous les auspices des fédérations contractantes, les règlements de la Fédération dans le pays de laquelle le match a lieu seront seuls en vigueur.

ART. 8. — Les règles de jeu de football association sont, dans les matches internationaux, celles de la Football-Association Co Ld.

ART. 9. — La Fédération internationale seule a le droit d'organiser un championnat international.

ART. 10. — Aucune fédération ne peut admettre une société d'une autre nation. Exception est faite en ce qui concerne la Bohème.

N.-B. — Par mesure transitoire, l'article 3 ne recevra d'application qu'à partir du 1er septembre 1905.

Administration. — La fédération internationale se réunit chaque année en un congrès dont la date et le lieu sont fixés par le congrès précédent.

Chaque fédération nationale n'a droit qu'à une voix au congrès.

La Fédération internationale est administrée par un comité de cinq membres nommés pour un an par le congrès et rééligibles,

International Football Association Board (IFAB). Finally, FIFA alone had the authority to organise an international football tournament. This was the origin of the World Cup.

The Dutch football association did not sign the treaty until early 1905 and the door was left open to those who had not signed: Sweden, Italy, Hungary, and above all the British. Guérin returned to London with Baron de Laveleye. On his previous visit in December 1903, the President of the Belgian football association had been frustrated by the language and the manners of the English. They learned that the FA had called a meeting of all European Associations in London in April 1905, thereby ignoring the existence of FIFA. Guérin was well aware that the FA was seeking to control the future of European football without joining the new Federation. When the representatives arrived in London for the meeting on the 1 April, Guérin sent his own invitations for the second FIFA Congress in June 1905.

In London the FA stated that 'the European associations were not yet national associations' and they could not yet be treated as such. In addition to this, the FA did not wish to take part in an international tournament. Any agreement at all seemed unlikely until Baron de Laveleye managed to break the deadlock. The British agreed to recognise FIFA, but they would not become members.

The second FIFA Congress was held in Paris between 10–12 June 1905. The same countries were represented as in the previous year and mainly by the same people. An international tournament was again planned down to the smallest detail, and the committee

> 2   BULLETIN OFFICIEL DE LA FÉDÉRATION INT
>
> soit : un président, deux vice-présidents, un secrétaire général et un secrétaire adjoint. Le président, le premier vice-président et le secrétaire général, forment le Bureau.
>
> Le Comité ne peut comprendre plus d'un membre de chaque fédération.
>
> La cotisation annuelle de chaque fédération est fixée à 50 francs, payable dans le courant de janvier. Les rapports entre les fédérations et la Fédération internationale, se font par l'intermédiaire des délégués officiels.
>
> Le présent contrat sera exécutoire à partir du 1er septembre 1904. Les présents statuts sont adoptés à l'unanimité.
>
> Par exception, le Comité fixera lui-même le lieu et la date du prochain congrès.
>
> Lu et approuvé, Paris, ce 23 mai 1904.
>
> Pour la France : Robert Guérin, A. Espir.
> Pour la Belgique : Mühlinghaus, Max Kahn.
> Pour la Hollande : Hirschman.
> Pour la Suisse : Schneider.
> Pour l'Espagne : A. Espir.
> Pour le Danemark : Sylow.
> Pour la Suède : Sylow.
> Sauf ratification de l'Union Néerlandaise.
> L'Allemagne a adhéré en principe par télégramme en date de ce jour.

7

remained unchanged. In addition Slavia Prague, an early version of the Czech FA, attended. Italy was still absent, as was Sweden. In Sweden two associations were requesting entry. Furthermore FIFA considered that the FA had joined *de facto* and stated that the Federation would only authorise matches between clubs that were affiliated via their FA to FIFA, a new gesture of goodwill towards the English. In mid-October Italy and Hungary joined FIFA, which made a total of 11 members, and signalled the end of the gestation period.

8

(1906-1908)
Crisis

By the time the third FIFA Congress met in Berne on 3 and 4 June 1906, the international tournament had again failed to take place and this led to the departure of Robert Guérin. At last the British delegation arrived with four members, one of whom, Daniel Woolfall, was elected President. Initially the British were concerned with establishing their rules as standard. A committee was put in place to revise the existing statutes. The main purpose of this was to achieve an agreement on the meaning of the term 'country', the problem of players who changed nationality, and

9

Fédération Internationale de Football Association.

Dear Sir,

I am pleased to inform you that the Emergency Committee of the F. I. F. A. have provisionally sanctioned the affiliation of the following National Associations:

Finnish Ball Association.
Finska Boll Förbundet.
WALTER FLANDER, Helsingfors, Kasärng. 14 B.

Irish Football Association.
J. FERGUSON, Belfast, 1 Adelaïde Street.

Norwegian Football Association.
Norsk Fodbold Forbund.
H. W. BENNECKE, Kristiania.

Please will you take notice of the following changed address:
ANDRÉ ESPIR, Paris, 20 Rue de Longchamp (16ᵐᵉ).

C. A. W. HIRSCHMAN,
Hon. Secr. treas. F. I. F. A.

AMSTERDAM, 15ᵗʰ November 1907.

all issues concerning the regulation of international matches. FIFA was capable of regulating but not organising football.

At the fourth FIFA Congress in Amsterdam on 19 and 20 May 1907, Austria and Spain were represented. The first article of the statutes read as follows: 'FIFA consists of Associations which control football in their respective countries'. It was clear that FIFA granted membership to associations that were alone in controlling football in their country, or, as in Sweden's case, were the most influential. One thing remained to be decided. What meaning should be given to the term 'country'? Should a country only be one integrated in a regional state or could it be a territory of a federal state, such as a colony or an ex-colony in an unclear state of autonomy?

It was under these circumstances that the question was raised of how Bohemia should be treated. The Austrian delegate, Hugo Meisl, had unsuccessfully called for the Bohemian FA to be excluded on the grounds that Bohemia was an Austrian territory.

In November the Executive Committee, consisting of the President and the General Secretary Hirschmann, provisionally admitted the Associations of Finland, Ireland and Norway.

At the Vienna Congress on 7 and 8 June 1908, the proposed membership of Scotland and Ireland was rejected. If Scotland and Ireland had been allowed to join, Austria and Germany had threatened to request membership for all their confederate states, 26 and 12 associations respectively. On these grounds Austria obtained the exclusion of Bohemia. This demonstrat-

8 Daniel Woolfall. Guérin's successor and the English FIFA President from 1906 to 1918.

9 European-wide interest in FIFA. The circular announcing the Irish Football Association's provisional membership of FIFA in 1907.

10 Sport and Politics. Emperor William II having difficulty dealing with a shot from the Royal Engineers' team. British caricature from 1914.

GOAL!

WHAT THE
R.E.'s
ARE GOING TO DO.

F.G.LEWIN

10

ed FIFA's application of the rule regarding recognised international states.

In Vienna, FIFA faced a crisis. It was started in July 1907 by the formation of the Amateur Football Association (AFA), a dissident English amateur group. With the support of the USFSA, which was opposed to both the FA's support for professionalism and British linguistic imperialism, the AFA requested membership of FIFA. All the representatives, except the French, voted to turn down the request citing article 1 of the statutes. Despite the threat of a split, the French representative, Billy, underlined the affinities of the USFSA with the AFA, united by their commitment to amateurism. In vain he asked permission to organise matches with the clubs of the AFA. Only the representatives of Switzerland and Italy hesitated to reject his request.

(1908-1919)
British ascendancy

Following this disappointment, Robert Espir lost his position as Vice-President and the USFSA left FIFA – its own creation. European football was threatened as the Swiss and Italian football associations could little afford to give up their matches with the clubs of the USFSA. An Extraordinary Congress was held in Brussels in December 1908. It provisionally accepted the candidacy of another French sporting association: the Comité Français Interfédéral (CFI) which consisted of youth clubs and smaller leagues. However, Switzerland and Italy continued to play matches against the teams of the USFSA and were threatened with expulsion.

During the Budapest Congress on 30 and 31 May 1909 the issue of the USFSA reappeared due to the Italian Association represented by Espir. The Frenchman called for the right of the Italians, in this exceptional case, to

DIE FUSSBALLSPIELER BEIM KRONPRINZEN   Empfang auf der Schloßterrasse (rechts — mit den Schildmützen — die Deutschen, links Engländer und Ungarn)

11

VIE AU GRAND AIR

LE GARDIEN DU BUT!

12

play the teams of the USFSA. He was supported by the Swiss. This request was refused along with another for the use of French and German for all business. Unsurprisingly, Hungary's requested authorisation to hold matches against UIAFA teams was also refused. UIAFA (Union Internationale Amateur de Football Association) was a breakaway federation formed in March 1909 and composed of the AFA, USFSA and Bohemia.

13

TRENCH GOAL FOOTBALL
BRITISH DESIGN   BRITISH MADE

CORNER   BEHIND   BEHIND   CORNER

COUNT ZEPPELIN   RIGHT BACK   THE KAISER   LEFT BACK   VON SANDERS

RIGHT HALF   VON DER GOLTZ   CENTRE HALF   VON MOLTKE   LEFT HALF   VON ENVER PASHA

INSIDE RIGHT   VON HINDENBURG   INSIDE LEFT   VON BÜLOW

OUTSIDE RIGHT   CENTRE FORWARD   VON KLUCK   OUTSIDE LEFT

LITTLE WILLIE   VON TIRPITZ

KICK OFF   REGISTRATION APPLIED FOR

During the Milan Congress between 14–16 May 1910, the Hungarian FA renewed their request to play any amateur teams but were refused for a second time. At the same Congress, the CFI was officially admitted to FIFA. The domination of the British FA within FIFA was borne out by the admittance, against the statutes, of Scotland, Ireland and Wales. But the membership of South Africa, the first non-European association, placed the Federation at the head of a 'universal game' as Hirschmann termed it . FIFA was finally establishing its authority over the game of football, despite its origins as a privileged gentleman's club with no headquarters and no jurisdiction over either the laws of the game or the competitions themselves.

At the Dresden Congress on 4 and 5 June 1911, the German representatives cautiously put forward the suggestion that FIFA should eventually become the regulatory body for the laws of the game. President Woolfall and the FA were not prepared to consider such an idea. The Germans then asked if the FA could at the very least invite one member of the FIFA to sit on the International Board. The British were not ready and they replied with a flat refusal. However, by arranging the participation of one team per country at the Stockholm Olympic Games in 1912, FIFA started along the road which would lead to the total control of the world football tournament. This was the outstanding achievement of FIFA's short history.

The last Congresses before the Great War revealed German moves against the British hegemony. During the Stockholm Congress, 30 June and 1 July 1912, the German representatives called for more discipline regarding the problem of affiliations, noting that the associations of Chile, Argentina and even the United States, and the former Australian colonies were all members of the FA. The British partially gave way to this pressure and Argentina left the FA to join FIFA.

11 Football and the high life. The Swedish crown prince receives the German, British and Hungarian teams during the Stockholm Olympics (July 1912).

12 The sports press enters the war. Cover of the French sportsmen's weekly *La Vie au Grand Air*, December 1916.

13 Trench Football. After dribbling past the crown prince, Hindenburg or Moltke, the Kaiser is the last man to beat in this game of pocket billiards.

LA SUISSE (BUSER) A PROPOSÉ LA RÉSOLUTION SUIVANTE AU NOM DU BUREAU INTERNATIONAL DE LA PAIX DE BERNE. « LE XIE CONGRÈS DE LA F.I.F.A. RÉUNI À CHRISTIANIA LES 27 ET 28 JUIN 1914 SE DÉCLARE DÉSIREUX DE SOUTENIR TOUTE ACTION VISANT À

rapprocher les nations les unes des autres

ET À REMPLACER LA VIOLENCE PAR L'ARBITRAGE DANS LE RÈGLEMENT DE TOUS LES CONFLITS QUI POURRAIENT SURVENIR ENTRE ELLES. » ADOPTÉE À L'UNANIMITÉ.

FIFA, PROCÈS-VERBAL DU 11E CONGRÈS TENU À CHRISTIANIA, 27 & 28 JUIN 1914, p.10.

14 Jules Rimet, French gentleman. 1919.

15 Footballers became the stars of the Olympic games. The Spanish goalkeeper Zamora punches the ball clear during the quarter final between Belgium and Spain (3-1) at the Olympic Stadium in Anvers (29 August 1920).

16 The grand duchy of Luxembourg took part in the Olympic football tournament in Anvers (1920). From left to right: Koetz, Elter, Hamilius, Schmit, Ungeheuer, Leesch, Metzler, Langers, Schumacher and Massard.

Hirschmann was pleased with the return of the USFSA to FIFA in 1913 following its membership of the CFI, and above all at the announcement at the Copenhagen Congress that the FA would welcome two FIFA members onto the International Board. He was also proud of the 11 international teams that took part in the 1912 Olympics and the growth of the finances: 2022 Dutch florins compared to 491 in 1908. In 1914 there would be 2665. During the Copenhagen Congress the British delayed the convening of a meeting of international referees for a second time and hindered the creation of an international referees' association.

For its tenth anniversary, FIFA held its Congress in Norway at the end of June 1914. In the presence of over 30 representatives, including two future Presidents, Jules Rimet and R.W Seeldrayers, the British reasserted their linguistic domination. Despite this, the FIFA delegates did obtain the right to put forward their own representatives to the International Board.

By 1914 FIFA had non-European member associations such as South Africa, Chile, Canada and the United States. Yet three European countries were still to join: Portugal, Greece and Romania. The authority of FIFA was now well-established and had not been contested since the return of the USFSA and the disappearance of the AFA in England.

With a premonition of the horrors to come, FIFA's 1914 Congress called for arbitration instead of military action. During the Great War that followed football was still played, even at the Front during breaks in the fighting, and Hirschmann ensured FIFA business continued as usual. By April 1919, the Federation's funds had grown to 3546 florins and the Executive committee was able to provisionally welcome the membership of Portugal, Uruguay, Paraguay and Brazil.

(1919-1931)
A Global Organisation

After the Armistice, the football associations of the victorious countries called for a Congress without the defeated Central powers. The Executive Committee, presided over by Kornerup from Sweden following the death of Woolfall, opposed this idea referring to the statutes. The FA decided to renew relations only with those associations that refused to play against the former enemy countries (September 1919). Hirschmann and Kornerup objected to this stance due to its lack of political neutrality.

Baron de Laveleye, the second Vice-President, proposed that Germany, austria and Hungary should be struck from the list of affiliated associations enshrined in Article 1 of the statutes. But delegates from the countries joined together to request the right to play any country they wished. The allied countries met in Brussels and decided to no longer recognise any football associations that authorised matches against the defeated nations. However, by May 1920, only the British maintained this stance. In protest they withdrew from FIFA.

Hirschmann sought to postpone the next Congress as he was waiting for the Central powers to join the League of Nations. Both victorious and neutral FIFA members came together at Antwerp on 27 August 1920 at a meeting which coincided with the Olympic Games. It was decided to allow the neutral members freedom to decide who they played. However, the football associations of the victorious nations refused to play against the neutral nations if they decided to play against the defeated countries. Matches against the British were sanctioned despite their resignation from FIFA. Jules Rimet was

15 >

16 >

L'ÉQUIPE LUXEMBOURGEOISE

17   18

provisionally named as President assuming the post officially on 1 March 1921 and Hirschmann retained his position as General Secretary.

The first post-war Congress did not take place until
May 1923 in Geneva. Germany and Austria were not
present but Hungary was represented. There was as yet
no settled membership of the Federation. After various
membership changes, the Football Association of Ireland,
linked to the independence movement, had rejoined. The
FA made it clear that as far as it was concerned this sig-
nified the end of an amicable relationship with the continental association. Congress also increased FIFA's funds
by fixing the annual membership fee at 10 US dollars,
and a guaranteed minimum percentage of the gross revenue from all international fixtures would also be passed
on to the Federation.

In his report for the year 1923–24, Hirschmann noted
that all the continental European countries had joined,
which meant an increase from the original 6 to more than
40 members. This confirmed FIFA's place as the largest

sporting federation in the world, bringing together the
greatest number of athletes. FIFA also accepted the return
of the British, even though they refused to pay FIFA a
percentage of the revenue from their international matches. The FA also rejected all intervention in the relations
between the British associations. The intercontinental
aspect of FIFA was highlighted when Hirschmann suggested the appointment of a Vice-President from each
continent. Ambassador Buero, the representative for
Uruguay, had already asked for an Executive Committee
position for Latin America. As Spanish was the main language in South America, Spain suggested Spanish as an
official language of FIFA to encourage other South
American countries to join.

But it was the question of amateurism that dominated
the Congress. Following the example of the International
Olympic Committee (IOC), FIFA and the individual
national associations were constantly searching for an
agreed definition of the term 'amateur status'. The traditional point of view was that the player should meet all

19   20

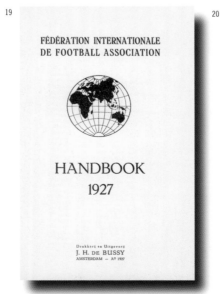

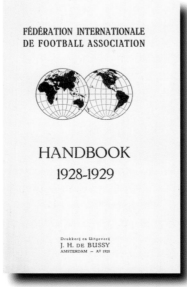

17 D. E. E. Buero,
Uruguayan ambassador
and FIFA Vice-President.

18 Monti, a powerful
midfielder, was an Italian-
Argentine who played for
Juventus and who won the
World Cup with the
Azzurri in 1934.

19/20 New FIFA logo in
1928. FIFA aimed to be a
global organisation and
wanted to inform the world.

21 Football's administrators
surround Jules Rimet, FIFA
President at the Amsterdam
Congress, 1928.

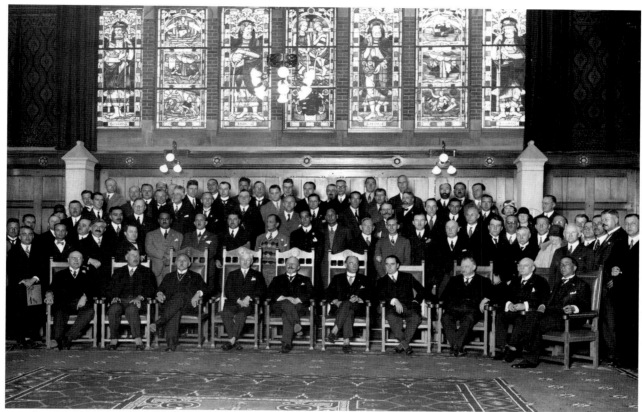

21

22 Starched collars and Persian rugs. An opulent setting to discuss the thorny issue of the definition of amateurism. Brussels, March 1926.

the costs of their participation. However Seeldrayers thought that playing football should not incur a material sacrifice, believing that this punished the poorly paid and he advocated payments for loss of earnings. FIFA agreed to recognise the professionalism that had developed in central Europe, but could not arrive at a definition of it acceptable to all members. The discussion was continued at future Congress meetings, but with little success. The debate was taken up with a vengeance in 1925, when finally Congress wisely chose to allow individual associations to decide the amount which could be paid for loss of earnings to their amateur players.

The IOC decided to turn a blind eye to these payments and allowed FIFA to organise the Olympic football tournament in Amsterdam in 1928. Football's importance was established during the tournament, which culminated in another victory for Uruguay following their success in Paris in 1924. The British stood firmly by their belief, restated during the Rome Congress in 1926, that a player was either entirely professional or amateur. They left FIFA again.

Exasperated by the potential consequences of this decision, FIFA created a commission to generate a plan for a world championships. This had the aim of estab-

lishing FIFA's independence from the IOC and the Olympic tournament and overcoming, once and for all, the question of amateurism versus professionalism. The first meeting of the commission was held in Zurich in February 1927.

During the 1925 Congress financial problems had become a pressing issue. Seeldrayers started by asking Hirschmann for a detailed statement of accounts and a budget proposal. Switzerland proposed that the Austrian Meisl should replace Hirschmann. At this point FIFA still did not have an office or any employees.

In 1927 FIFA continued to grow globally. The arrival of Cuba and Costa Rica gave the Federation a foothold in Central America. In 1928 FIFA accepted the creation of continental confederations such as that of South America. On the cover of the second edition of the FIFA Handbook (1928), instead of the usual one, two sides of the globe were depicted. From this point onwards all continents would be included. FIFA had also earned political recognition, shown by the welcome given to the representatives at the Amsterdam Congress in 1928 by a Dutch government minister.

Discussions between FIFA and the FA revealed that the British were not interested in rejoining the

Vom Fifa-Kongreß in Berlin

Obere Reihe: (von links) Eicher (Schweiz), Ing. Fischer (Ungarn), Rimet (Frankreich), Kartini (Süddeutschl.), Johanson (Schweden)
Untere Reihe: Linnemann (DFB.), Dr. Xandry (DFB.), Dr. Mauro (Italien), Meisl (Oesterreich), Duran (der Sprecher Spaniens)
(Für den Kicker gezeichnet von Fritz Lunzer) **25**

23 FIFA's first ladies. The wives of FIFA directors at the Budapest Congress in 1930.

24 Delegates pose for a photograph at the Berlin Congress, May 1931.

25 Typical FIFA Congress delegates as caricatured by the artists of *Kicker* (2 June 1931).

< 23

< 24

Federation, and intended to govern world football via the International Board (IFAB). FIFA rejected the idea that this authority, that is to say the British associations, should become the true governing body of world football. Seeldrayers was of the opinion that FIFA had already shown too much weakness in accepting the FA's management of the laws of the game.

FIFA recognised that the absence of the British was no longer an obstacle to becoming world football's governing body. Congresses became events; the Amsterdam Congress brought together 80 people. The souvenir book for the 25th anniversary in 1929 paid homage to the founders of the Federation and reviewed the achievements so far.

From the start of the 1920s, Congresses were inundated with issues that required resolution. The control and legislation governing the international movement of footballers was the primary function of FIFA. With the increasing migration of professional players from central Europe and later from Latin America, the development of new rules was necessary.

Undoubtedly, 1930 was a turning point for the Federation. The British associations continued to be a major problem as the other football associations could not ignore their existence. The FA did not openly make demands but by playing on internal differences within FIFA they unsettled the core of the Federation. At one point they demanded a special statute to cover the relations with the British associations and the ex-British

colonies, but they 'did not wish to join FIFA, under any conditions'.

At the Budapest Congress in June 1930 another debate about the functions of the Executive Committee took place. Meisl called for a complete restructuring of the Executive supported by Dr Pelikan (Czechoslovakia) and Dr Mauro (Italy). Mauro added that he thought there should be one single leader at the head of FIFA. The process was set in motion and other suggestions flooded in. Linnemann (Germany) proposed that FIFA should remain a community of interests for the national football associations and not a federation which issued orders to its members. He continued to suggest that FIFA should

26

26 Ivo Schricker, FIFA Vice-President in 1928. As full-time General Secretary Schricker became FIFA's key employee in November 1931.

27   28

only intervene on issues pertaining to the regulation of international matches, player transfers and the question of amateurism. Linnemann also called for the associations to be represented in relation to the number of their registered members. Mauro advocated the appointment of a permanent Secretary in Zurich and closer relations with non-European football associations (Executive Committee 15 March 1931 in Paris).

The Berlin Congress in May 1931 confirmed that FIFA was satisfied to be a union of independent football associations, and would not get involved with the internal affairs of these associations.

A shake-up occurred in December when the directors of FIFA learnt that it had suffered major financial losses as the result of speculation by Hirschmann. Hirschmann himself had been ruined by the Depression and resigned his position. The Dutch association sought to make up the financial shortfall. FIFA did not pursue any legal proceedings in view of Hirschmann's previous voluntary work for the Federation, and even saw fit to pay him a life annuity. This serious episode hastened the restructuring of the Federation. Ivo Schricker, a skilled German ex-player and the then Vice-President, was named as provisional Secretary from the 1 November 1931. It was the end of an era.

27 FIFA started to settle in Zurich.
FIFA's first headquarters
from 1932 to 1954 was
77 Bahnhofstrasse. A modern
office in a large building.

28 Roman grandeur.
The opening of the Rome
Congress at the Capitol, 24 May
1934.

(1931-1939)
Maturity

The Stockholm Congress in May 1932 implemented major changes to the Statutes. The Executive Committee would henceforth be made up of a President, two Vice-Presidents, and six members, one of whom had responsibility for the Federation's finances. Two financial auditors would independently check the accounts, which until this time had been held at various banks. Stringency was the order of the day. To reduce costs, Congress would only meet every two years. The headquarters would be situated in Zurich due to its central location, good rail connections and Switzerland's neutrality. The headquarters were modest, only two rooms for Schricker and his deputy who now served 50 associations. Even though the office was small, the building was situated on the prestigious Bahnhofstrasse. FIFA had eventually become a regulatory organisation driven by a principle of decentralisation and independence of the member associations.

The Rome Congress in May 1934 was a more sedate affair. Times had changed and the representatives discussed the financial report for an entire session. The accounts had been put in order following the receipt of 1% of all international match revenues; this equalled 17,902 Swiss francs in 1932 and 25,000 in 1933.

The number of international matches was growing: 73 in 1934 without including those of the World Cup in Italy, and 106 in 1935. The World Cup earned FIFA 55,778 Swiss francs and the matches of 1935 only 50,000. The financial importance of the World Cup was already apparent and was confirmed by the 1938 tournament. Because of the global depression, FIFA found it increasingly difficult to obtain the payments due from member associations, including annual subscriptions. Nevertheless, the

29

30

29 A relaxed atmosphere at the Paris Congress in 1938.

30 An international group. The FIFA Executive Committee, 1934.

31 Football hostage to the Spanish Civil War. Players of the nationalist team play Salazar's Portugal team. 16 December 1937.

bank balance increased to almost 80,000 Swiss francs in 1935, which was invested in gold, and international bonds in various western European financial markets.

The Executive Committee was asked to prepare an overhaul of relations with the South American confederation where problems still existed. They also approached the issue of the intrusion of agents and other intermediaries during the transfer of players and organisation of matches. The Berlin Congress in August 1936 decided to ban their involvement.

After this Congress a representative from the South American football associations was admitted to the

Executive Committee. But when he suggested the creation of five autonomous continental confederations FIFA rejected the idea. The Federation suspected that this would divest the organisation of its powers. Apart from this, discussions with Latin America were strained as internal disagreements there were rife: Argentina left the Confederación in 1937. At the Paris Congress in 1938 the Argentinian representative joined the Executive Committee.

Throughout the 1930s Congress and the Executive Committee spent most of their time discussing and examining the problem of international player transfers, which had taken precedence over the issue of amateurism. FIFA eventually established the principle that no association could qualify a player from another association unless that player was in possession of a transfer certificate provided by the association they were leaving. There remained however, countless contentious and unique cases for FIFA to examine.

Over these years the board of FIFA, a sort of gentlemen's club, was stable with Jules Rimet, Mauro and Seeldrayers as uncontested President and Vice-Presidents respectively. The other members formed a very stable phalanx. Bauwens the German and Delaunay the Frenchman were permanent members of the International Board. As for Schricker, he was secretary

31

32

33

32 Caricature in the French weekly *Football* 16 March 1933, before a match between Germany and France. Reproduced a week later in *Kicker*.

33 Keeping a fair distance or turning a blind eye? Schricker, FIFA's General Secretary and his deputy Rijnink in front of the FIFA flag during the Second World War.

to 55 associations in 1939. No important dispute had faced the men whom Rimet had skilfully assembled with his legendary way with words. Nevertheless, it was possible to see a certain impatience from Seeldrayers and Mauro regarding his role. They were reticent about Rimet's solitary journey to Latin America in an attempt to establish an agreement with that increasingly influential stronghold of world football.

(1939-1945)
FIFA and the Second World War

From this point, political issues were an increasing problem due to German aggression. Football associations were created and dissolved while others fragmented. The fact that FIFA was based in Switzerland allowed the organisation to continue its business to a certain extent but it owed much to the neutral perseverance of Ivo Schricker. His copious correspondence with the members of the Executive Committee did not make the slightest reference to the events of the war. Meetings in Zurich were exceptional. Bauwens, the representative of the country that controlled the movement of people and traffic around Europe, did not seek to favour FIFA, so Congress could no longer convene. Sporting activity was limited to 28 international matches in Europe in 1940 and 18 in 1941. From 1941 onwards, mail took many months to arrive at its destination and communication became increasingly difficult. By 1944 FIFA was paralysed and its resources were exhausted.

At the end of the war in 1945 there had been no contact with the football associations in eastern Europe since 1940. Associations outside of Europe, in countries at war such as China, Japan and the Philippines

34

were also no longer contactable. FIFA's funds had fallen to 130,016 Swiss francs in December 1944 due to the loss of membership fees, revenue from international matches, and the cancellation of the World Cup in 1942. More importantly, the South American confederation sought to profit from the situation by attempting to take control of the heart of FIFA. The meeting of the Confederación in January 1945 appointed Augustin Matienzo as their representative to FIFA. As such, he became a statutory member of the Executive Committee. In fact he became the only legitimate member of FIFA's highest authority as the South American congress pointed out that the mandate for all the other members had expired in 1942. The Confederación therefore insisted that Matienzo should be the provisional President of FIFA until the next Congress could be held. Following this, Matienzo asked Schricker for the addresses of all the associations with the intention of inviting their representatives to meet in Montevideo. Furthermore, he placed the suggestion that Brazil host the 1950 World Cup on the agenda of this congress. The South American Confederation also desired the amalgamation of the three existing American confederations.

Other disruptions were to be expected in this year (1945) and those that followed.

FIFA AND THE DAWN OF PROFESSIONALISM

Following the First World War, players around Europe began to receive payment for playing football.

1

2

The practice of shamateurism (whereby amateur players received payment under the counter for playing football) spread and professional leagues were soon set up in central European countries following the British model. These professional leagues were a clear success, being established in Austria in 1924, and over the following years in Czechoslovakia and Hungary. With the arrival of a large contingent of cheap yet well-known and skilled English players, the effects of market forces on football spread like wildfire across Europe. National professional leagues were created in Italy (1929), Spain (1930) and France (1932). In Germany the plan for a professional league was abandoned after Hitler came to power. Despite major internal power struggles,

Argentina, Uruguay and Brazil also established professional championships during the 1930s.

In a few years, just about everywhere football players became public figures. The professional leagues that had developed around the globe were widely reported on by newspapers and a radio hungry for sensation. Generally, professional football had been a national concern, but the creation of professional leagues in countries with no history of football soon necessitated the intervention of the international authorities. In the face of the somewhat chaotic development of professionalism, FIFA was forced to intervene and occasionally to deal severely with clubs whose directors often seemed to ignore the Federation's Statutes.

1 Reunions after the trials of war. The first Executive Committee meeting in Zurich 10 December 1945. From left to right: Eir (Denmark), Lotsy (Netherlands), Schricker (General Secretary), Rimet (France), Seeldrayers (Belgium), Pelikan (Czechoslovakia).

2 Jules Rimet contemplates his life's work at the start of the 1950s.

3 Supporters celebrate Independiente winning the Argentinian championship in 1939.

3

4 Despite the depression, Brazilian stadiums were full. Fluminense's stadium in 1935.

The Colombian experience

In Latin America by the end of the Second World War, football had achieved unprecedented popularity. As Europe tore itself apart, South American crowds crammed into stadiums to cheer on their idols. In Argentina, matches between the big clubs were a spectacle watched by tens of thousands of spectators. The construction of new stadiums at the start of the 1940s and the arrival of teams who played attractive football, such as the *Máquina* of River Plate, ignited this new passion for football. With a forward line composed of Muñoz, Morena, Pedernera, Lanbruna and Loustau, River Plate ran like a well-oiled machine. Elsewhere the popularity of the game and the Argentinian style spread across the whole subcontinent.

Regular use of aeroplanes for transport to fixtures and a desire to play the Argentinian stars, prompted many South American directors to organise friendly matches with the professional teams from Buenos Aires. This was why, on 18 January 1948 in Bogotá, 12,000 spectators, a record attendance for the country, were able to watch the victory of a local club from Santa Fé against Vélez Sarsfield from Buenos Aires. The success of the fixture gave local businessmen the idea to recruit foreign players to create a Columbian professional league. They saw that sporting entertainment could become a profitable activity.

In 1948, Colombia was going through one of the darker periods of its history. The liberal caudillo Jorge Eliécer Gaitán was assassinated in April. The repression which followed, known as Bogotazo, took the lives of many tens of thousands of people. Despite all this,

the project to create an independent professional league took shape and began a few months later.

The Colombian football association (Adefútbol) had its headquarters on the Atlantic coast at Barranquilla, while the Liga Mayor de Fútbol (Dimayor) chose the capital Bogotá. Initially ten clubs signed up to the new league. To make the project workable, its directors managed to persuade the Colombian national airline, Avianca, to allow the Dimayor a special rate of fifty-five per cent off the normal fares.

The first championship of the Dimayor started in August 1948 and was a popular success, mainly due to strong support from both the newspapers and radio. As all political reporting was banned, professional football became the favourite subject of the media: *'contribuyó a evitar la disolución de la patria, en momentos de una grave crisis interna. Cataplasma providencial en la herida (…) congeló pasiones fratricidas y abrió ante un pueblo despesperado, estadiós de paz.'* (Football is helping to avoid the dissolution of the country in these times of serious internal crisis, and is a healing agent… allowing fratricidal passions to be temporarily put aside, and opening stadiums of peace to a desperate population.) The Senate of Colombia, aware of the impact of football on public opinion, decided to award the championship winning team a prize of 10,000 pesos. Strengthened by public support, the Dimayor sought to confirm its established position by importing recognised overseas players.

At the same time in Argentina and Uruguay, professional football was rocked by an unprecedented dispute. During the autumn of 1948 professional players went on strike demanding improved working conditions, better pay and, above all, freedom of employment. Due mainly to the intransigence of the league bosses the dispute was

drawn out. When the Argentinian manager of the Millonarios de Bogotá offered Adolfo Pedernera, one of the stars of Porteño, the chance to join him in Columbia the affair generated a great deal of attention. In a few weeks more than fifty Argentinian professionals who were in dispute with their clubs had arrived in Colombia. Although the Dimayor offered the foreign players it recruited legally binding employment contracts it showed no respect for FIFA's rules. No compensation was paid to the clubs for whom the players had been originally contracted to play, and no international transfer papers were requested, both of which FIFA required. In the spring of 1949, the relations between the Dimayor and the Federation reached the point of no return. The clubs, believing their players were under contract only to them, refused to release them to participate in the South American championship (Copa America) which was due to take place in Rio de Janeiro.

As a result, the Colombian football association decided to expel the Dimayor. At the congress of the South

7

8

American Confederation (CONMEBOL) in Rio, Bernard Jaramillo, the representative of Adefútbol, justified the expulsion on the grounds of indiscipline, refusal to take notice of FIFA statutes and because their vision of football was the pursuit of profit rather than the good of the sport. The very same day, the continental federation decided unanimously to follow the lead of the Colombian association and expelled the Dimayor saying: *'la insólita actitud configura plenamente un acto de insubordinación, lo que non se puede tolerar'*. (This strange attitude represents an act of intolerable insubordination.)

Far from resolving the situation, the expulsion freed the clubs of the Dimayor from all statutory constraints and intensified their recruitment from abroad, destabilising several national associations. The league initially had ten teams, but by 1950 there were eighteen and the number of foreign players in Colombia was growing. Before the expulsion the Dimayor had had thirty-two foreign players; only two years later there was ten times this figure – the league did not impose any restrictions on the number of foreign players per team. In contrast to this laxity and in an attempt to improve the quality of the spectacle, the players were made to wear numbered shirts, professional English referees were employed

and two substitutes per match were authorised.

In Colombia this period of football was evocatively known as *'El Dorado'*. The dazzling version of football played was symbolised by the *'Ballet Azul'* of the Millonarios of Bogotá. In the playing ranks alongside Pedernera were two of the best footballers in the world at that time: Alfredo Di Stefano and Nestor Rossi. Although idolised in the stadiums and the Colombian press, FIFA saw the players of the Dimayor as outlaws. The Independiente de Medellín, rechristened *'Danza del Sol'* (Sun Dance), had twelve of the best Peruvian players in their team. Fifteen Hungarian players, who were disqualified by the Hungarian FA for leaving their country clandestinely, were nevertheless signed by Deportivo Samarios of Santa Marta. Alfredo Di Stefano recalled that: *'Era curioso ver cómo, dependiendo de las nacionalidades, nos distribuián por ciudades: las uruguayos en Cucutá, los argentinos sobre todo en Bogotá, los Brasileños en barranquilla, los peruanos en Cali y los engleses en Santa Fé. En el Universidad de Bogotá eran todos ticos, constarricences, y jugaban de maravilla la pelota.'* (It was strange how the players were distributed in towns according to nationality: the Uruguayans in Cucutá, Argentinians mostly in Bogotá, Brazilians in Barranquilla, Peruvians in Cali

dération Internationale de Football Association

Dear Sirs,

Suspension of Players.

We would inform you that the National Associations set out below have suspended the following of their former players:-

Names of Players	Former Clubs

Asociaciòn del Futbol Argentino

1) Laureano R. Feliciani	-----
2) Miguel A. Lettieri	-----
3) Alejandro Mur	-----
4) Enrique M. Pesarini	-----
5) Elger Poelo Alarcon	-----
6) Eusebio Chamorro	-----
7) Roberto Martinez	

Federaciòn Nacional de Futbol, Costa Rica

1) Isaac Jimenez (5 years)	C.S. Cartagines

The Football Association

1) C. Mitten (31st December 1951)	-----
2) G. Mountford (3rd September 1951)	-----

Federazione Italiana Giuoco Calcio

	A.G. Nocerina, Nocera Inferiore
1) Busidoni Mario	A.C. San Donà di Piave
2) Piccoli Ugo	" " "
3) Sandrin Silla	" " "
4) De Paulis Renato	" " "
5) Momesso Alessandro	" " "
6) Cibin Amedeo	" " "

Oesterreichischer Fussball-Bund

	First Vienna F.C.
1) Ernst Sabetitsch	" " "
2) Rudolf Strittich	

In accordance with Art.18 of the F.I.F.A. Statutes, suspension by National Associations must be strictly observed and players who have been suspended cannot be registered with any other club.

9 FIFA became involved in the Colombian crisis: A circular letter written on 80 August 1951, suspending foreign players from the rebel Dimayor league.

10 1948, Amsterdam. An enlarged Executive Committee welcomes the British and Russian representatives. From left to right: H.E. Manuel Bianchi (Chile), K.J.J. Lotsy (Netherlands), L. Frederiksen (Denmark), A. Drewry (England), R.W. Seeldrayers (Belgium), J. Rimet (France), I. Schricker (General Secretary), R.A. Kirkwood (Scotland), W.A. Granatkin (USSR), M. Andrejevic (Yugoslavia), J. Krebs (Switzerland), V. Valousek (Czechoslovakia).

10

and the English in Santa Fé. At the University of Bogotá all the players were Ticos from Costa Rica who played beautifully on the ball.)

What was happening in Colombia threatened to spread, as is shown by the correspondence with other national associations such as the Mexican football association. However, during 1949 the FIFA Executive did not seem to be aware of the effect the rebellion in Colombia was having on the rest of the American continent. European issues such as the membership of Saarland and the readmission of Germany to FIFA occupied all of its energies. Relations at the heart of the Federation between the Europeans and the South Americans had been strained since the war. The return of the British and the arrival of the Soviets, who were immediately given two of the four Vice-Presidencies was taken as an insult by the CONMEBOL. Football in Latin American had never been so popular and it was felt that the loyalty of the region to FIFA during the war had contributed largely to FIFA's survival. At a time when the associations needed total support from the international federation to re-establish their authority over the opposing faction in Colombia, the South American federation felt that FIFA wasn't doing enough.

Officially, FIFA showed its support by suspending the rebel players and imposing a ban on matches between the teams of the Dimayor and teams affiliated to FIFA.

However, the Federation delayed direct involvement in the resolution of the situation. In protest, Argentina, supported by the Peronist government and considered by many to be one of the best teams in the world, refused to take part in the qualification matches for the World Cup due to take place in Brazil the following year. Peru, unable to select its best players, refused to play its match against Uruguay. All the while, the Dimayor continued to prosper. The star club, Millonarios de Bogotá, played fantastic football that was enjoyed by ever-increasing crowds. Ivo Schricker wrote to Rimet: 'In Colombia the Bogota DiMayor league, with the Millonarios club, have left the Colombian FA and are organising spectacular matches – almost all of the best players from Argentina and other countries have left their Associations to become well-paid performers in the Bogotá circus'.

Even ignoring the commercial element of the Dimayor, which would have shocked the FIFA chiefs who were still committed to the ideal of amateurism, FIFA had never been faced with such a schism. When the members of the Executive Committee arrived in Brazil for the World Cup, they were able to appreciate the level of trauma caused by the Colombian rebellion. By this time the Colombian problem had spread beyond South America. Even some English professionals, such as the international players Franklin and Mitten, had joined the ranks of the dissidents. Finally, in 1950, when three Uruguayan

< 9

11 The arrival of Nestor Raul Rossi and Alfredo Di Stefano in Colombian 'Eldorado', 1949.

12 Ottorino Barassi. The Italian dealt with important matters for FIFA, and here he checks the weight of the balls to be used for the World Cup in 1934.

13 An expensive trip. On his return to Great Britain in 1950, Neil Franklin is suspended for four months after leaving his club, Stoke City, to play in the Colombian league.

11

12

players, recent winners of the Jules Rimet Cup, left Uruguay to join the rebels in Colombia, FIFA felt duty bound to intervene. During the meeting of the Executive Committee in Zurich in December 1950, the Colombian problem was investigated for the first time. It was decided to send three representatives to Bogotá *'to resolve the differences between the "Division Mayor de Fútbol profesional de Bogotá" and the Federación Colombiana de Fútbol. The associations of South America appreciate the intervention of FIFA which aims to restore unity in Colombian football.'* The three-man delegation comprised the Brazilian Vice-President of FIFA, Aranha, the Chilean President of the CONMEBOL, Luis Valenzuela, and Barassi, the Italian engineer.

The intervention was even more justified as the isolation of the Dimayor had started to reveal signs of weakness. Following the expulsion of the La Paz professional league and its international players from the Bolivian Football Association, these players invited the top Colombian clubs to the Bolivian capital, where they were subjected to a demonstration of attacking football which was acclaimed by the spectators in the sold-out stadiums. On his return from Colombia, Barassi presented his findings to members of the Executive Committee in Barcelona: *'The Dimayor has agreed that from now on it will ensure that its clubs respect FIFA rules regarding the transfer of players. It is hoped that an arrangement can be made to ensure that the compensation requested by the club of origin is not excessive with regard to transfers that have already taken place.'* By seizing the initiative and assuming the role of mediator, FIFA reaffirmed its position in South America. Determined to take control of the proceedings, the Executive Committee gave its three negotiators a mandate to resolve the conflict permanently. In August, Barassi had to dampen the optimism of his colleagues: *'Few players have been presented following the signing of the memorandum in Colombia. No emissary from the Dimayor has gone to Argentina. However, Argentinian players have been sought and transferred by the Argentines who are already playing in Colombia. The situation is no better in Argentina and little money has been received by the clubs.'*

Eventually, due to the mediation of FIFA, an agreement was signed on 11 September 1951, and was ratified at an Exceptional meeting of the CONMEBOL in Lima in October of that year. Under the terms of the agreement, the Dimayor was reintegrated into the Colombian FA. The players would remain with their Colombian clubs until the end of 1953, at which date they would have to rejoin their former clubs. The Colombian clubs were not allowed to collect compensation in the event of further transfers, this would be paid to the club of origin.

13

FIFA had resolved its most serious crisis yet. Time and time again, the national associations had made moves to withdraw from FIFA and had asked for an independent federation of South America. In Europe it is clear that the Scandinavian associations, for example, were focussed on East-West relations and did not understand the importance of the Colombian situation, nor that of South American football more generally. In 1953 a top-ranking Finnish official wrote to Gassmann, the new Secretary General of FIFA, *'I hope that you will reduce the excessive influence of the South Americans'*.

In the midst of the crisis, a split seemed inevitable. By moving away from its Eurocentric focus and by becoming directly involved, FIFA was able to establish its legitimacy in South America. FIFA had to draw lessons from the Colombian experience and force national associations to control effectively their professional leagues. Dr Mauro considered that *'the events in Colombia are an advance warning of possible conflicts with professional football. FIFA should defend itself against this danger and put in place measures to counter the threat.'*

Hungarian Dissidents

At the same time as these events, the transfer of the Hungarian international Laszlo Kubala to FC Barcelona had started a 'cold war' in the transfer market for professional players. Laszlo Kubala, a Czechoslovakian, had moved to Hungary where he played for the Hungarian National team. In 1949 he left Hungary clandestinely to go to Spain via Italy. Accused of borrowing large sums of money from his previous club – Vasas of Budapest – Kubala was suspended for life by the Hungarian association and in his absence was sentenced to imprisonment for fraud. This started a tug of war between the Spanish and the Hungarian Football Associations with FIFA as referee. The case was a delicate one. Article 18 of the FIFA regulations stipulated: *'National Associations being members of the Federation shall recognise each other's suspensions without examining the reasons thereof'*. Arguing that *'la suspension a été prononcée uniquement pour des raisons politiques'* (the suspension was made for purely political reasons) the Spanish FA *'refuse catégoriquement de se*

14

soumettre à l'article 18 des statuts de la FIFA' (categorically refuses to comply with Article 18 of the statutes). The Hungarians responded on ethical and moral grounds, describing Kubala as a man *'aux moeurs dépravées, noceur, batailleur, qui a délaissé sa patrie, son club et ses parents sans aucun travail ou aide matériel* (sic)' (a depraved and immoral individual, who leads a debauched and violent life. He left his country, his club and his family without hesitation). Despite the international suspension which was imposed, he signed for FC Barcelona and was supported by the Spanish government. As a naturalised Spaniard, he also played for the Spanish national team in friendly matches. Summoned by FIFA to explain the situation, the President of the Spanish FA stated that Kubala was qualified to play by *'autorisation supérieure et sans que nous eussions aucune puissance morale pour nous y opposer'* (a higher authority that we have no moral power to oppose). Taking into consideration the complexity of the affair and the quality of the player, who had rapidly become one of the finest players of the time, FIFA hesitated. Although the Eastern European associations requested the suspension of the Spanish FA, which was guilty of ignoring international transfer rules, FIFA refused. The

15

14 Kubala puts a penalty past the English goalkeeper Gil Merrick. Despite protests from the Hungarian FA, Kubala featured in the FIFA team that faced England in the match played to celebrate the 90th anniversary of the English FA on the 21 October 1953. The match finished 4-4.

15 A Cold War drama. Poster for the Spanish film '*Kubala! Champions looking for peace*' made in 1955.

16 Kubala at work, playing for FC Barcelona during the return leg match in the Inter-Cities Fairs Cup against Basle 6 January 1959. FC Barcelona won 5-2.

17 Di Stefano (right) and Kubala (left), naturalised Spaniards and part of the Spanish national team, juggling a football during a training session in the Colombes stadium, before a match against France, March 1958.

16

boundaries between sport, politics and economics had become confused and FIFA was compelled to become involved in the arbitration of disputes for which it was not properly prepared. The Kubala affair was full of contradictions. While it remained unresolved, Kubala was chosen to play for a FIFA XI against England in 1953. However, he was still not allowed to participate in the qualification matches for the 1954 World Cup, during which Turkey eliminated Spain. The day after this defeat, the Spanish member of the Executive wrote an antagonistic letter to President Rimet accusing FIFA of '*ne pas avoir autorisé le joueur et anti-communiste Ladislao Kubala à participer à ces rencontres pour ne pas se brouiller avec*

l'Association hongroise, les raisons économiques de la participation de la Hongrie en Suisse ayant été plus fortes que la réparation d'une injustice' (not having authorised Ladislao Kubala, the anti-communist player, to participate in these matches to appease the Hungarian FA, as the economic importance of Hungary's participation in Switzerland was more important than righting an injustice). Clearly annoyed, Rimet refused to consider the issue from a political perspective: '*Vous dites "l'anti-communiste" Kubala. Je ne vous suivrai pas sur ce terrain, pas plus que je n'ai suivi telle Fédération de l'Est qui demandait l'exclusion de l'Espagne "fasciste"*' (You say that Kubala is an 'anti-communist'. I will not enter into a debate about this issue, as

17

18

I have not spoken to any Eastern European FAs regarding the possible exclusion of 'fascist' Spain.) Rimet reiterated the moral argument *'Kubala, joueur de qualité reconnue, aurait simplement recherché hors de chez lui des avantages d'ordre matériel qu'il était assuré d'obtenir à l'étranger.'* (Kubala, a player of recognised quality, has left his country of birth to seek material gain). Following the Kubala affair, Congress met in Berne and FIFA adopted new statutes to modify Article 18 and oblige football associations to justify any suspensions which they imposed.

In 1956, the problem of Hungarian exiles arose again after the Soviet invasion of Hungary. There were 240 football players from the first and second divisions among the Hungarian refugees. All the players from the Honved team, the elite of Hungarian football, were now outside Hungary. Initially, Arthur Drewry, the FIFA President, asked the General Secretary to remain calm. *'I feel it is too soon to circulate our associations on this matter'*. However, a few weeks later the affair became more serious. Requests for certification arrived in Zurich from more than fifteen countries. Gassmann hesitated to make a decision: *'je n'ai engagé la*

FIFA d'aucune façon pas plus que moi personnellement'. (I have not committed FIFA any more than myself.) Honved, summoned to return to Hungary, organised a tournament in South America. Despite opposition from FIFA and the Brazilian football association, Honved played matches against Flamengo and Botafogo in order to demonstrate their opposition to communism in front of the President of the Brazilian Republic and various members of the government.

The United Nations High Commissioner for refugees was frequently consulted. While the Hungarian football association refused to provide transfer certificates, it was necessary to differentiate between the genuine political exiles and the players who had 'taken advantage' of the troubles to escape Hungary and sign lucrative professional contracts in western countries. Among the fugitives were many finalists from the previous World Cup, such as Puskas, Czibor and Kocsis, all three recruited without transfer by Spanish clubs Barcelona and Real Madrid.

Eventually an agreement was made which imposed a one-year suspension on the Honved players for having

19

organised a tournament against FIFA's wishes, and another year of suspension for failing to possess transfer certificates. All other exiled players from the first and second division were suspended for one year and, in an exception to FIFA's rules, exiled players from the regional Hungarian leagues were qualified from July 1957. Once again, FIFA had sought to uphold its rules, but had been forced to accept political and economic reality.

18 The Honved team during a period of Hungarian success (1952).

19 Five Stars. The Real Madrid forwards in June 1959. From left to right: Kopa (France), Rial (Spain), Di Stefano (originally from Argentina), Puskas (exiled Hungarian) and Gento.

20 Material and family success for an exile. Puskas with his daughter in his apartment in Madrid.

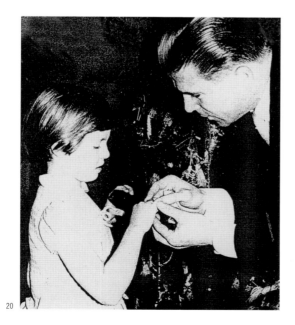

20

Australian 'Emigrants'

In 1959 an affair similar to that in Colombia developed in Australia. The formation of an independent league in New South Wales that recruited Austrian, Dutch and Israeli professional players without transfer certificates immediately provoked the FIFA Executive to impose its authority. Alerted by complaints from the home football associations of the emigrés, FIFA ordered the Australian FA to resolve the problem as soon as possible as the Federation had no control over the activities of a dissident league. Strengthened by its experience with the problems in Colombia, FIFA took drastic action and excluded the Australian FA at the 1960 Rome Congress *'aussi longtemps qu'elle n'aura pas rétabli l'ordre dans son association et donné au Comité Exécutif la déclaration écrite de respecter à l'avenir les Statuts et le Règlement et de s'y conformer sans réserve'* (until such time as order has been restored within the FA, and the Executive Committee is given written assurance that in future it will respect the Statutes and rules without exception). The leadership of the Australian FA was quick to explain that the newly arrived players were 'genuine migrants' who had arrived in Australia to start a new life, and that playing football was their secondary occupation. Secretary General Käser commented that in FIFA's rules, nothing justified the attitude of the

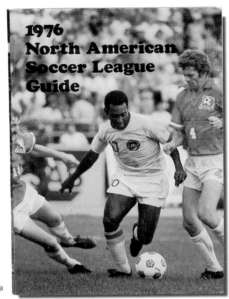

21 a

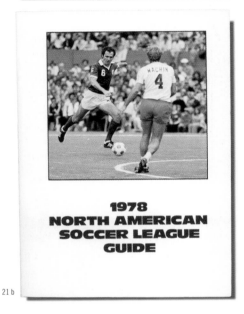

1978
NORTH AMERICAN
SOCCER LEAGUE
GUIDE

21 b

Australian FA. *'The questions of all the transfers are governed without exceptions by the Statutes and Regulations of FIFA as far as a player's change from one National Association to another is concerned… It would be an error on your side to believe that only Australia has immigrants. There is one more thing: the Austrian and Dutch players – to mention only these – did not immigrate to Australia and incidentally become members of a football club. On the contrary, you wanted to recruit good football players in Europe and made them look like immigrants. Thus you thought you had the the right to overlook the existing regulations.'* As can be seen in the note from the Secretary of the Austrian FA, *'Der gegenseitige Spielerschutz ist das Fundament der FIFA'* (reciprocal protection of players is the very foundation of FIFA). Dr Barassi, still Vice-President of FIFA, called a meeting in Zurich in August 1961 to iron out the differences. It was not successful. The return of the majority of the migrant players to their original associations the following year resolved an incident that had threatened to embarrass the new President of FIFA, Sir Stanley

Rous. He was close to the Australian FA and had no desire to exclude a Commonwealth Association from FIFA.

Questions related to professionalism occupied many other national associations. In Mexico, despite the often difficult co-existence of both professional and amateur players within the association, the Mexican FA strove to achieve *'un gran armonia entre los dos elementos que trabajan por el engrandecimiento del fútbol mexicano'* (harmony between both professionals and amateurs who work towards the growth of Mexican football). In 1956, Gassmann, the FIFA Secretary General, received two curious questions from the Thailand football associations. Should an amateur footballer who had fought as a professional boxer be classed as a professional? Also, how should a professional actor be treated? As a performer should he be treated as a professional?

In his reply Gassmann, obviously surprised by the questions, placed the ball firmly in the national associations court: *'Our amateur definition does not provide for this case. We do not think, however, that he should be considered to be a professional, as he did not get money for playing football. In view of the fact that there is no provision for this case in the definition of FIFA, it is up to your association to decide'.* Surprisingly, he specified with regard to actors that: *'if the player has received money for playing football in a film then he must be considered as a professional football player'.*

In the 1950s, many small football associations had understood the FIFA message and attempted to establish their own professional leagues rather than fall prey to 'rogue' leagues which had the potential to destabilise them and in extreme cases prompt their expulsion from FIFA. Requests for information about how to set up professional leagues were received from Costa Rica, Guatemala and Hong Kong. In order to avoid internal conflicts, FIFA advised these associations to contact other national associations who ran professional leagues. Disputes between professional leagues and the national FA were one of the characteristics of football in the United States where Soccer had experienced difficulties in becoming established and where the FA had no control over the development of the game.

American peculiarities

Since the 1920s many professional leagues had been created in the United States independently of the national FA. In addition to non-payment of international transfer fees, the American leagues had developed their own interpretations of the rules of the game.

For a long time professional teams were almost exclusively made up of foreign players, which was not approved of by Stanley Rous: *'Coaching the natives until they are sufficiently good to earn their living or become part-time is the answer'*. FIFA asked the national associations to suspend all players that had moved to America to play in 'rogue' leagues. *'In bezug auf Spieler und Trainer, die zu diesen wilden Profis gehen wollen, liege es in der Macht des norwegischen Verbandes, die Spieler... zu sperren und diese Suspension gegebenfalls durch die FIFA auf alle anderen Verbände auszudehnen.'* (The Norwegian association reserves the right to suspend players and coaches who wish to join these rogue leagues, and to inform all FIFA members of any such suspensions). Käser publicly disapproved of the American approach: *'It is purely money. The sport has no value at all. It is show, it is a commercial approach.'*

From the copious correspondence between FIFA and the Americans, it is apparent that FIFA was annoyed with the American way, yet keen to see football develop in the United States as around the rest of the globe. In Zurich, no one could understand the incessant desire of the American leagues to modify the rules of football to make the game more attractive and more American. From widening the goal and increasing the number of substitutes allowed during a game, to the creation of a special offside line thirty yards from the goal line, the Americans systematically infringed the universal rules until the 1990s. Even Henry Kissinger, the former American Secretary of State, tried to justify the American peculiarities. Kissinger was passionate about football and became Honorary President of the American professional league.

Relations between FIFA and the United States FA improved after the success of the football tournament at the Los Angeles Olympic Games in 1984, the successful growth of women's football and, towards the end of the twentieth century, the creation of a professional league (MLS) which involved many home grown players. Following decolonisation, the question of professionalism had made relations with African countries very difficult. On the one hand, the African football associations were hostile to official payment of players and had complained to FIFA regarding the lack of cooperation from the European associations that refused to

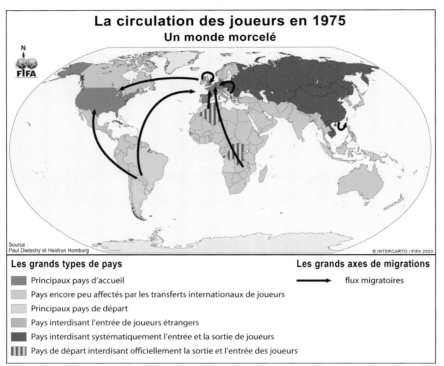

La circulation des joueurs en 1975
Un monde morcelé

Source :
Paul Dietschy et Heidrun Homburg

© INTERCARTO / FIFA 2003

Les grands types de pays

- Principaux pays d'accueil
- Pays encore peu affectés par les transferts internationaux de joueurs
- Principaux pays de départ
- Pays interdisant l'entrée de joueurs étrangers
- Pays interdisant systématiquement l'entrée et la sortie de joueurs
- Pays de départ interdisant officiellement la sortie et l'entrée des joueurs

Les grands axes de migrations

→ flux migratoires

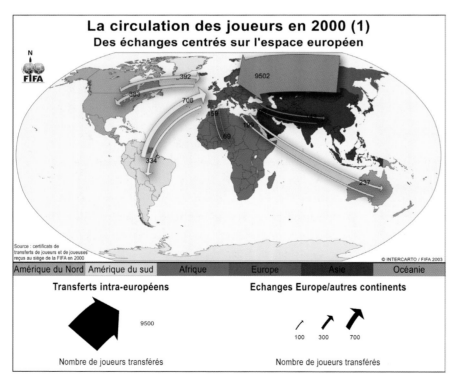

La circulation des joueurs en 2000 (1)
Des échanges centrés sur l'espace européen

Source : certificats de
transferts de joueurs et de joueuses
reçus au siège de la FIFA en 2000

© INTERCARTO / FIFA 2003

| Amérique du Nord | Amérique du sud | Afrique | Europe | Asie | Océanie |

Transferts intra-européens

9500

Nombre de joueurs transférés

Echanges Europe/autres continents

100 300 700

Nombre de joueurs transférés

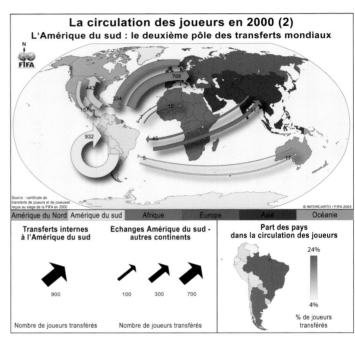

La circulation des joueurs en 2000 (2)
L'Amérique du sud : le deuxième pôle des transferts mondiaux

Source : certificats de
transferts de joueurs et de joueuses
reçus au siège de la FIFA en 2000

© INTERCARTO / FIFA 2003

| Amérique du Nord | Amérique du sud | Afrique | Europe | Asie | Océanie |

Transferts internes à l'Amérique du sud

900

Nombre de joueurs transférés

Echanges Amérique du sud - autres continents

100 300 700

Nombre de joueurs transférés

Part des pays dans la circulation des joueurs

24%

4%

% de joueurs
transférés

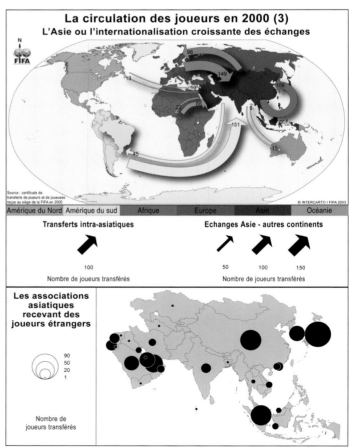

La circulation des joueurs en 2000 (3)
L'Asie ou l'internationalisation croissante des échanges

Source : certificats de
transferts de joueurs et de joueuses
reçus au siège de la FIFA en 2000

© INTERCARTO / FIFA 2003

| Amérique du Nord | Amérique du sud | Afrique | Europe | Asie | Océanie |

Transferts intra-asiatiques

100

Nombre de joueurs transférés

Echanges Asie - autres continents

50 100 150

Nombre de joueurs transférés

Les associations asiatiques recevant des joueurs étrangers

90
50
20
1

Nombre de
joueurs transférés

make African professional players available to play for their countries. On the other hand, the African associations often objected to the transfer demands that came from Europe. Throughout the 1960s and 70s, Algeria systematically refused every international transfer request.

The situation changed a great deal from the end of the 1980s. After the acceptance of professional players at the Olympic Games football tournament in Los Angeles, in 1984, the question of professionalism ceased to be an issue in most countries.

The fall of the Berlin Wall had, among other consequences, the effect of ending the State amateurism model in Eastern Europe and establishing in its place standard professionalism. Finally, the Bosman ruling in 1995 removed the ability of European clubs to refuse to grant authorisation for players to transfer at the end of their contracts if the clubs did not receive what they saw to be an adequate transfer fee. This had major repercussions for the nature of FIFA. The first and most important change was a considerable increase in the international movement of players. FIFA processed 1478 inte national transfer requests in the year 2000 alone.

As one would expect, the lion's share (seventy per cent of international transfers were in Europe. However, it is interesting to note that football associations in countries such as Turkmenistan, Kazakhstan, the Maldives and Vietnam, to mention just a few of the members of the AFC, were also affected. In 2000, 115 professional or semi-professional Brazilian players moved to Asian clubs.

Today, professional leagues have been established by more than fifty national football associations, and disputes between leagues and associations have ceased. The growth of the international market for football players has increased FIFA's role. Its legal services have to check that authorisation from the originating football association is in place for each international transfer. Since its creation, the consistency and regulation of the international market for football players and overseeing international matches, have been two of the Federation's main prerogatives.

At the start of the twenty-first-century FIFA has more control than ever over player movements between member associations. This essential role is not visible to the general public, but has always been an essential regulatory activity of the Federation. Recent developments would suggest that FIFA's role in this area will continue unabated into the future.

1904-1938

ORIGINS
AND EARLY DAYS
OF THE
WORLD CUP

To the non-specialist, the existence of FIFA is linked to the World Cup as its acronym reappears every four years during the World Cup Finals competition. The founders of FIFA had several objectives. In the first Statutes (1904) the idea of a world competition only appears in article 9 which proposed that: 'The International Federation is the only organisation with the right to organise an international competition'.

< 1

1 The construction of
Wembley Stadium's twin
towers in north London,
1923.

2 Aerial view of the Colombes
Stadium, taken on the day of the
final between Switzerland and
Uruguay, which Uruguay won 3-0,
9 June 1924.

3 Mazzali the Uruguayan
goalkeeper saves an Argentinian
shot during the Olympic Games
final.

4 Arguably the most important
event of the Games. A corner stand
of the Amsterdam stadium during
the first Olympic final between
Argentina and Uruguay 1-1,
10 June 1928.

5 The last days of amateurism.
The Uruguayan football team take
the Olympic Oath at the Colombes
Stadium, France, 1924.

FIFA's control of the Olympic tournament

In the course of the second Congress in June 1905, the idea was again brought up for discussion and was set out with more accuracy: sixteen national teams would play each other in four groups. This finals tournament was to take place as part of the third FIFA Congress in Switzerland (1906). The participants of the Congress predicted a good financial return and hoped to generate interest from the national associations. Along with the length of time required to travel to the event, the cost of organisation was a major obstacle for the success of the idea. Access to important matches was already assured to the best teams. The importance of money had been established at the very beginning. The competition planned for 1906 did not take place. The governing body was not strong enough, and material circumstances were too unfavourable. Even the International Olympic Committee (IOC) showed itself to be incapable of staging a genuine football tournament during the Games of 1900 and 1904.

The Olympics did stage the first international football tournaments, but without assuming responsibility for all the organisation. During the London Olympic Games in 1908, the Football Association staged a football competition involving five European teams. At the Stockholm Games in 1912, affiliation to FIFA was a requirement for the ten participating teams. It appeared that a trend was emerging. FIFA sought to take control of the organisation of the Olympic Games football tournaments, a desire which was not opposed by the International Olympic Committee.

During the FIFA Congress of 1913, the Dutch association proposed that the football tournament due to be

2

3

Mazzali, en estupendo esfuerzo, cede corner en el match final, salvando su arco.

JEUX OLYMPIQUES DE 1924 _FOOTBALL
LA PRESTATION DE SERMENT
ÉQUIPE D'URUGAY
318
AN
PARIS

played at the Berlin Olympic Games in 1916 should be considered as FIFA's international competition. FIFA arranged the football tournament for the Paris Games in 1924. The success revealed to the FIFA chiefs that a world football competition was possible 'without one single Football Association official, or British journalist, professional manager or British spectator...'. But a desire to break away from IOC control was expressed, a return to the letter of the FIFA Statutes.

The debate regarding true amateurism and the question of loss of earnings payments to amateur players intensified. This caused a split within FIFA, the more tolerant associations clashing with the IOC's strict requirements. Even though the football tournament for the 1928 Games in Amsterdam was to be organised by FIFA, the unending debates led some of the FIFA members to look for an alternative solution: a competition under the exclusive control of FIFA, and which involved the best teams regardless of the professional status of the players.

6

First discussions

Two facts prompted FIFA to move towards the creation of its own football tournament. Initially, although to a lesser extent since the success of the 1924 Olympic tournament, the determination of the Football Association to insist upon a strict distinction between the professional and amateur players, had a paralysing effect on all developments. But the departure of the Football Association from FIFA gave the organisation freedom to act. Secondly, in 1926 four central European countries – Czechoslovakia, Austria, Hungary and Italy – announced that they planned to stage an international tournament. This disturbed the Executive Committee, who felt powerless to intervene. Banning the tournament would be futile as it would take place regardless, as was already the situation in Latin America. On 10 December in Paris, the Executive Committee declined to oppose the Central European tournament but were aware that they needed to present an alternative competition. More importantly, the disqualification of professional players from the Olympics and the deterioration of their relationship with the IOC forced FIFA to act. The Executive Committee initiated a survey of affiliated associations regarding the creation of an international competition. A special commission was put together, made up of the Swiss Gabriel Bonnet, the FIFA Vice-President Hugo Meisl, Henri Delaunay, Ferreti and Linnemann. Lastly, the national associations were invited to reply to six questions about the structure of the proposed competition.

This commission met under the chairmanship of Bonnet and in the presence of Jules Rimet in Zurich during February 1927. It would appear that Jules Rimet had caught a glimpse of the opportunities that an international championship would bring to football and FIFA. He solemnly declared 'FIFA is now facing a new era'.

After lively debate, the Commission was united by Delaunay's vision of a 'world competition' and the commission decided to put forward three suggestions to the Executive Committee. The first two, those of Meisl and

Delaunay, were very similar. Meisl's idea was for a European competition, Delaunay's for a World Cup every four years. The system of grouping teams, and the attendance of non-European teams was mentioned. The third proposition was that of the German, Linnemann. He suggested that there should be a competition for amateurs, if possible during the Olympic Games, and another every two years for professional players. In sum, Delaunay's suggestions, supported by Bonnet, seemed decisive.

The Helsinki Congress in June 1927 was impressed by the proposals, and Jules Rimet was able to announce that the Executive Committee proposed the organisation of an

7

6 The Mitropa Cup
played for between
1927 and 1960.
A solely European
competition between
Austria, Hungary, Italy,
Switzerland,
Czechoslovakia and, in
the final tournament,
Yugoslavia.

7 The cover of Jules
Rimet's book, *Histoire
Merveilleuse de la Coupe
du Monde*, 1954.

8 Henri Delaunay,
Georges Bonnet and
Hugo Meisl (left to
right) were the
promoters of a global
event. Here they
discuss the creation
of a World Cup. Geneva,
January 1929.

8

international competition starting in 1930, with the venue yet to be decided. Each association was expected to play their strongest team. Congress could not make any further decisions, as the three propositions from the commission in Zurich had not been circulated to the national associations. The failure to pass on the commission's suggestions was Hirschmann's fault, but we do not know if he acted deliberately or if his negligence was simply accidental.

The dossier was added to the agenda for the 1928 Congress in Amsterdam which took place at the same time as the Olympic Games. Jules Rimet underlined that the decision to stage a World Cup was a response to the differences in opinion between FIFA and the IOC on the question of amateurism. Henri Delaunay proposed the creation of an organising committee for the 1930 World Cup and Congress agreed by twenty-three votes to five. Bonnet became the chairman of this committee, which was therefore under the control of the Executive. Meisl, Delaunay and Linnemann were to help Bonnet.

The World Cup Organising Committee

When this committee met again on 8 September in Zurich, Jules Rimet's presence showed his interest in the project. The committee was to put together a plan which he would take back to the next Congress to be approved. When once again, Linnemann protested that professional and amateur players should not play against each other, he was in the minority. Eventually the commission proposed one competition to take place every four years, which would be called the World Cup. The matches would be played between 15 March and 15 June, the teams having been matched by drawing lots. Where possible, all the games would take place in a single country. Qualifying matches for the competition would only be played where there were more than thirty-two participants.

The question of how the money generated would be distributed remained undecided and the discussion was continued in Geneva in January 1929. The Italian association had already put forward its candidacy on condition that they received thirty per cent of the revenue.

9

9 Following their
Olympic victory against
the Swiss, the
Uruguayan players
complete their lap of
honour. 19 June 1924.

10 The people of
Montevideo await the
result of the Olympic
final from the other side
of the Atlantic, 1928.

On the division of revenues the committee put forward
three proposals. The first to give twenty per cent to FIFA,
twenty per cent to the participating teams and forty per
cent to cover other costs. The second and the third proposals gave only five per cent to FIFA. The committee
drafted a plan for the general organisation of the event and
called for candidates to come forward.

Yet financial problems remained unsolved, despite
another meeting. The members of the committee remained
in disagreement and Article 17 of the tournament rules
was reserved for clarifying the distribution of profits.

At the Congress in Barcelona in May 1929, debate
focused on the same question of money. This led
Seeldrayers to worry that '*Le football a déjà été si souvent
accusé d'être mené par des considérations financières que
nous devons efforcer de ne pas donner prise a ces idées.*'
('Football has already frequently been accused of being
led by financial considerations so we must be careful not
to give fuel to such ideas'.) After the rejection of one plan,
another committee was formed during a suspension of
the session. Presided over by Seeldr ayers, it also included the Uruguayan ambassador from Brussels, Buero. The
decision was made quickly, and it was decided that the
future organising association must accept the risk.

The choice of Uruguay

The committee proposed that the organising country
should assume responsibility for all of the costs, including the travel and any eventual deficit. FIFA contented
itself with ten per cent of the gross revenue. Also FIFA
authorised friendly matches before and after the tournament from which part of the revenue would go to the
teams involved.

The committee also noted that some associations threatened not to take part if an American country was chosen
to hold the first World Cup. This implies that Uruguay,
the final choice, was already being considered. As soon as
the decision regarding the finances was made, the
Netherlands, Sweden, Hungary, Italy and Spain, who up
until this point had been candidates, withdrew. Argentina
spoke out in favour of Uruguay and the Uruguayan association made many promises, mainly financial, based on
an expectation of the massive crowds that would attend
the games. Uruguay's bid was successful, helped, no
doubt, by having won the Olympic competition in 1924
and 1928.

Even early on in FIFA's history politics played a part.
The state of Uruguay looked for international recognition

10 >

and sought to capitalise by organising the World Cup to coincide with the centenary of the country's independence. This is the main reason why Buero showed such enthusiasm when presenting to Jules Rimet the plans for the stadium, El Estadio Centenario, to be built in Montevideo. The main guarantee that convinced the Executive Committee was the promised backing by the government who agreed to underwrite the cost of the event.

While few teams considered sending teams to Latin America the following year, the choice of Uruguay at Congress was unanimous. Jules Rimet immediately took up his pilgrim's staff to go to sway the associations who were undecided about participating. A letter to Buero dated 14 December 1929 shows that he had sensed a general apathy. Despite the withdrawal of the UK, Denmark and Sweden, he remained optimistic. For his part, Buero was also active encouraging the associations who had embraced professionalism to take part. He promised payments to the players if their clubs refused to pay those who left to compete. However, visits that Buero made to the associations in question, including the Football Association, proved fruitless. The rumour that in future Latin American countries would boycott events staged by European associations spread across Europe to little effect.

11

11 The Goddess of Victory, the first world cup trophy by French sculptor Abel Lafleur. Made in solid silver and gold plate on a lapis lazuli stand, it was renamed the Jules Rimet cup in 1946.

12 Jules Rimet on board ship with the Belgian, French, Romanian and Yugoslavian teams, bound for Montevideo.

12

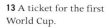

13 A ticket for the first World Cup.

14 Dorado scores the first Uruguayan goal in the 1930 World Cup final between Uruguay and Argentina (result 4-2).

15 1934 - Mussolini's World Cup. Players and managers carry the '*Coppa del Duce*' presented to the winners by Italy's leader.

16 The formidable presence of Il Duce. Mussolini attends the 1934 World Cup final, won by… Italy.

The first World Cups (1930, 1934, 1938)

The first World Cup was only a moderate success in the eyes of the Europeans, but it showed the potential for the future. It was only a few weeks before the start of the competition that Belgium, Yugoslavia, Romania and France decided they would take part. Their teams set sail on the same boat for the long voyage. Held back by their professional obligations, many players selected by their association declined the invitation to play. During the tournament a certain slackness prevailed. The rules of the game were not very well-respected and the referees were not well qualified and sometimes quite eccentric.

The true sporting success of the tournament was reflected by gripping contests between the nine South American teams. 90,000 spectators attended the final and

17

watched Uruguay beat Argentina 4-2. The hierarchy previously established at the Olympic Games in 1928 was confirmed. Some of the characteristics of future competitions made their first appearance at the Uruguayan World Cup. Tens of thousands of people accompanied the South American teams to their games. This heralded the beginning of a sporting tourism that would continue to increase. 20,000 Argentinians arrived in Montevideo aboard specially chartered boats. The final balance sheet also foretold the future. From a healthy profit, the Uruguayan association was able to reimburse the travel expenses of the participating teams. For the first time FIFA received a considerable sum of money. For a long time to come the World Cup would be FIFA's main source of income. Other more negative aspects also provided an indication of what was to come. Nationalist demonstrations and violence accompanied some of the

matches. At one point police intervention was required to protect the Argentinian team. The World Cup was already a mirror to the contemporary world reflecting political, economic and social conflicts. From now on national teams would take their place alongside club teams in the hearts of supporters.

In 1934 the Italian World Cup in Italy took on a political dimension as desired by the fascist regime. The matches were affected by this political pressure. Either implicit or explicit pressures were exerted on the referees who favoured the Italian team which eventually triumphed in an atmosphere of almost national hysteria. Jules Rimet could only look on from his position behind the ostentatious presence of Il Duce. France in 1938 was a return to relative calm. It seems that the competition was played in a sporting or a political atmosphere according to the political circumstances in the organising country.

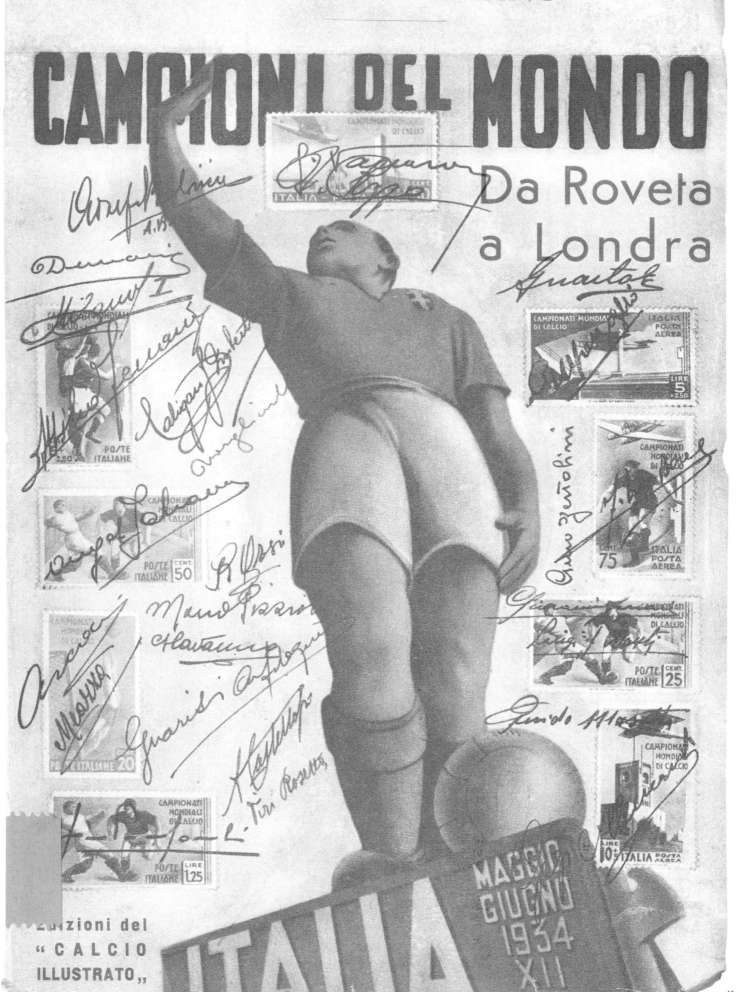

19 The Seoul World Cup stadium which hosted the opening game and a semi-final of the 2002 World Cup.

20

20 A game where the stakes were raised beyond sport. The quarterfinal between France and Italy played at the Colombes Stadium, 12 June 1938. (result 1-3)

21 Republican protocol: the Italian players (left) and the Hungarians (right) are introduced to French president Albert Lebrun before the final of the World Cup, 19 June 1938.

22 90 minutes later the Italian captain Giuseppe Meazza makes the fascist salute before receiving the World Cup from the hands of the president of the French republic.

Stadiums, World Cups and sport policy

Stadiums became a key issue when FIFA decided to organise a World Cup. The experience of the Olympic Games had made FIFA aware of the need to ensure that the enclosures in which the competition was to be held could accommodate a large public. Technical innovations and public order were also taken into account. Reflecting the era, the stadiums that hosted the first World Cups were on a huge scale. It was the development of television that drew the attention of the organisers away from the fashion for increasingly large stadiums and towards considerations of comfort, security, access roads and parking or the construction of stadiums that could

be used for purposes other than for sporting events.

Modelled on the Coliseum in Rome, the construction of large sporting arenas went hand in hand with development of modern sport. The national importance of stadiums was itself linked to the revival of the Olympic Games from 1896.

At the Olympic Games in Stockholm in 1912, the first at which the football tournament was run by FIFA, the Olympic Stadium built for the occasion had a capacity of 90,000 spectators and offered the potential for substantial revenue to the organisers. The 1920s marked a turning point in the vision of stadiums on continental Europe; the wooden structures that dated from the start of the century were replaced by concrete cathedrals. In Vienna, where football already attracted huge crowds, a large

21

22

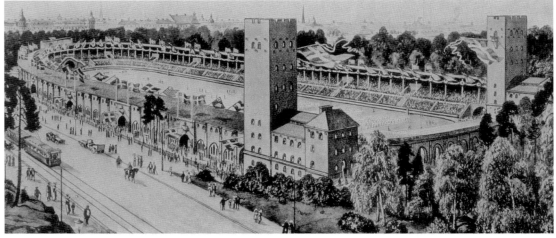

23

modern stadium was built in the amusement park in Prater right next to the big wheel. In 1924 a stadium was built in Wembley, northwest London for the British Empire Exhibition, a capacity crowd of 125,000 inaugurated the stadium at the 1923 FA Cup Final. With its symbolic twin towers, Wembley stadium, where the 1966 World Cup final would be held, was soon re-christened the 'Mecca of Football'. The Stade de Colombes was built for the 1924 Olympic Games in Paris and four years later in Amsterdam the Olympisch Stadion, designed by the young architect Jan Wils, hosted the Uruguayan team as they won the competition for the second time in front of 40,000 enthusiastic spectators. Football at that time was the most popular event of the Olympics, and the one that enabled the Olympic Games to make a profit. For both the Paris and the Amsterdam Games public money was necessary to finance all, or almost all, construction work, which in the case of Amsterdam, took more than three years.

Also, when the 1929 FIFA Congress in Barcelona decided to grant the organisation of the first World Cup to the small South American republic of Uruguay, Rimet's adversaries criticised the choice of a country where the infrastructure was particularly poor. The organisers had less than a year to build an arena capable of hosting a global event.

Because of the poor state of repair of the two existing stadiums in Montevideo, the Central Park and the Pocitos, the construction of a new ground was essential. The chosen architect, Juan Scasso, planned the

24

25

26 Two modern
myths combined:
football and the
car. Wembley
stadium during the
1966 World Cup.

construction of an elliptic stadium built using 14,000 m²
of reinforced concrete, with the capacity to hold 70,000
spectators. The structure was equipped with huge car
parks that occupied 450,000 m² in the José Battles Park
on the outskirts of the town. In a race against the clock
the whole country mobilised to finish the building work
in time, three teams working in relay 24 hours a day.
Despite their efforts, the stadium was not finished in
time for the start of the competition. Nevertheless, the
competition still took place before a huge crowd and this
monumental structure is still regarded as one of the
principal symbols of Uruguayan national identity.

The Uraguayan stadium created a template that would

be followed by other World Cup hosts throughout the
century. Firstly, its name was politically inspired.
'Centenario' celebrated one hundred years of Uraguayan
independence. Secondly, the stadium was constructed
at the edge of the city. Thirdly, it was constructed a considerable distance from the pitch (as opposed to the
British stadium style where the distance was minimal.
And finally, the stadium took longer to build than originally projected.

For the first World Cup all the matches were played in
the same stadium, which was not the case at the second
World Cup in Italy. When the Fascist regime of the 1930s
sought to organise the competition it was quick to

27

28

29

understand the crucial importance of the stadiums. In a climate of world economic crisis the Italian government followed the example of Roosevelt's New Deal in the United States, and launched large-scale construction projects of which the football stadiums are a good example but from 1925 the regime had sought to modernise its sporting infrastructures. The construction of the Littoriale Stadium in 1925, one of the grounds that hosted World Cup matches in 1934, had marked the beginning of this policy. The stadium in Florence, built for the World Cup by the engineer Pier Luigi Nervi, linked technical innovation, the importance of the spectators' view and elements of political propaganda. The creator, influenced by the futurist movement, planned a stadium with 45,000 seats. Built entirely of reinforced concrete, access to the arena was via helix-shaped external escalators that combined aesthetics with functionality. The use of entrances at the top of the stands was an original idea that allowed quick entrance for spectators. As a specialist remarked in the 1920s, the crowds tended to gather in the lower rows thus obstructing the flow of spectators whose seats were situated higher up. Even more original was Nervi's idea of a central covered stand, the roof of which was supported, without pillars, by the the

arch, thus allowing perfect visibility for all the spectators. Today considered an historic monument, the Florence stadium is a magnificent example of technical innovation, architectural harmony and the integration of sporting architecture into the urban fabric enabling the stadium and peripheral buildings to blend in with the Florentine town centre.

An element of political propaganda was always present. The stadium built in Rome in 1927, was named PNF stadium (National Fascist Party) and the Florence stadium was named after Giovanni Berta, a militant fascist raised to the status of a martyr (today the stadium bears the name of Artemio Franchi, former president of UEFA and vice president of FIFA). The stadium in Turin was named simply the Mussolini Stadium. With its 70,000 capacity, as the largest and most modern of Italian stadia, the aim was to reflect the status of 'il Duce'. The regime did not skimp elsewhere on expenses and built other stadiums in Naples and Trieste especially for the Olympic Games. The 1934 World Cup was a truly national event and took place in eight different stadiums all several hundred kilometres apart. The railway, another jewel the Italian fascists boasted of, transported players, journalists and supporters from one region to another. The regime

27 A 'futurist' enclosure: the stadium dedicated to Berta, the 'martyr of the fascist revolution' built in Florence in 1932.

28 A full and almost completed stadium. The Centenario in Montevideo on the day of the 1930 World Cup final.

29 The Mussolini Stadium. Built in 1933 it was one of the few Italian buildings named after il Duce.

30 The fascist regime also designed modern stadiums of more modest proportions, such as the one in Trieste by Licteur, built in 1932.

saw this World Cup as the opportunity to show the whole world its modernity and organisation: 'The success of this event is thanks to the collaboration that fascism has created throughout Italy between transport companies, printers and privately owned businesses who have demonstrated their generosity, zeal and honesty'. The success of the competition suggested a model style of organisation, of stadium and infrastructure construction.

France took notice of this when organising the next World Cup in 1938, and there was a fear of comparisons between the French competition and the Italian success. This prompted the headline in the daily paper *Excelsior* on the eve of the competition, 'A truly huge test for our small stadia'. New velodrome-stadiums, linking the two sporting passions of the French, were built in Bordeaux and Marseilles. In this period of extreme diplomatic tension, expectations did not involve much optimism.

The financial results of the 1934 World Cup had proved the efficiency of the Italian administration, but the organisers of the 1938 event feared a lack of French sporting enthusiasm. Nothing would have been worse than the competition taking place in front of empty stands. However, even though the financial gains were lower than those of the previous World Cup, the event was a success and, in the long term, it equipped France with football stadia.

In 1947 when FIFA confirmed that Brazil would organise the World Cup three years later, the government and the municipality of Rio de Janeiro decided to build a stadium worthy of the event. The Maracana, a 150,000 capacity stadium drew the attention of the Cariocas. The *Jornal dos Sports* even gave an account of all the stages of construction from the hiring of builders to the work itself. It went so far as to publish serialised stories

30

31 Monumentalism in football; the inside circular view of the Maracana, July 1950.

32 An unfolding national drama, the second and winning goal for Uruguay in the Maracana Stadium, Rio, 16 July 1950.

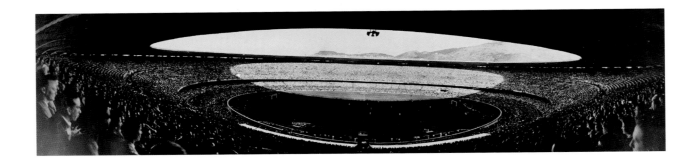

31

showing the progress of the building and encouraged its readers to visit the site. The stadium was opened a week before the start of the competition and was the pride of the nation. It represented the modernisation and the democratisation of Brazil and in a few weeks' time it was the scene of a true national tragedy: the victory of Uruguay in the deciding game of the competition. The final took place in front of nearly 200,000 spectators, the largest crowd in football history. The Maracana had even

more of an effect than the Centenario de Montevideo on South America's popular passion for football, the World Cup, and the importance of national teams as a constituent element of a modern nation. In Belgrade in the 1950s when Tito's government decided to build a great stadium it was nicknamed '*The Marakana*' reflecting the symbolic importance of the Brazilian stadium. At this point football association and football club revenues were made up almost entirely of entrance money paid by spec-

32

36

33

34

35

33 A dual attraction:
the television broadcast
of a World Cup match in
Germany in 1954

34 Officials check
the crowd numbers in
the Wankdorf Stadium
at the start of the World
Cup, 1954.

35 A more modest and
less costly enclosure
for the World Cup Final
in 1954.

36 Packed to the rafters,
the Nou Camp in
Barcelona, 1982

tators, so the Maracana and its vastness offered the assurance of significant income. FIFA itself benefited greatly from larger stadiums thanks to the percentage of gate money that it received. After the unprecedented success of this World Cup Schricker was able write to President Rimet 'we are rich!' For ten years he had had the greatest difficulty collecting subscriptions and this arrival of ready money was most welcome.

The peak of the Maracana's success also marked the end of the monumentalist model. While some of the largest stadiums in the world such as the *Nou Camp* in Barcelona date from this era, the end of the 1950s, saw the emergence of television and the rise of the virtual spectator. The 1954 World Cup in Switzerland was played in much smaller stadiums. The final between Hungary and Germany in the Wankdorf Stadium in Berne, played in pounding rain, was attended by less than a third of the number of spectators at the previous final. Nevertheless, by means of radio and television the whole of Germany followed the match live, as is testified by the final images of Rainer W. Fassbinder's film *The Marriage of Maria Braun*. Elsewhere, Western nations showed themselves to be more reticent about undertaking such large-scale construction of stadiums that were rarely filled. The World Cups in Switzerland, Sweden in 1958, and Chile in 1962 marked the return to more modest proportions as the priority became the convenience and comfort of spectators.

37

Modern stadiums: technology and security

It may have taken until 1974 for World Cup matches to be held at night, but today the stadiums selected to host World Cups are the object of numerous and meticulous inspections. Although capacity was once the principal concern of architects, a new concept of sporting enclosures took shape in the 1960s. Disasters that occurred during major matches in Lima and Glasgowhad shown the crucial importance of security issues and the need to impose exacting standards on the organisers. Also, the tragedies at Heysel and Hillsborough in the 1980s led FIFA to take very strict measures aimed at avoiding any sort of violence in stadiums during its competitions.

Thus, since the 1990 World Cup in Italy, the stadiums selected to host the competition only had allocated seating, to improve the experience of spectators, prevent crowd movement and control ticket sales. For all countries applying to organise a World Cup, the question of security in stadiums is of paramount importance, 'in no case can security be marginalised or avoided in any way whatsoever, to satisfy other requirements'. At the same time the question of comfort is central to stadium quality. Press rooms, massage rooms, changing rooms, disabled access for spectators, transport for fans from city centres to stadiums, and the proximity of airports are essential criteria in the choice of locations for FIFA competitions.

To host a World Cup final today a stadium must be

37 The St-Denis Stade de France, the heart of the 1998 World Cup.

38 A grandstand with all mod cons. The royal box in the King Fahd Stadium in Riyadh, Saudi Arabia, 1989.

39 Bank of screens. Late 20th Century sports-media technology.

38

39 >

able to accommodate 2,000 journalists, 350 photographers, an equipped press centre, 1,000 telephone connections and four television studios. Of course currently there are few affiliated associations capable of satisfying the numerous requirements for organising an occasion as important as a World Cup and of hosting thousands of players, officials and journalists and hundreds of thousands of spectators. But as the World Cup in Japan and Korea proved without doubt, the future lies in joint organisation and in modern, functional stadiums such as those built for the 2002 competition.

The world of stadiums

Countries that had regained their independence in the 1950s considered the construction of an imposing national stadium as high a priority as their FIFA membership. In Malaysia in celebration of their independence on the 31 August 1957, the Prime Minister Tunku Abdul Rahman opened a national stadium in Kuala Lumpa for an international football tournament. The Mauritian FA, in its membership request, indicated to FIFA that it owned the main stadiums on the island and that the largest could hold 15,000 spectators. In Kenya in 1966, the Nairobi municipal council proposed building one of the biggest stadiums in the world. 'The stadium when

completed will hold about 200,000 people. We are planning for the future and in about fifty years we anticipate drawing crowds to fill the stadium.'

National football associations in countries that were gaining independence often found a lack of infrastructures to be one of the main weaknesses. In 1953 in an official publication the Indian football association apologised 'to the football loving public as to why there had been no Stadium yet in the great city of Calcutta' pointing the finger of responsibility at political institutions. In Madagascar, climate makes the island's six stadiums practically unusable during the rainy season.

In recent membership requests the question of sports arenas has always been the focus of attention. In the republics emerging from the former USSR there are numerous, huge stadiums. Kazakhstan has 150 stadia of which five have a capacity of more than 25,000 and the small republic of Kyrgystan with a population of four million is equipped with twenty-six stadiums each with able to accommodate more than 3,000 people. However, other associations such as Grenada are less well off. In their membership request, the secretary had to add, 'Please note that we have no stadium in Granada, only open parks where football fields can be marked and the game played'. It was not without pride that he wrote to Zurich two years later to announce that his association

40 The Freetown National Stadium, Sierra Leone photographed in 1994.

41 The legacy of colonisation. The King Badouin stadium in Léopoldville, Kinshasa, built in 1953.

42 At the desert gates: the King Fadh Stadium in Riyadh, 1997.

40

41

Association National Stadium Capacity Membership

Federation	Stadium	Capacity	Membership
Belize	Marylebone Cricket Club Ground	15,000	1,044
Bostwana	National Stadium Gborone	20,000	17,000
Rwanda	Nyamirambo Kigali National Stadium	25,500	31,000
Dominique	Windsor Park	15,000	1,645
Kirghizistan	Spartak Bishkek	25,000	28,954
Cook Islands	National Stadium	3,600	2,350
Guam	Mangialo Stadium	6,000	2,112
Tonga	Tongan National Stadium	10,000	38,48

42

now had a genuine 18,000 capacity stadium for a population of 110,000 habitants.

In associations belonging to the CONCACAF and the OFC the capacity of national stadiums is often greater than the membership, but these constructions are often makeshift, without grass pitches, floodlights for night matches, or adequate changing rooms.

In Singapore where space is particularly lacking, football is a special spectacle, and in 1976 the national stadium Kallang already had a capacity of 65,000 and all the latest facilities. In the Gulf States huge modern stadiums have been built since the 1970s, such as the Sultanate of Oman's 45,000 capacity El-Shuta Stadium. Football stadiums everywhere are ideal gathering places and constitute an important means of identification and representation for communities. The stadium, more than any other modern building, focuses a feeling of patriotism and popular passion. Large stadiums that have been a part of of World Cup history have even attained an almost sacred dimension. As symbols of the evolution of football they are visited today like modern-day cathedrals. If a century ago they were merely the exclusive theatres of sport, today they have become the home of globally significant events.

LAWS OF THE GAME AND REFEREES

Modern football was invented before FIFA. By 1904 most of the main features of the game were in place: the football pitch was marked out as we know it today save for the arc at the point of the penalty area; goal nets were attached to the goal posts on all major grounds; the corner kick, free kick, penalty kick and throw-in had been in use for over a decade; flags usually marked the four corners; special football boots and shinguards were used in the majority of organised games and the referee was in sole charge of the game, assisted by two linesmen (although they were not in uniform yet). Players could still be offside in their own half of the field and goalkeepers could handle the ball there and they could also still wear shirts of the same colours and pattern as the rest of the team. Football was already a modern phenomenon in Britain: a crowd in excess of 100,000 had watched the 1901 FA Cup Final at Crystal Palace.

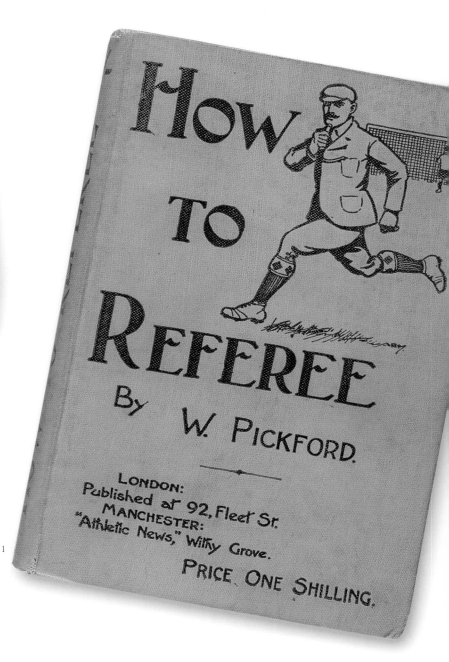

adjourned Special

**Minutes of Meeting Held at 42, Russell Square, London,
Friday, April 4th, 1913.**

Present:—Mr. T. E. Thomas (Football Association of Wales), in the chair, Messrs. J. R. Stephens (Football Association of Wales), C. Crump and W. Pickford (Football Association), A. M. Robertson and D. Campbell (Scottish Football Association), H. Hegan and J. MacBride (Irish Football Association).

There were also in attendance:—Messrs. T. Steen (Scottish Football Association), F. J. Wall (Secretary, Football Association), J. M'Dowall (Secretary, Scottish Football Association), J. Ferguson (Irish Football Association), and T. Robbins (Secretary, Football Association of Wales), who acted as Secretary to the Board.

Apologies for absence were received from Mr. R. T. Gough (President, Football Association of Wales), and Mr. D. B. Woolfall (Football Association).

The following Proposals of The Football Association, that the Rules be altered as hereinafter mentioned, were carried:—

RULE I.—This Board shall be called the INTERNATIONAL FOOTBALL ASSOCIATION BOARD. The Football Association, the Scottish Football Association, the Football Association of Wales, the Irish Football Association, and La Federation Internationale de Football Association, shall each be entitled to send two representatives, who shall constitute the Board.

RULE IV.—The Board shall meet annually, on the SECOND SATURDAY IN JUNE. The meetings shall be held in rotation, in England, Scotland, Wales, Ireland, and Paris, at the invitation of each Association in order of seniority. The invitation for the year 1913 shall be given by Ireland, and for 1914 by The Federation Internationale de Football Association. One of the representatives of the Association convening the meeting shall preside, and the other shall act as Secretary.

RULE VI.—Business shall not be proceeded with at any meeting unless Four Associations are represented.

RULE VII.—Alterations in the Laws of the Game shall only be made at the Annual Meeting in June, and no alteration shall be adopted unless agreed to by at least four-fifths of the representatives present and voting. All other resolutions, whether submitted at the Annual Meeting or at a Special Meeting, must be agreed to by at least four-fifths of the representatives present and voting.

3

RULE VIII.—Omit the word "four" in the eighth line.

RULE IX.—The decisions of the Board shall be at once binding on all the Associations, and no alterations in the Laws of the Game shall be made by any Association until the same shall have been passed by this Board.

The following Proposal submittid by The Scottish Football Association was unanimously carried:—

That the English, Scottish, Welsh and Irish Associations petition Parliament to take measures to repress "Ready Money Football Coupon Betting."

It was further decided that The Football Association take up the matter and circularize Members of Parliament for them to support the measure.

A vote of thanks was tendered the Chairman for presiding.

(Signed) **T. ROBBINS,**

The Football Association of Wales,

Acting Secretary.

H Hegan
14 E June 1913

4

The laws of the game

The first major overhaul of the laws of football took place in 1891. It was undertaken by the International Football Association Board (IFAB) which had met for the first time on 2 June 1886. It comprised two representatives from each of the football associations of England, Ireland, Scotland and Wales and met once a year to 'discuss and decide proposed alterations in the laws of the game and generally any matters affecting Association Football in its international relations'. Two FIFA representatives were admitted to the IFAB in 1913. As any change in the law required a three-quarter majority they were always in danger of being out-voted by the British. But in fact, relations between the representatives of the four British associations and the two FIFA members seem to have been cordial even after the British had withdrawn from FIFA in 1920.

By 1923 FIFA had its own committee to look at the laws of the game, the *Comte consultatif des règles du jeu et de l'arbitrage*. It would later become the Referees' Committee and so we shall call it throughout. The committee was keen to discover from affiliated football associations how they were organising their referees and how they appointed them to international matches. They were also prepared to answer questions from national associations about the laws and their working. This was to be one of their major activities. In 1925 the Referees' Committee included some important FIFA officials, including Bauwens, Delauney, Hirschman, Meisl, Mauro and Verdych – several of whom were active and experienced referees.

Each national association could nominate up to six referees whom they felt were competent to take charge of international matches. It was stressed from the beginning that referees in such fixtures should be selected from neutral countries. But probably the most important task of the Referees' Committee – indeed one of the major aims of FIFA when it was formed in 1904 – had been to ensure that the laws of the game were followed by all member associations. A crucial aim was to achieve a

1 How To Referee by William Pickford (1906), the bible for European FAs and referees. Pickford founded the Association of English Referees in 1893 and was briefly FIFA Vice-President in 1927-28.

3 / 4 Minutes of the first International Board meeting in 1886 written by John K. McDowall (Scotland). Subjects included IFAB Statutes and football footwear.

uniform interpretation in all countries and at all levels of the sport – not easy in an organisation that soon had members from five continents. Moreover, this was complicated by what became known as 'spirit' of the law, more of which later.

The question of whether or not the substitution of players should be allowed was a long-running issue over which opinions differed. There was no mention of the word 'substitute' in the Laws before 1923 but there was obviously a growing practice of using them in many places so IFAB decided that 'except in a match played under the rules of a competition, substitutes may be allowed to replace players receiving injuries during a game, subject to this arrangement being agreed upon by both teams before the start of a match'. But this change did not settle the matter. The United States Soccer Football Association (USSFA) tried to persuade FIFA's Paris Congress in 1924 to recommend to IFAB that dur-

ing the first 75 minutes of play either side may withdraw one or two players and make substitutions. Congress was not persuaded. Nor was the Referees' Committee convinced of the need for a change in 1938 when the four Scandinavian associations asked to be allowed to substitute injured players in competitive matches with each other.

That the law was being flouted by many of the affiliated national associations was very clear after 1945. The USSFA, for example, was told that if they wanted to remain in FIFA the rules of their national cup competition had to be changed. But their Secretary objected to the proposed elimination of the substitute rule for local games on the grounds that they 'we have Sunday players who work all week and cannot expect to have conditioned players as they do in Europe. Our fans demand a full team at all times. Soccer promotion today is difficult enough without adding additional burdens.' He stressed

5 / 6 Two examples of dangerous play according to the *FIFA Universal Guide for Referees* (1953)

7

that they only wanted exemption for local games and would follow FIFA rules in internationals. But even in international matches the rule was being ignored. When Switzerland met Brazil in April 1956 both sides agreed that the goalkeeper and two other players, if injured, could be replaced. Brazil had actually wanted to replace up to four players whether injured or not. For the match Austria v Brazil, also played in April 1956, it was agreed to replace the goalkeeper and one other player, if injured, up to half-time. These substitutions were actually made. But then it all got a little out of hand and confused. In the first half Sabetzer (Austria), who was not injured, was replaced by Buzek. The spectators protested because Sabetzer played well. Late on, Hanappi (Austria), who was not injured, left the field of play of his own free will to be replaced by Sabetzer who a few minutes before had been himself replaced by another player. The Austrian goalkeeper was replaced as well as two Brazilians.

It was alleged that in the United States four players could be replaced and later return and that matches were divided into four periods of twenty-two and a half minutes each. It was also known that in Central and South America substitutes were freely used. In 1957 the Argentinian FA actually asked FIFA's Executive Committee if in their World Cup qualifying matches against Bolivia, both sides could substitute three uninjured players in the games in Buenos Aires and in the high altitude of La Paz. They were told to travel early so the players had time to adapt!

Stanley Rous argued at a meeting of the Referees' Committee that a questionnaire on the substitution issue was sent out to all national associations in membership in 1955 and had only been returned by half of them. Could the laws be changed if half the associations did not know what they wanted? It is not entirely clear what lay behind all this. Clearly FIFA could not accept that

7 Substitution of a player during the 1962 World Cup in Chile.

8 'Fair charge but goalkeeper is not in possession of the ball' *FIFA Universal Guide for Referees* (1953)

9 'Fair charge when goalkeeper is in possession of the ball' *FIFA Universal Guide for Referees* (1953)

10 When can a shoulder charge be used? *FIFA Universal Guide for Referees* (1953)

some affiliated associations were ignoring the laws of football. On the other hand, if enough of the membership found the present laws unpersuasive then that was a strong argument for changing them. The British were reluctant to accept substitutes even though injuries had spoiled their own Cup Finals in 1952, 1953 and 1955. The cause of this reluctance is not clear as their argument was never spelt out. Perhaps they liked the (rare) triumph of ten against eleven? More probably it was partly a distrust of change initiated overseas and partly the feeling that substitutes would allow unspecified but sinister malpractice to disfigure Britain's gift to the sporting world. In the event, the FIFA Executive Committee sent out a second questionnaire to the national associations. This time seventy per cent responded and it was clear that a change had to be made. It was but it was a cautious one: an injured goalkeeper could be substituted at any time during a competitive international and one injured player could be substituted up to half-time. Even the Executive Committee accepted that allowing more substitutions would lead to abuse – though they did not say what might be. The law would be further, but gradually, liberalised over the next three decades.

Notice that it was the injured goalkeeper who was first given the privilege of automatic substitution. The goalkeeper has always been privileged as the only player allowed to use his hands. His is an important position, the last line of defence, the one whom it is easiest to blame if things go wrong. He is first mentioned in the Laws in 1878 and then in 1893 when the first piece of protective legislation was passed. In the British game it had become a popular tactic to knock the goalkeeper over as a ball was passed into the immediate vicinity of the goal. This was forbidden in 1893. The goalkeeper could be charged but only if he had or was in the act of playing the ball or obstructing an opponent. An amendment in 1901 also allowed him to be charged fairly once he had move outsided his small goal area.

The British game was an aggressive one of hard tackling linked to manly shoulder charges which could become excessively violent even for British tastes. In 1905 Law 9 was amended to emphasise that, though charging was permissible, it must not be violent nor dangerous. But in football matches in Europe's offshore islands, charging was an important part of what was thought of as a game that combined skill with force. And it was enshrined in the laws of the game. But in much of Europe and in South America, for example, it was not liked. It became a rule that was effectively discarded in many countries. In central Europe by the 1930s, if a forward charged the goalkeeper even when the man in the green jersey had the ball it 'invariably irritated the public.' An article in *Football World* in January 1939

11

emphasised the need to apply all the laws fixed by the IFAB and waxed somewhat lyrical when asking if anything in football was more 'spectacular, athletic and lively than sending both goalkeeper and ball into the nets by means of a nice correct and loyal charge?' But referees in South America and Europe increasingly penalised it. By the 1950s it was a cause of some confusion leading to ill-feeling. A member of the council of the Hong Kong Football Association wrote to FIFA in 1956 wondering whether Law 12 (4) covering charging the goalkeeper when in possession of the ball was still in force. Teams from the continent, and he named Austria, Sweden and Yugoslavia, insisted that the goalkeeper must not be charged when holding the ball. What were they to do? FIFA's reply was that his visitors were wrong and he should send them the names of the teams!

Meanwhile at the home of the manly shoulder charge, the English were having doubts. In the 1957 Cup Final an Aston Villa forward made a reckless challenge on the Manchester United goalkeeper which led to his being carried from the field. As substitution of an injured player was not permitted in a competitive match, United had to put an outfield player in goal. They lost the match and with it the Cup and League double, which had not been achieved for sixty years. The English international referee, Arthur Ellis, asked the manager of the England team, Walter Winterbottom, if he did not think it was time to protect the goalkeeper 'as they do on the continent'.

But the law would remain in force for several decades, not reflecting the growing reality of non-compliance. Law 12 (4) would eventually disappear but even in the 1999 edition of the *Laws of the Game* the implication is that charging an opponent is within the rules so long as it is not decreed by the referee to be 'careless, reckless or of excessive force'. But if seems safe to say that in practice the era of charging the goalkeeper is over.

The referee has always had a lot of discretion because so many issues are a matter of split-second judgement. Does what he has seen deserve his intervention or not? One issue that tested the referee's judgement and inter-

in FIFA. But the organisation of the domestic American game was limited by its participants being mainly immigrants – Germans, Irish, Italians, Scots, Brazilians – and the fact that it had to compete for support and resources with longer established sports such as baseball. Professional leagues had struggled to survive and an International League, largely using foreign professionals had folded in 1965. But in 1966 US television broadcast the World Cup taking place in England and this may have stimulated local businessmen to have another go at bringing professional football to the world's richest nation. Soon two leagues had been formed. The United Soccer Association was licensed by the USSFA whereas the National Professional Soccer League was an independent body outside the control of FIFA. Both lost money and in 1968 merged to form the North American Soccer League (NASL). It was soon clear that the new organisation was not going to be satisfied with the laws of football as the IFAB and FIFA had come to know them. FIFA's Secretary was checking the constitution of the NASL when he had discovered that teams could make three substitutions to their starting elevens, contrary to Law 3 which clearly stated two. Jimmy McGuire, President of the USSFA, made an impassioned plea for exemption. The NASL had to play in the summer – partly to avoid competition with American football – partly because only then could they get a television contract – and American summers were hot.

As we have seen, the Americans had other difficulties with the universal interpretation of the laws. The North American Soccer League wanted experiments with a view to law changes. The International Board had been thinking about this as goals per game declined everywhere and defensive attitudes among coaches appeared to be in the ascendant. They had actually organised a match

in Edinburgh in 1968 with a line drawn to the touchline level with the penalty spot as the boundary of the offside zone but decided that it did not work. Now the NASL wanted to continue the experiment in their own championship. FIFA's Secretary was strongly opposed. 'I feel that a new experiment in the United States would … bring unrest to the football world and would be prejudicial to FIFA's efforts to bring about the universal interpretation of the laws of the game.' Two entrenched and opposed positions seemed to be developing. On the one side, FIFA and the International Board who had overseen football becoming the world's most popular sport but recognised that all might not be well, yet were unsure what to do about it. On the other, a young, brash organisation which was struggling for sporting survival in a country apparently most inhospitable to football.

Phil Woosnam, a former British professional with Leyton Orient, West Ham and Aston Villa (he also played seventeen times for Wales) was now Commissioner of the NASL and pleaded their case. After explaining the importance of structural change, administrative modernisation and the need to capture the interest of the six to eighteen age group, he suggested that the biggest drawback for soccer football in the USA was its lack of scoring. His four years in the States studying American sports and their willingness to make rule changes for the sake of a better spectacle had convinced him that football would benefit from the same approach. The NASL, he believed should be allowed to experiment for a complete season with whatever rule changes the IFAB might recommend aimed at increasing the rate of goal scoring. Two such changes immediately came to mind. First, a relaxation in the offside law and second an increase in the size of the goal from eight feet (2.44m) by eight yards (7.32m) to nine feet (2.74m) by nine yards (8.23m). He

14

14 Dramatisation of a foul. Azizi (Iran) brought down by Regis (USA), Iran v. United States (World Cup 1998).

15 The red card, used to punish severe fouls or a second yellow card offence.

16 How to choose between red and yellow cards? *Futuro* refereeing lessons in Haiti, 1998.

was also in favour of points for goals. Helmut Kaser, the Secretary of FIFA replied agreeing that football's grass roots in America required attention, but he was opposed to any law changes and unsympathetic to the idea of making profits out of football. This was the old FIFA up against the New World with a vengeance!

Woosnam did get permission from IFAB via the USSFA and FIFA to conduct an experiment in the latter part of the 1972 season limiting offside to the area between the goal line and an extended eighteen-yard line. But, like so many similar experiments, few were convinced that the change made any difference to the way the game was played. Clearly, the NASL thought football was not attractive enough in the competitive sporting market of the United States. The league was soon back with a request for another experiment in 1974: five rather two substitutes in NASL matches and free substitution. This was partly designed as a way of giving more young American nationals the chance to play. Most of the teams were made up of experienced European and South American professionals, but it was essential for the future to bring young native-born players through. If FIFA had some sympathy for this idea, they were less impressed by another request to enlarge the size of the goals. The aim was six a game, as against the current 2.5 in England, 2.1 in Spain and 1.87 in Italy. Kaser told Kurt Lamm, the Secretary of the USSFA, that neither proposal had much chance of being approved.

In 1975, desperate for network television exposure, the NASL wanted either to insert commercials when the ball went out for a goal kick or find another opportunity to stop the game for a thirty-second advertising slot.

Kaser was quick to point out that this would be 'absolutely contrary to the Laws of the Game and ... to decisions of the competent FIFA Committees.'

But these issues would not go away. Two years later the Secretary of the United States Soccer Federation, as USSFA had now been renamed, wrote again requesting permission to experiment with the offside area, enlarged goals and shoot-outs. He pleaded with FIFA not only to recognise the intensity of the struggle that the American federation and the NASL were having but also to show some leadership in a changing world. But the Referees' Committee unanimously refused to grant permission to increase the size of the goals. Such changes 'merely cause a lot of insecurity throughout the world, make the game more and more complicated and what is worse completely destroy the current universal interpretation and application of the laws ...' While recognising the difficulties NASL faced, they felt the answer was not experiments with the laws but improved fitness and ball skills.

Of course, FIFA *was* engaging in some experiments of its own. Short corners, a kick-in instead of a throw-in and the temporary expulsion of players had been tried in a number of youth tournaments. These were the only kind of experiments that would be tolerated, ones that might lead to alterations in the 'mentality of clubs and certain players'.

Yet the American problem refused to go away. IFAB began experiments with the offside law in 1978 and the NASL was delighted to be able draw a line across the field thirty-five yards from each goal line to create the offside zone. But while the Board and FIFA discontinued the experiment after a year, the NASL kept it going. In December 1980 they were informed by the FIFA

15

must stop signifying the end of their games by firing a starter's pistol!

Twenty years later the President of the São Paulo Football Federation in Brazil also tried to enhance the game's popularity by a radical change of the laws. During the 1990s he introduced three-minute time-outs in each half, two referees and a white spray for them to use to mark the point from which free-kicks should be taken and defensive walls stand. In 2001 he abolished drawn games. Goalless matches meant no points for the teams and score draws were settled on penalties with one point going to the losers and three to the winning teams. There were critics, including the former 1970 World Cup star Tostao who argued that as there was more to football and life than just winners and losers, the draw was democratic and healthy. One has to learn to share, he said. FIFA banned President Eduardo José Farah from transferring his rules to the regional and national leagues.

In the 1990s, FIFA made several adjustments to football's rules. Referees were instructed to be firm on tackles from behind and Law 12 was updated to make clear

16

Executive that if they had not undertaken to adhere to the laws of the game by 15 January 1981, the USSF would be suspended. This precipitated some exchanges between Switzerland and the United States that were more exciting than most football matches. These included a personal letter from Dr Henry Kissinger, President of the NASL to FIFA President Havelange requesting that the NASL be permitted to retain the thirty-five yard offside zone. FIFA replied with a denial that such permission had actually ever been given. Eventually a compromise was reached. The FIFA Executive agreed that the NASL be 'exceptionally permitted' to use the thirty-five yard offside line and three substitutes instead of two up to the end of their 1981 season. After that the league must fully comply with the laws of the game as decided by the IFAB and published by FIFA. A further American proposal to set up a study group on the results of the offside changes and the impact of three substitutes was turned down by FIFA even though the Americans had offered to pay for it. The new FIFA Secretary, Mr Blatter, also insisted that the USSF inform the NASL that they

Telegram: "SOCCER"

All-India Football Federation

Patron-in-Chief:
Dr. RAJENDRA PRASAD,
PRESIDENT OF THE REPUBLIC OF INDIA

President:
PANKAJ GUPTA, Esq., B.A., M.B.E.

Hony. Secretary:
K. ZIAUDDIN, Esq., B.A., B.T., J.P.

Hony. Treasurer:
Capt. B. R. K. TANDON, M.A.

1, West Range, Calcutta-17.
Phone: P. K. 332.

Office: 92, Hornby Road, Bombay.
Phone: 26906.
Residence: 13, Regi House, Lady
Jamshedji Road, Mahim, Bombay.
Phone: 62824.

Office: Bareilly College, Bareilly.
Phone: 116.
Residence: Mandir Dunji, Bareilly.
Phone: 63.

No...........................   31st March 195 4

The Hon: Secretary,
F. I. F. A.,
Bahnfostr 77,
ZURICH (Switzerland).

Eingegangen
-6 APR 1954

Dear Sir,

        I am enclosing a copy of the Referee's
Report forwarded to us by one of our Constituents,
the Western India Football Association, Bombay.
        This pertains to one Mr. J.N. Morris who has
been playing as Goalkeeper for an affiliated Club.
The Referee during the game noticed that the player
had an artificial leg with iron plates and bars.
        I shall thank you kindly to let us know
if the player is eligible to take part in the games
under Law 4 of the Referees' Chart.

                        Yours faithfully,

                        (K.Ziauddin)
                        Hon: Secretary.

17

that contact with the opponent before touching the ball is foul play. Perhaps most significant, was a shift in emphasis in the offside law whereby the referee's assistants, formerly linesmen, were instructed to keep their flags down when a player was technically offside but not involved in the play. As attackers were also not to be given offside if level with the last defender, the balance of the game was altered in favour of the attack. Three substitutes were finally now allowed.

On the experimental side, the Belgian Second Division failed to escape its natural obscurity by substituting the kick-in for the throw-in. Commercial imperative appears to have been behind a trial introduction of the time-out in both the Women's World Cup and Under-17 World Championship in 1995. Each team was allowed one ninety second break in each half. Most supporters of the game, referees and journalists were opposed and as only a third of the possible time-outs were used the experiment remained exactly that. The 1990s also saw the completion of a thorough revision and streamlining of football's laws. The seventeen basic rules had become so cluttered with amendments, footnotes and explanations of IFAB decisions that it had become the antithesis of the simple game. The new edition came out in 1999.

Such a revision was important in its own right. One of the regular tasks of the FIFA Secretariat and the Referees'

Mr. G. M. Morris,
C/o. THOS. COOK & SON (CONTINENTAL AND OVERSEAS) LTD.,
    Hornby Road,
    BOMBAY - 1.

                                    23rd June, 1954.

The Hon. Secretary,
Western India Football Association,
Club House, Cooperage,
BOMBAY.

Dear Sir,

        I thank you for your kind communication of the 26th of
May 1954, which still does not advise me whether I shall be banned
from Football under the auspices of the Western India Football
Association or not. However, I presume that in view of the fact
that the sole decision has been left with the referees, my ban
is still maintained.

        In this case I wish to appeal to the Western India
Football Association to take up the matter once again and this time
at least give me a sporting chance to place before them my own
case.

        From the papers it appears that all that was sent forward
to the different bodies was Mr. Ambalam's report advising you that
I was playing with an artificial leg with iron plates and bars.
This, to say the least, is a very crude description of my artificial limb and it amazes me that the Referees' Association on
receipt of this report did not call upon me to appear before them
and state my case or alternatively appear before them in Football
kit. If you had resorted to either of these courses, and my
case given a fair hearing, you would have seen that the Referee
Ambalam's report, which likened my appearance on the Football
Field to Knights of old proceeding to battle complete in armour
from head to foot, was not at all the case, and that apart from
the hinges and the stays holding the hinges to my limb, no metal
is attached to the orthopedic appliance. You have also failed
to point out that I have played for 4 years without doing any
harm to another player.

                        Yours faithfully,

                        Gen. Secretary of Cooks Sports Club.

    c.c. to: The Hon. Secretary,
            Federation Internationale De Football Association,
            Bahnfostr 77,   ZURICH (Switzerland).

        c.c. to: The Football Secretary of Bombay Gymkhana Ltd., BOMBAY.

        c.c. to: The Hon. Secretary, All India Football Federation,
            BOMBAY.

18

19

17 The case of the goalkeeper with the iron leg (India FA 1954). Act I, the All India FA explain the case to FIFA. According to the referees report, Morris, the goalkeeper, played 'with a steel artificial leg'

18 The case of the goalkeeper with the iron leg (India FA 1954) Act II. Defence of the accused stressed that the goalkeeper did not resemble a 'cavalier wearing armour from head to toe'.

19 The case of the goalkeeper with the iron leg (India FA 1954). Act III, FIFA's decision. 'In accordance with Law 4 of the game, Mr Morris is not authorised to take part in a football match'

Committee has been to answer queries on the rules from national associations and it was crucial to make them as clear as possible. Of course, a game that knew no geographical boundaries was bound to produce uncertainties of interpretation given that all possible contingencies could hardly be covered by seventeen laws. Moreover, the original laws were in English and may not always have translated clearly into other languages. It also took a long time for the laws of football to be translated into some languages. The first version in Malay, for example, was not produced until 1970.

FIFA occasionally received unexpected queries regarding bizarre refereeing decisions. Two cases show their complexity. In July 1935, Fenerbahce played Besiktas to decide the Turkish championship. The first two games were drawn. In the third, with the score level at one goal each, and ten minutes left to play, a linesman, obviously with other commitments, left the field. No substitute could be found and the referee decided that the last ten minutes should be finished with only one linesman. In that time Fenerbahce scored the winning goal. Following Besiktas' protest, the President of the Turkish football association decided to ask for Schrciker's advice. He replied that he had never heard of anything like it in forty-two years of football. The second involved a goalkeeper in western India who in 1954 had played for four years with an artificial leg but was then sent off by a referee for being a danger to other players. He complained that it was unfair, asking FIFA to reconsider his case.

In 1947 the recently formed Burma Amateur Football Association were presented with a problem in a local match which they thought required the aid of FIFA. The Post and Telecoms goalkeeper had taken a goal kick to his full-back who was standing outside the penalty area. The full-back returned the ball to the goalkeeper but inadvertently sent it into his own goal. The referee should have awarded a goal but instead gave a corner. The game ended in a 3-3 draw. Should that result stand even though the referee admitted his error? Or should the goal disallowed by the referee be awarded to Civil Suppliers, the other team, who would then win 4-3? Or should the game be replayed? Even FIFA got confused, first saying that the game should be replayed, the referee having admitted that he applied the law incorrectly and wrongly awarded the goal — which of course he hadn't. The files are silent on FIFA's second reply.

Nor was it only new and relatively inexperienced associations who regularly asked for FIFA's views on tricky issues of what the laws said or meant. The Netherlands football association had been preparing a new edition of the *Laws of the Game for Referees* and 'studying the text of the English edition issued in 1978' they thought that they had discovered a few anomalies. Law 10, for example, Method of Scoring, laid down that the team scoring the greater number of goals during a game shall be the winner. But what about own goals? So, as they said 'to avoid misunderstanding' the text might read 'the team scoring the greater number of goals into the opponents, goal during a game shall be the winner'. FIFA's reply to this does not seem to have survived. And it was a match in the Dutch League between Ajax and Helmond Sport in which a rather unorthodox penalty kick was taken. Instead of shooting directly for goal, the kicker (Johan Cruyff) passed to a player running into the penalty area from his left who then dribbled the ball forward before returning it to the original kicker who scored. But was it fair? The answer was yes, so long as the ball had been originally played forward, the receiving player had come from outside the penalty area and his colleague had stayed behind the ball and was therefore onside. In the same year the Dutch also wanted to know what the referee's decision should be if a defending player in his own penalty area with a shinguard in one of his hands hits the ball with it and prevents it from entering the goal. The answer was a penalty as the shinguard is considered as an extension of the hand. It is not surprising that the

KNVB enjoyed the sections in *FIFA News* given over to articles and questions on the laws of the game and were sorry when they were discontinued.

The Scandinavian football associations were also regular correspondents with FIFA on the laws of the game and contributed to the outlawing of the so-called 'professional foul' in 1990. In 1985, the General Secretary of the Norwegian football association, asked for an interpretation of a Law 12 subsection which stated that 'a player shall be sent off the field of play if he is guilty of violent conduct or serious foul play.'

'Serious foul play,' wrote the Norwegian General Secretary, 'what is that? In our opinion one of the most serious fouls a player can commit must be when he intentionally ... by holding, tripping or pushing, stops an opponent outside the penalty area who has a clear path to goal, and a good possibility of scoring ...' By outlawing the professional foul they hoped a friendlier game and more goals would result.

Earlier members of the international football establishment had thought that, if football could develop and spread across the globe, as it had, it must be mainly due to the rules having been perfectly drawn up in a manner that ensured their correct application.

20

20 A case study in a school for referees in London, approximately 1937.

21 The toss before the 1920 Antwerp Olympics football final between Belgium and Czechoslovakia. The match was short and bad tempered.

21

Compared to rugby, football had fewer laws, was much simpler to play and potentially more attractive to watch. On the other hand, there was plenty of room for differences of opinion about what happens on the field and what, if anything, should be done about it. The people whose job it is to both know the law and exercise their judgement in applying it are the referees. Nobody likes them but it is clear that football could not do without them. They are supposed to be seen but not noticed. They are crucial to the game at all levels. Hardly anyone has written about them save for the self-satisfied autobiographies of a few dozen celebrity officials who have risen to the top in their national associations and become FIFA international referees. Refereeing may await its historian, but it certainly has a history.

22 John Langenus, the Belgian international referee at the who refereed the first World Cup final on 30ᵗʰ July 1930.

Referees

As we have seen, one of the reasons for setting up an organisation to oversee the progress of football across national boundaries was the importance of developing a uniform interpretation of the laws of the game. The production of good referees was clearly a most crucial part of this process. Their recruitment and training was the responsibility of individual national associations. FIFA wanted to encourage this and thought setting up a Referees' Committee would be a good idea. When this was proposed to the FIFA Congress in 1913 the well-known English referee, John Lewis, founder member of Blackburn Rovers and FA Councillor, thought the idea a waste of time and money. He claimed that, although a referees' union had been formed in England, conditions there were no better than twenty-five years ago and that many English referees had no deep understanding of the game. This was the same John Lewis who at the age of sixty-five, refereed the final of the Olympic football tournament of 1920 in Antwerp between Belgium and Czechoslovakia. The Czechs disagreed with so many of his decisions that, after he had awarded a second goal to Belgium in the second half, they walked off the field and refused to continue.

In spite of this British referees were thought of as being the best for a long time. In fact, until the Second World War their superiority was unchallenged worldwide. In 1938 the Argentinian Football Association recruited Issac Caswell, a retired football league referee from Blackburn, to help improve standards in a league which placed massive pressure on referees from players, spectators, club

23

officials and owners. Standards of refereeing in the growing football world improved only slowly. British referees were still controlling almost a quarter of all full and 'B' internationals between the beginning of 1951 and the end of 1952. The first FIFA conference for international referees was held in Prague in May 1925. FIFA publications were increasingly used to underline the importance of improving refereeing standards and an article in *Football World* in 1938 declared it one of the problems of the contemporary game. Referees were urged to confront the 'lack of courtesy' in many international matches and apply the rules by delivering cautions and sendings off. Not only were referees low on experience; they were often not physically fit enough. This mattered more after 1925 when the game speeded up following a change in the offside rule. Many referees could not keep up with the game and were generally vague about which position they should take up in relation to the play. There were often language difficulties in international matches between the referee and the players and often between the referee and his linesmen. International football was inevitably bound up with national prestige and the emotional intensity often made matches difficult to handle. No wonder the IFAB experimented with two referees in trial matches at Chester and West Bromwich in 1935, but the results were disappointing. As we have already seen, referees also had to cope with inconsistencies in the interpretation of the rules that were developing in different parts of the football world. FIFA did not have the resources to deal with these issues by putting on courses for the best referees.

24

Given all these factors, it is not surprising that the refereeing in the first three World Cups was weak. Although only six players were sent off in these tournaments, one of them was the wrong Peruvian in their match with Romania in 1930. It cannot have helped that the players' shirts were unnumbered. Referees were only selected from those countries competing in the finals, which meant that there were only three from Europe in 1930 and none from South America in 1934 or 1938. Inevitably there were allegations of incompetence and worse but it must be stressed that apart from the Olympic football tournaments this was a new experience for a group of relatively inexperienced people. Two factors pointed the way to practice. The idea of a FIFA badge to be awarded to the best international

25

referees was first broached by the Referees' Committee in 1939, although it would be ten years before it was taken up. More importantly, Stanley Rous developed the diagonal system of control after, according to the Belgian referee John Langenus, he had seen Belgian referees making a similar attempt at scientific positioning on the field. This was destined to become the blueprint for all refereeing. It was featured in a long article in *Football World* in 1939 and involved the referee moving around an imaginary diagonal line drawn from one corner flag to another with the two linesmen patrolling the touchline farthest away from the referee's route.

In the decades which followed the end of the Second World War, FIFA was able to start tackling the important problem of refereeing standards in two main ways. Firstly, the post-war World Cups were popular and made money. What better than to spend some of it on improving the standards of referees worldwide, especially in those newly inde-

pendent countries whose enthusiasm for football was so clear. Secondly, in Stanley Rous FIFA had a man of whom it could be said that refereeing was a central life interest. For Rous, the referee was not simply the one figure without whom organised football could not take place, he was also a moral paragon, a man steeped in the ethics of fair play, even-handed in his judgements, honest, an example of the virtues of self-discipline and self-control with the skills to manage the behaviour of others in vigorously physical and emotional situations. The referee was the true guardian of the spirit of the game. Rous believed strongly in the value of training courses for referees and he not only helped organise them in all the new Confederations but he himself travelled thousands of miles to lecture on them. He took charge, for example, of the first FIFA referees' course in Asia, in Tokyo in 1958, held to coincide with the football tournament at the third Asian Games. Twenty-four referees from fourteen countries took part.

25 Participants at a FIFA refereeing school held in Costa Rica in 1959.

His courses gradually developed a syllabus that mixed the practical with the theoretical, used films as well as books and by the mid-sixties had been translated into eight languages. Subjects explored included how to become a referee, co-operation between referee and linesmen and the positions to be adopted at various phases of the game such as corners, free kicks and penalties. There were also demonstrations and discussions around the more contentious interpretational issues such as obstruction, advantage, time wasting and other abuses of the laws. The importance of physical fitness and how to achieve it was also stressed. A good example of what was achieved was the course in Central America over twenty-two days in July and August 1965. It was run by the well-known Spanish former referee Pedro Escartin and he was assisted by Alvar Macis, the Secretary of the Central and North American and Caribbean Football Confederation (CONCACAF). The course began in the relatively unpromising territory – for football that is –

of Panama and finished in Guatemala via Costa Rica, Nicaragua, Honduras and El Salvador, all places where football had become, or was in the process of becoming, the most popular sport. Refereeing was of a high standard in Costa Rica and some contribution to that had doubtless been made by an earlier course six years earlier. Nonetheless, sixty-two referees turned up for three days of afternoon and evening sessions and 350 referees, trainers, players and other interested parties attended the film shows. A tape recording was made of the course to be used in other local football organisations. Costa Rica then, and probably now, had the highest standard of football in Central America, if Mexico is excluded. In Honduras and El Salvador suggestions were made about referee recruitment and training. In every location the course was ended by a fifteen-minute discussion about the conduct of the referee in which delicate subjects were raised – not simply about presentation and good manners – but of also not

accepting too much hospitality and of not mixing with players, trainers or officials in the bars. Escartin was convinced that his 24 landings and take-offs had been worth it and it would be churlish to disagree.

In Africa, the process of formal decolonisation may have been almost complete by the 1960s but the loss of European expertise in a range of fields could not be quickly rectified. Football refereeing was one of them. An English referee who accompanied the Middlesex Wanderers on their tour of East and Central Africa in 1965 found local standards poor with intimidation and violence against referees common. There may have been some post-imperial *schadenfreude* at work here but there was also evidence of referees with eccentric notions of their powers. At Ndola in Zambia, as one side had not arrived the referee insisted that the home side should kick off. When they 'scored' he blew his whistle for the end of the first half, then repeated the procedure for the second half. The 'match' lasted two minutes. Then, the opposing side arrived, after a journey of 185 miles. After their protests, the referee agreed to play the game, which the visitors won 4-2. But in his report, the referee said the result was 4-4 having counted the two unopposed 'goals' he had allowed before the proper game had begun.

The sensitive nature of African-European relations were also revealed after Ghana had defeated Nigeria in Lagos in October 1960. The match had been refereed by an Englishman, Ken Aston, who had had to report that after trying to leave the stadium, the coach containing the Ghana team was stoned, windows were smashed and some of the passengers were injured. He also offered the opinion that there was nothing in the behaviour of the Ghana players which could have provoked such a reaction but there had been an 'anti-Ghana' atmosphere among the public and in

the press for several days before the match. Aston also complained about the travel arrangements, the accommodation and the poor hospitality. The Nigerian football association's representative admitted that the crowd control arrangements after the game had been inadequate but concluded:

... it is our desire to play football according to the rules of the game. It is for this reason that we have at all times endeavoured to seek the assistance of FIFA and the English Football Association in sending out to this country first-class referees to officiate at our matches. These requests are made because we feel that we can learn quite a lot from Europeans who have more experience in refereeing then our local referees. It is therefore essential that when we ask FIFA to send us a referee we should be sent men who are tolerant and sympathetic and who

26 At the end of the stormy match between England and Argentina during the World Cup. Police Officers escort Kretlein, the German referee, 23 July 1966.

27 The limit of human perception. Only the referee can decide if the ball crossed the line. At 3-2 in England's favour the Jules Rimet trophy is getting closer.

28 Red cards were distributed generously during the Mexico Olympics. Mexican referee, De Leo, sent off three Bulgarian players during the final, which was won 4-1 by Hungary (26 October 1968).

appreciate our difficulties ... [Mr Aston's] comments on the accommodation in the army barracks suggests a prejudice which had it been known to us before his arrival would have compelled us to refuse his services.

Mr Aston refuted the charge of prejudice, pointing out that he had commanded 'large bodies of Indian troops during the last war'. But when the Nigerian football association sent a telegram asking FIFA to appoint a referee for the next match against Ghana the preference was for one from western Germany or Italy.

More serious were suggestions of political interference and attempts to influence the outcome of international matches by offering travel expenses or fees to referees which were in excess of those guidelines issued by FIFA or the African Football Confederation (AFC). There were also allegations that if the home association did not like the way a referee had performed in an international match they would

28

29 What hit the referee? Van Gemert, the Dutch referee, was hit by the ball during a match between Germany-Brazil in June 1973.

refuse to pay his expenses or use a currency that was difficult to exchange.

Rumours that referees might have been influenced to favour one side would exacerbate the feelings against them by administrators, players and crowds. Footballing relations between Europe and South America deteriorated following some of the refereeing in the 1966 World Cup. Rous had to call two secret meetings in London in 1967 to rebuild the relationship with South America and to admit that the image of FIFA there had been damaged. International football was clearly bound up with the prestige of states, and rivalries between some countries could be fierce. Moreover, as we have seen, it was a relatively easy way to foster a sense of national identity and modernise a state. But referees could sometimes find themselves at the centre of alarming events, the complex causes of which they could hardly be expected to appreciate.

D.S.K Amengor from Ghana had such an experience after he had refereed a match between Mali and the Ivory Coast on 19 June 1977.

After the game which Mali won 1-0, the Head of National Security in Mali, Lieutenant Colonel Tiegoro Bagayoko, entered the dressing room with some soldiers and policemen armed with guns, sticks and belts. My linesmen, Messrs J.O. Odai and Matthew Ossi-Tutu, were beaten by Captain Sylla who is the chairman of the Referees' Committee of Mali. The soldiers continued to beat us savagely for a long time on the instructions of Lt Colonel Bagayoko, even after he had left the dressing room ... Even the First Secretary of the Ghana Embassy who was in the dressing room with us, was also beaten up by the soldiers ... A piece of Bagayoko's walking stick which he used in assaulting me and which got broken in the process is being mailed to you as an exhibit. I wish to add that I sustained injuries, bruises and abrasions on my head, face, left shoulder, back, buttocks, right fore-finger and thumb. We managed to see the Match Commissioner and lodged an official complaint with him. He advised that my match report should not be posted in Mali and that this is why the report is late.

Being a referee could turn into a nightmare even on the most illustrious of stages, as the World Club Championship of the 1960s and 1970s clearly demonstrated. These matches brought out the worst in everyone concerned and the only surprise was that it took until 1980 to decide that they should be played as a single match in neutral Tokyo.

The 1970 World Cup was a defining moment for FIFA and world football in many ways. Moreover, not one player was sent off and the number of cautions, marked by the issue of the new Yellow Card, was the lowest on record. The work of the FIFA Referees' Committee appeared to be vindicated, the training courses, the films, the articles in various FIFA publications, the determination to produce a consistent interpretation of the rules, and a week of preparation before the finals for the thirty referees had produced a show that everyone could enjoy. It wasn't perfect but it had shown that increasing indiscipline on the international football field was not an inevitable consequence of the increasing intensity of competition as many had thought.

But that was too optimistic. Another defining moment was Italia 1990 with its cynical fouling and tedious football. International football and the way the game was played continued to change. Players continued to get bigger and stronger and their rewards for success became greater. The game got even faster. Just look at the films of even the giants of 1970 and note how relatively slow they seem!

30

This made it harder for referees to keep up with the play and to concentrate 100 per cent all of the time. Ophthalmic specialists in Spain in the 1990s concluded that because the human eye could not focus quickly enough to see players rapidly changing positions, linesmen were unable to judge offsides accurately. Moreover, the media coverage of international football grew more insatiable and less restrained. Perhaps reflecting a wider world that had become less respectful of authority, and in football terms, less willing to accept the mistakes of referees and linesmen which could be analysed in slow motion and picked over countless times. In 1980, George Joseph refereed the final match in the Olympic qualifying tournament in Baghdad between Iraq and Kuwait. Afterwards, he was taken to a TV studio, shown a film of the match several times and forced to admit he made some wrong decisions and sign the referee's report accordingly.

Referees have become more professional in their outlook and preparation, both physically and mentally. Some from Brazil, England and Italy have even become full-time salaried officials. The laws have also been changed in ways unthinkable in 1970. The so-called professional foul was outlawed in 1990 and 1991. In 1992, the goalkeeper was banned from picking up the ball when it was passed to him by one of his own team mates and the tackle from behind, when contact is made with the player first, was made illegal in 1998.

There are certainly more referees now than ever before. In 2000, there were over 720,000 worldwide and 417,000 in Europe. The best referees are no longer all Europeans. Perhaps they are no longer all men. Perhaps the time has come to select the best referees irrespective of gender. We still know little about the social composition of referees or why they do it.

31

Recent research from Britain suggests that referees may suffer from 'illusory superiority', which means that they think they know better than everyone else – even other referees. They never blame themselves for the hostility of players and crowds. Perhaps without this confidence they could not function. Eventually the adoption of new technologies could jeopardise both their authority and their confidence.

The rules of football are universal and it is the role of referees to apply them universally. The interpretation of the rules has often been reflected differently in the same way that different cultures have not only practised football but invested it with meaning.

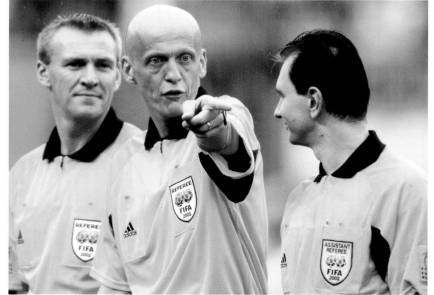

32

JUAN DEPORTISTA
LA FURIA ESPAÑOLA
De la Olimpiada de Amberes à la de Paris

RENACIMIENTO

NATIONAL STYLES, TECHNIQUE AND TACTICS

In the first three decades of the twentieth century the emergence of national leagues and especially national teams contributed to a broader recognition of national distinctions.

NATIONAL STYLES, TECHNIQUE AND TACTICS

2

3

explored in the first part of this chapter. What does seem to be true is that most of those who have discussed national styles over the years have certainly thought that they were talking about something real.

Once regular international football began and especially after the start of the Olympic Games football tournament and the World Cup, it was not surprising that countries began to express their own particular idea of what football was. In the early twentieth century all football was compared to the British game. But British football itself was evolving. The original game of individual rushes had

4

As the historian Eric Hobsbawm has pointed out 'the imaginary community of millions seems more real as a team of eleven named people' especially if it is playing in an international competition like the World Cup. Many writers, and not only football specialists, have noticed the way particular countries express themselves on the football field by adhering to different styles which, it is often asserted, show a real continuity over time. In international football, teams represent the culture of a nation and play the game in a way that reflects the values of that culture. So Argentina has always offered high skill but suspect temperament, Brazil have been generally flamboyant and inventive while Cameroon have combined technical virtuosity with ruthless defence. The English meanwhile, have been characterised as phlegmatic but predictable while Italy have produced teams which were both physically assertive and technically sound. Does any of this tell us anything about the real virtues and vices of nations or are we simply using the language of stereotypes? Some of these issues will be

Player Portraits

Diego Maradona

+ 'Only once during my career did I feel as though I had really reached the heights of the game. It was the day I made my debut in the Argentine first division... I was so happy because I felt that my life was moving on to another level. The sun was shining, the stadium was packed with fans... That Sunday would have been perfect if we had won. But it wasn't to be and Talleres beat us thanks to a goal from Luduena.'

+ 'The overriding feeling when I lifted the World Cup was the need to share the moment. Share it with the people of Argentina. It's hard to imagine what the victory meant to the vast majority of them.'

Michel Platini

+ 'It was during the World Cup that I realised I was representing something more than just France.' + 'My philosophy is simple: to return to football everything that the game has given me' + 'I have seen life from every angle thanks to football – as a player, coach, director and as co-chairman of a World Cup organising committee. The experience players gain during their careers can also play an important role in the administration and development of the game.'

George Weah

✦ 'Of course, I am very religious. I have God to thank for my gift for playing football and I will never forget that.'

✦ 'In Liberia, a country that has experienced great hardship, my success on the football field has provided a glimmer of hope.'

Bobby Charlton

✦ 'I have always been faithful in football, just as I have in life.' ✦ 'Football might have changed – it is certainly faster nowadays – but it is still the showmen who capture the public's imagination. In my day, it was Di Stefano and Pelé. Today, it is Ronaldo, Zidane and Beckham.'

Alfredo Di Stefano

✦ 'Football and ballet have a great deal in common. The game is founded on skill, balance and imagination. Every player has to concentrate on technique, speed and teamwork. A great player cannot be selfish. Even if people say that football is a sport that is not intuitive because you don't use your hands, it is still an art form, a kind of poetry. Thinking that football is just kicking a ball is a sign of ignorance.'

Cha Bum

✦ 'When I was playing in Germany, I thought about what could be done to make Korea one of the top teams in international football. I knew that I had to do something and work for the future.'

Eusebio

+ 'Throughout my life, I have had a double identity. I have two hearts: one for my home and the other for Portugal.'

+ 'While I sometimes had to take a zig-zagging course on the football pitch, I have always followed a straight path in life.'

Roger Milla

+ 'In Africa, I have ceased being Cameroonian. For African people, I am a representative of the entire continent.'

+ 'Like many other footballers, my destiny is split between two continents – Africa and Europe. And that is not always easy. Footballers should work more in campaigns against illiteracy and AIDS, because children will listen to them more than other people.'

Franz Beckenbauer

+ 'Football is one of the world's best means of communication. It is impartial, apolitical and universal. Football unites people around the world every day. Young or old, players or fans, rich or poor, the game makes everyone equal, stirs the imagination, makes people happy and makes them sad. And best of all, a person's skin colour, language, education or bank balance makes no difference inside a football stadium. As an international organisation, FIFA has an important role to play in bringing people together.'

+ 'Fame does not only bring benefits, but also many responsibilities. Players have the opportunity to work for football and for all those who love the game. That is one of the reasons that motivated me to make a commitment to the 2006 FIFA World Cup™ in Germany. Football has given me so much that I feel obliged to give something back.'

+ 'I had one of my most wonderful experiences in New York when I playing for the Cosmos. It was amazing to play alongside Pelé. The pitch was much smaller than in Europe and I had some problems with the artificial turf because the ball always bounced up to knee-height. Pelé had already adapted to it because he had two years' more experience than me. But it had been hard for him as well at the start. He used to talk about how he had come to the USA in 1975 and how a special match had been organised at

Randall's Island Stadium to mark the occasion. It was the first time that ABC – one of America's biggest TV channels – had broadcast a football match live. After the game, when Pelé had returned to the dressing room and taken off his boots, he had a nasty shock. His feet were green. Immediately, he thought that it was a sign from above and wanted to return to Brazil straight away.

The Americans had a simple explanation. With the match being televised across the nation, they thought it would be a good idea to cover the pitch with green paint – thankfully, it washed off!'

Roque Maspoli

+ 'In Brazil in 1950, we started the match as underdogs. But we knew a lot about the Brazilian team. We knew their strengths and we also knew their weaknesses. It was our selfless style and formidable team spirit that drove us to victory in a stadium that was suddenly silenced.'

Nelson Mandela

+ 'Robben Island imprisoned our bodies and not our minds. We turned the bastion of oppression into a cradle of our hope for a non-racial democratic South Africa. FIFA in first suspending (1964) and then banning (1976) South Africa strengthened the overall drive in realising that goal. The creation of a new society on the southern tip of the African continent has been achieved through the struggle of our people and the contribution of the international community. We pay tribute to football leaders such as Havelange and Sepp Blatter as we celebrate our tenth year of democracy in 2004.'

Jules Rimet

+ 'Of all the sports in the world, and perhaps all human activities, football is the one that most frequently forges contact between young people from different nations. Today the game is the most effective instrument for cultivating international accord and friendship. It encapsulates all the elements required for amicable exchanges.'

Johann Cruyff

+ 'The 1974 FIFA World Cup™ Final stays with me wherever I am in the world. Just after our 2-1 defeat, I still couldn't believe it. It was only later on that I started to realise that, although we had not won, we had still left the greatest impression on the fans. I am still very proud that almost thirty years later people all around the world, whether in Asia, South America or Africa, still congratulate me on the football that we played back then.'

Pelé

+ 'I recently received an invitation from the Queen of Denmark. It said that she would be especially honoured to meet the only 'king' who had been crowned by the people.'

+ 'It's not always easy for me to explain to my youngest children that I am not a king. Once they even asked me where I'd hidden my crown.'

+ 'Maybe I owe my longevity to the fact that I was born in a town called Três Corações ('three hearts')...'

+ 'When peasants with nothing seized land of their own, they preserved the stadiums to show how much respect they had for football.'

+ 'A friend of mine who is a priest told me that the name Pelé appears in the Old Testament and that it means 'good fortune'.'

Player Portraits

5

been transformed by the 1880s into a more collective game with the short pass among combining forwards being a particular feature. But it was always a very physical game with the shoulder charge and the tackle at its core. While the balance of the Scottish game may have tended more towards the skilful, Britain's highly competitive professional league increasingly placed a premium on speed and strength. It is clear that it was the British game overall that was copied, adapted and then largely rejected by many Europeans and most South Americans and this process began very early. British amateur and professional teams, for example, went on tours to Argentina, Brazil and Uruguay before 1914. Although they showed the virtues of regular training and practice their play did not impress their hosts. In particular they disliked the violent charging. It was notable that when a team from Argentina visited Brazil in 1912, home supporters were much more impressed with their game compared with that of the English Corinthians. Although amateur, the Corinthians played a physically vigorous game especially in defence.

The Argentinians, on the other hand, offered sophisticated ball control and a more delicate inter-passing game without the charging. By the 1920s, Argentinian sports writers would be talking about a distinctive style of play which had little or nothing to do with the British game.

In 1924 Uruguay took the European football world by surprise when they descended on Paris and won the Olympic football tournament. Commentators were surprised by the marvellous virtuosity of their players in receiving the ball, controlling it and using it. Such technique allowed players time to see where their best placed teammates were. When this was added to a mastery of the feint, the swerve and a dribbling ability of the highest order, ecstatic French critics could not resist comparing these Uruguayan thoroughbreds to English carthorses. Unfortunately, the English were not there to test the veracity of this insult. Uruguay repeated their victory in 1928, beating Argentina in the final, and the same two teams would contest the final of the first World Cup two years later with the same result. Uruguay and Argentina had been playing against each other

NATIONAL STYLES, TECHNIQUE AND TACTICS

6

7

since 1902 and between them had invented a new style which admirers called 'River Plate Football'.

The young men from Brazil also began their assault on European footballing sensibilities in the years between the wars. The São Paulo team had toured successfully in 1925 but it was the appearance of the Brazilian national team at the 1938 World Cup finals in France which produced an outbreak of excited praise for their superior technique and overall distinctiveness. This was partly based on the ball juggling and athleticism of Leonidas, an early performer of the bicycle kick, and the elegant defence of Domingos da Guia. The dexterity of some of the first black players seen in Europe was thought to be the product of a tropical climate and hard grounds which required a different level of skill to master the unruly 'female' ball. A leading Brazilian intellectual, the anthropologist and historian Gilberto Freye exclaimed that Brazilians had turned an ordinary British game into a 'dance of irrational surprises.' The dance metaphor would reappear many times in the work of scholars and sports journalists in the years to come as Brazil became the world's leading football nation and the favourite team of many enthusiasts. The development of television in the late 1950s bought the team many more fans.

Meantime, football in Central Europe had also begun to make claims for a style of its own to which some journalists eventually attached the label 'Danube School.' Austria, Hungary and Czechoslovakia (Bohemia before the Versailles Settlement) had all started playing before the First World War and this network of footballing relations and rivalries was further strengthened after it when allied countries refused to play with them. In 1927 the Danube nations established the Mitropa Cup, a club competition for the leading side in the above-mentioned three countries togeth-

er with that of another new state, Yugoslavia. Exchanges of ideas and people between the football capitals of Vienna, Budapest and Prague led to what contemporaries thought was a more technically refined game than that of the British with sophisticated ball skills providing the basis for a more tactical approach. Ironically some of this was due to the coaching of Englishmen and Scotsmen – although how much remains difficult to say. The most famous British coach was probably Jimmy Hogan who worked in several Central European countries but was particularly associated with developments in Hungary and the Austrian Wundermannschaft of the early 1930s. Hungary actually beat England just before the 1934 World Cup and Austria had a string of famous victories including one over Italy in Turin in 1934 and an extremely unlucky defeat against England in December 1932. Unfortunately, they failed to live up to expectations in the 1934 World Cup. Perhaps the players were past their best or just suffering from overwork. In 1933 Hugo Meisl's Austrian team, masquerading as Vienna Select, lost 4-2 to Arsenal in 1933. Meisl felt they

8

Die österreichische Nationalmannschaft
die am vergangenen Sonntag gegen die Tschechoslovakei 2:2 spielte

9 Mathias Sindelar a 'Complete centre forward, creative genius and formidable finisher' (Jacques De Ryswick), playing in the Mitropa Cup match between Austria and Ferencvaros (July 1935).

10 Hugo Meisl's 'Wunderteam' in their heyday. March 1930.

11 Before the invention of the Swiss bolt formation in 1935, the Swiss goalkeeper Pasche finds himself in a tricky situation in a match against Hungary in Budapest, 1931.

were overdoing the short passing, they needed more speed and their defensive covering had to be improved. He also made two other points which would be often repeated over the decades. The first was that the best clubs in Britain were stronger than the national teams. And the second expressed a low opinion of the aesthetic of British football. Central European football, on the other hand, was admired on several continents as Austrian and especially Hungarian players and coaches were influential in many countries.

One such admirer was Italy although how much influence they had there is not clear. The Fascist government wanted all Italians to be special – as befitted the age of the new Roman Empire – and the Italian sporting press applied this notion to its footballers. They were supposed to be strong, quick and clever and to play in a style which could reflect the new Italian identity. Some authorities have suggested that the basic Italian 'metodo', later to be refined

as the 'sistema', was Central European skills allied to a robust physicality of almost British dimensions. Helped by a new generation of players from Argentina, impressive technique and sophisticated short passing were allied to strength in the air to produce a team with a formidable defence which won both the second and third World Cups.

As international football developed and as FIFA promoted both the Olympic football championship and the World Cup it was not surprising that they became interested in the different ways in which different countries apparently played the game. Commentators in Europe and South America were talking and, more importantly, writing about different approaches to football they saw at international matches. Hanot in France, the Meisl brothers in Austria, Pozzo in Italy, Ivan Sharpe in England, Ricardo Lorenzo ('Borocoto') in Argentina and Mario Filho in Brazil all made powerful claims for

Der Sturm — einst

Früher in der alten Zeit,
Ja, da wurde angegriff.
Herrgott, war das eine Freud.
Kam der Sturm dahergepfiffen

Der Sturm — jetzt

Heute gibt es das nicht mehr,
Denn man schießt so zart und lind,
Und der Sturm braust nimmermehr,
Leise säuselt nur ein Wind.

13

12

national distinctiveness, and often, superiority of the way football was played in their countries. Sporting papers and magazines like the *Athletic News*, *El Grafico* and *Miroir les Sports* regularly explored these issues which were also increasingly the subject of the expanding space given to football in both the popular press and on radio. Some of the journalists who contributed to these debates were FIFA Executive Committee members. Books also explored this seductive subject such as Juan Deportista's *La Furia Espanola* and Luis Mendez Dominguez *Los Diablos Rojos*. Football for most countries was a foreign import but everywhere it was adapted to suit local circumstances – what was liked was kept and what was disliked was rejected. Of course, discussions about style were largely initiated by intellectuals searching for clues to national identity and on the lookout for deeper meaning. But in the years between 1920 and 1960 it seems clear that although such debates *were* about ideas and perceptions they were also about something more: a footballing phenomenon which seemed to many people to be real enough. It was widely recognised that one of the pleasures of football's internationalism was that different countries played it differently, a difference underlined by the fact that none of them could be seen doing it very often in a world without television.

Tactics

Despite the different national styles the tactics of the game were not thought to be particularly complex. Each team had a defence, a midfield and an attack and it was crucial to maintain contact between them in a game of continual movement and increasingly quick tempo. But in 1925 an important change was made to the offside law and its impact has been a matter of controversy ever since. Before 1925, a player receiving the ball in his opponent's half was offside if three defenders were not between him and the opposition goal line. This was a severe rule which meant that a successful long pass was difficult as forwards could not

12 Hungarian team, World Cup Finalists in 1938, improve their fitness under the watchful eye of their coach Schaffer, in the suburbs west of Paris.

13 Warriors or ballerinas? Caricature of the changing nature of forwards in the early 1920s (Germany 1924).

14 The nickname 'Red Devils' was given to both the Belgian and Spanish national teams at the start of the 1920s. (Los Diablos Rojos 1931)

15 >

16 >

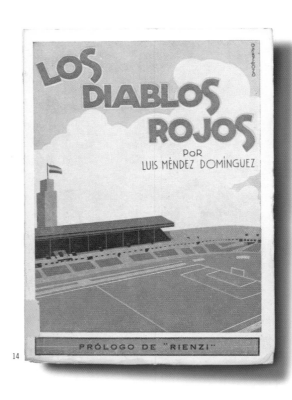

LOS DIABLOS ROJOS

POR
LUIS MÉNDEZ DOMÍNGUEZ

PRÓLOGO DE "RIENZI"

14

15 Incident in the match between River Plate and Independiente (Argentine 1932).

16 Platzer diving to no avail. The 'Wunderteam' lose to the Azzuri in the World Cup semi-final in 1934.

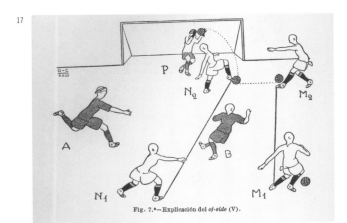

17

Fig. 7.*—Explicación del *of-side* (V).

18

35

No. 1. OFF-SIDE.

CLEAR PASS TO ONE OF SAME SIDE.

A has run the ball up, and having ⸏ in front passes to B. B is off-side because there are not two opponents between him and the goal-line when the ball is passed by A.

If B waits for ⸏ to fall back before he shoots, this will not put him in play, because it does not alter his position with relation to A at the moment the ball was passed by A.

No. 2. NOT OFF-SIDE.

CLEAR PASS TO ONE OF SAME SIDE (*continued*).

A has run the ball up, and having ⸏ in front passes across the field. B runs from position 1 to position 2. B is not off-side because at the moment the ball was passed by A he was behind the ball, and had two opponents between him and the goal-line.

---

loiter far up the field. It had helped to bring about the development of the short passing game in Britain, which was later largely adopted by the rest of Europe and South America but increasing use by professional defences in Britain of an offside trap led to a reduction in the number of goals scored and a decline of interest in football as a spectacle. As a result, IFAB reduced the number of defenders who had to be between the player receiving the ball and the opposition goal line from three to two.

The short-term effect was that the number of goals scored in English League football reached levels that, it can safely be said, will never be surpassed. But teams took defensive countermeasures. The full-backs, formerly central defenders, were pushed wider to mark the wing-forwards. The centre-half, formally a midfield player, was withdrawn to become a third back. It is not clear who invented this new formation but it *is* certain that the Arsenal team managed by Herbert Chapman used it to create a most effective method of retreating defence and counterattack. Alex James became the link between defence and attack often sending long passes inside the opposing full-backs onto which fast direct wingers such as Cliff Bastin and Joe Hulme could run. These new methods were not taken up everywhere. In the World Cups of the 1930s only Germany played this way. But the WM formation, as it became known, would become the standard method.

The new ruling had its critics. Yes, the game was quicker and an accurate long pass could be devastating but where was the combination passing and thoughtful movement into position? The old game's anticipation, craft and teamwork had been replaced by speed, power and caution. Jimmy Hogan, the Englishman who had coached so successfully in Austria, Germany and Hungary, thought that the WM had made British football static and that the very positions taken up by the players on the field forced them into adopting a high-kicking game. On the other hand, R.W. Seeldrayers, an influential member of the FIFA Executive Committee, wrote two articles in *Football World* at the end of the 1930s pointing out that the changes were not so important. It was a 'minor adjustment to the role of the centre-half', although he did recognise the increased pressure on the four midfield players who might have both attacking and defensive responsibilities. Yet both he and Hogan were right. Hogan was complaining about the stereotyped, inflexible approach of most British teams and Seeldrayers was suggesting that the WM was just a basic framework within which intelligent adjustments could be made. The country who made the most devastating adjustments in the first post-war decade was Hungary.

The first thing to remember is the powerful football tradition of Hungary, as we have already seen. The second important point was the 1948 takeover of the government by the Communist Party. This involved the application of state power to all sectors of society including football. It meant focusing on the production of a good national team at the expense of the domestic league. Resources, including the best players, were concentrated in a few clubs. Of the eleven who normally played for Hungary, eight played for Honved and three for MTK. League games were suspended before important internationals such as the one

Gyertek fiúk ti is előre, ne maradjatok ki ebből
a gyönyörű tüzijáték-körforgalomból!

19

17 Before the reform of the law in 1925, an explanation of the offside rule in a Spanish football manual (1925).

18 Explanation of the new offside rule in a referees manual published by the Football Association (1928-29).

19 National heros. Caricature of the Magical Magyars who defeated the English team twice in close succession, 6-3 at Wembley (November 1953), then 7-1 in Budapest (May 1954).

against England in November 1953. The national side was a collective project run by Gustav Sebers, coach and also Vice-President of the National Physical Culture and Sports Committee. The players were state-supported professionals who trained scientifically and practised relentlessly with the aim of bringing them to a peak of form for the most important matches. It should also be said that this policy coincided with a crop of players certainly unsurpassed in Hungary's football history and perhaps in that of most other countries also.

The basis of the Hungarian team's play was the WM but as one of their leading football trainers, Gyula Mandi, wrote, 'we play it elastically'. Hungary won the Olympic football tournament in 1952 and were unbeaten for two more years during which time they inflicted the heaviest defeats England have ever suffered, 6-3 at Wembley and 7-1 in the Nep Stadium. England's defence was woeful on both occasions, the marking non-existent. Kocsis and Puskas played as the spearheads of the Hungarian attack with the supposed centre-forward, Hidegkuti withdrawn into midfield. This puzzled the English centre-half who did not know whether to follow him or stay back and ended up doing neither. Meanwhile Boszik provided the other link between the defence and the attack. The system was thoughtful and flexible, making the best use of the exceptional attacking talent that Hungary had. But they were surprisingly beaten by West Germany in the 1954 World Cup Final. It was a major shock and not easy to explain but Puskas was not fully fit and perhaps should not have played – today he would probably have been a substitute – and the German players marked much more tightly than the English had done. Hungary probably

invented what football journalists began to call 4-2-4 but it was really only an intelligent version of the WM, it was a broad outline of how to play with all the players taking up positions within reach of the man with the ball. After the failure of the 1956 revolution the team broke up and never had another opportunity to renew their battle with Brazil.

It was not so much the tactical innovations which distinguished the Brazilian national teams of the fifty years or so after 1945 but the individual brilliance of their players. The promise of the 1930s was finally realised in the 1958 World Cup, the first time that Garrincha and Pele played together. Brazil never lost an international match in which both appeared. The team for the first match of the tournament only included one black player, Didi, but by the final there were three black players and two of mixed race to make Brazil the first multi-racial team to win the Jules Rimet trophy. They would win again in 1962 and most memorably in 1970.

It is a myth that the Brazilians were not interested in coaching and the application of knowledge to football. Aware of their failures in previous world championships, in 1958 they not only chose their training camp with care but brought a psychologist to ensure the team was mentally prepared. It was alleged that his tests on Garrincha showed an aggression level of zero and that Pele was 'infantile' – he was only seventeen after all. Nor is it true that the Brazilians largely ignored the defence. They had an excellent goalkeeper in Gilmar and two powerful full-backs in Djalmar and Nilton Santos. They did not concede a goal until the semi-finals. Tactically, they had adopted the fashionable 4-2-4, withdrawing a half-back to play along-

20 Attack and defend. Santos (Brazil) stops Ivanov the Russian forward. World Cup 1958.

20

side the central defender but also using Zagallo on the left as an extra midfielder. But inevitably it was the five goals Brazil scored against France in the semi-finals and the repeat performance they gave against Sweden in the final which had all the commentators struggling for words to describe football so excitingly original. How could the ordinary cope with the extraordinary?

The Italians had an answer. They had always welcomed foreign coaches. Moreover, the Italians were fascinated by the possibility of tactical and technical innovation. They embraced the tension of a football match, the almost unbearable anxiety of the close game and with a very competitive domestic league it was stopping goals more than scoring them that was the aim of both the *metodo* and the *sistema*. This philosophy reached its apogee under Helenio Herrera who built his Inter Milan team in the 1960s around what has come to be called *catenaccio* or the lock. He reinforced the defence by adding a fifth player, a free man who would play behind the back four with the aim of 'sweeping up' any attacking player whom they had missed. This way of playing was soon widespread in Serie A and was also adopted by the Italian national team. One of the most famous Italian football commentators, Gianni Brera, went so far as to christen it *Il gioco all'Italiana*, the Italian game. This was football based on the idea of passionate defence and the three principles of simplicity, seriousness and sobriety. Inter won two European Cups by entangling the opposition in the centre of the pitch and either scoring from quick breakaways or set pieces. No clearer clash of footballing styles has been seen than when Inter met Glasgow Celtic in the 1967 European Cup Final and the World Cup Final of 1970 between Brazil and Italy. *Catenaccio* was the loser on both occasions but not in Italy where neither the leading clubs nor the national team set it aside for long. Not only has it

often been successful but how else could the likes of Brescia hope to challenge Juventus without it?

Brazil once appeared almost unbeatable although the loss of a generation of outstanding players found them struggling to match past performances in the decade after 1970. They were replaced by Holland who became a football superpower barely twenty years after the introduction of professionalism there. There was, of course, some history. The Ajax team from Amsterdam had developed a reputation for attacking football based on skilful control and passing before 1945. Coached for many years by an Englishman, Jack Reynolds, they not only had good technique but discipline too. Reynolds also laid the foundations for Holland's now well-known youth policy. Another Englishman, Vic Buckingham, who had two spells as manager from 1959, also liked what he saw and tried to develop it. He too prized thought and skill and was impressed by Dutch football. 'It wasn't a rough-tough, got-to-win things mentality. They were gentlemen.' Long-ball football was too risky, believed Buckingham: 'Most of the time what pays off is educated skills.' By the 1960s Ajax was something of a Dutch institution. Its stadium was close to twenty pitches on which teams of players from different age groups played fifteen matches every week. Ajax won the Dutch championship in 1960 averaging 3.2 goals per

game and they would also win in 1966, 1967, 1969 and 1970. But it was two games in December 1966 that suggested that something special was afoot. Ajax knocked Liverpool out of the European Cup, a 5-1 victory in Amsterdam followed by a 2-2 draw at Anfield. In the second match a young man called Cruyff scored both goals. This was a harbinger of 'total football'.

In 1955 Willy Meisl wrote a book entitled *Soccer Revolution* in which he predicted that the future of football lay with a less stereotyped approach. Defenders must be able to attack, attackers must be able to defend. Players needed to acquire the skills that would make them all-rounders. There were clear signs of this in the 1960s in countries other than Holland. Beckenbauer for both Bayern Munich and Germany seemed equally comfortable in defence or going forward. Even in Italy, the Italian left back Facchetti was prone to making dangerous forward runs. As we have noted earlier, the minority of footballers who thought about it were adapting the basic system, looking for more flexibility. The phrase 'total football', *totaal voetbal* in Dutch, seems to have been first used to describe the Ajax style and then the Dutch national team in the

1974 World Cup. Players were given responsibilities in both defence and attack, they switched positions and, especially in the cases of Ajax and Holland, they attacked a lot.

But when Rinus Michels became the manager of Ajax in the sixties he had first built the defence signing Vasovic from Partizan Belgrade to play as the *libero* or freeman. Michels was very keen that attacks should come from deep but when players moved forward with the ball it was important that teammates should cover for them. It was not so much the positions which changed but the players who occupied them. Once a move had ended then players were expected to return to their usual positions as quickly as possible. But everyone had to think offensively. 'Come out', 'push up', 'make space', 'move into space', these were the new phrases in the coaches' usually limited vocabulary. And when you did not have the ball, you harassed the opposition relentlessly to get it back. Ajax won the European Cup in 1971, 1972 and 1973 attacking cleverly and continuously switching positions and apparently winning an emotional and intellectual victory as well as a physical and tactical one over the ultra-defensive Inter Milan in 1972.

People always ask who invented the passing game or who invented the third back game? They also want to know who invented total football? Alas, there is no simple answer to any of these questions. Obviously, both players and managers have a part to play. Michels was always trying different things in training and it is hard to believe that players like Krol, Neeskens, Vasovic and above all Cruyff, were not influenced. But good players, and these were very good players, do much of their work almost by instinct. By the early seventies, both Ajax and the Dutch national side had been together for five years and had played, and talked, a lot. Like the Hungarian Golden Team

NATIONAL STYLES, TECHNIQUE AND TACTICS

23 The end of the lesson in Brazilian football given to the Italian team in the World Cup Final (Mexico, 21 June 1970). Fourth goal scored by Brazil's captain Carlos Alberto.

24 Beckenbauer, the Kaiser opposite Cruyff, the master of 'total football'. World Cup final 1974.

that we discussed earlier, the Brilliant Orange one was adept at playing the ball into space for a fast running colleague. They attacked as a team with defenders, for example, moving quickly up the field as soon as the ball was cleared, making it relatively easy to catch the opposition offside. When possession was lost, forwards moved back and harassed opponents. They tried to use all of the pitch, spreading the play wide, seeing every run and movement as a way to increase and exploit available space. Then, when they lost the ball, they worked hard to deny space to the other team. Some thought must have gone into where and when to run and when to stay. The aim was to give the ball quickly and accurately to the player who had the most time… and, of course, to keep possession.

It is interesting to look at a contemporary report on the 1974 World Cup written by the Director of Coaching of the Football Association. He thought that the Dutch played with two more or less orthodox wing-forwards with no typical centre-forward. Cruyff was essentially an attacking midfield player who, like all other members of the team, sought to move forward into attacking positions. It is clear how similar this was to the Hungarians although by 1974 everything was done much more quickly. Cruyff though was as important to the Dutch as Pele was to Brazil, Puskas to Hungary and, later, Maradona would be to Argentina. If there was a rebirth of attacking, adventurous play Cruyff was the figure most associated with it in 1974. Commentators in particular wanted to believe that the play of Poland, West Germany and Holland was a sign that football was becoming less defensive. So they invented the phrase 'total football' which sounded modern and clever and, more to the point, like the way the Dutch team appeared to be playing. But strangely enough, also like Hungary, the Dutch could not win the World Cup. They lost in two finals in the 1970s and did not reach any of the three European championship finals held that decade.

FIFA was also interested in how football was evolving, particularly the complex relationship between defence and attack. The Technical Development Committee (TDC) was particularly interested in monitoring the development of the game at the highest level and this meant the World Cup. From 1966 the TDC produced a report by a group of present and former coaches in which they tried to analyse what they had seen in the World Cup Finals. The group grew in size over time and became more geographically representative. In 1966 it had consisted of three Englishmen, Ron Greenwood, Harold Hassall and Walter Winterbottom, two Russians, Valentin Granatkin and Gavril Katchaliev and a Swiss, Roger Quinche. By

25 >

26 >

25 Cruyff directs play in the World Cup final 1974, Germany v. Netherlands.

26 Gerd Muller, 'Der Bomber', scoring the winning goal for Germany after 43 minutes in the World Cup Final in 1974. Germany v. Netherlands (result 2-1).

NATIONAL STYLES, TECHNIQUE AND TACTICS

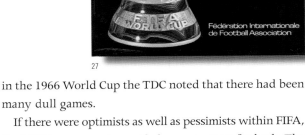

27

1986 it comprised Erich Vogel from Switzerland, José Boneti (Brazil), Dettmar Cramer (Germany), Ivan Toplak (Yugoslavia), Jozef Venglos (Czechoslovakia), Terry Neill (Northern Ireland) and Andy Roxburgh (Scotland). In 2002 Roxburgh and Venglos were still there along with Abedi Pele (Ghana), Carlos Alberto Parreira (Brazil), Frank Farina (Australia), Lin Chin Chon (Malaysia), Francisco Maturana (Colombia), Holger Osieck (Germany), Ivica Osim (Bosnia-Herzegovina), Alvin Corneal (USA) and Anghel Iordanescu (Romania).

As we have already seen, many football commentators by the 1960s were aware that the balance between attack and defence was shifting in favour of the latter. As football became more competitive the accent fell on defence, which led to more personal contact and more fouls. Organising the defence seemed so much easier than devising new ways to attack. The game could be slowed down, especially once a team got in front, in defence and midfield by deliberately passing the ball from player to player with no intention of making progress, and passing back to the goalkeeper who then took his time to clear. Petty fouling on the edge of the defence was becoming more common and the use of a central defender as sweeper meant that the other defenders could take more risks when tackling. None of this was improving the spectacle and

in the 1966 World Cup the TDC noted that there had been many dull games.

If there were optimists as well as pessimists within FIFA, the 1970 tournament provided some support for both. The Brazilians were just amazing and showed what individual skill could still achieve with their chest control, wall passes and swerving shots. Everyone was so relieved that the altitude and the heat of Mexico were apparently so easily overcome. Then there was the success of the referees and the new red and yellow cards. On the other hand, Italy had won their group despite scoring only one goal and Morocco, perhaps more understandably, had kept five defenders back on their own corners.

But the growth of international football and the increasing importance attached to it was leading to a reluctance to take risks. Moreover, there were many more opportunities to watch others play as television and video enabled

28

27 The picture supports the text. Official report of the World Cup finals 1974.

28 A tough match played by Argentina to win the World Cup Final 1978 at home. Foul by Dutch defender Poortvliet on Bertoni (Argentina).

29 Clash of styles leads to a tight match, French inspiration versus German control. Platini (France), Trésor (France) and Hrubesch (Germany) in the World Cup semi final, 1982.

30

31

coaches to collect information on and note the strengths and weaknesses of their opponents. And as we have seen, it was easier to stop good players than to devise new offensive tactics. In 1974 the TDC thought that only Germany, Holland and Poland played to win: the rest played not to lose. By 1978 most critics agreed that defensive arrangements had improved much more than offensive ones and the gap between the two was widening. The pressure to win had brought not only an increase in close marking but in intimidation, violent tackling and petty fouling — six to eight players would get behind the ball when possession was lost.

Yet interpretations still fluctuated between optimism and pessimism. The 1982 World Cup was a major encouragement for the optimists. Brazil recovered their desire to play *arte futebol*. Algeria and Honduras were said to have played in their own way, supervised by national coaches who knew how to adapt 'inborn' qualities of temperament and physical stamina to fitness, tactics and technique. Yet neither of the two best teams, Brazil and France, reached the final. Instead, it was the teams with the best organisation in defence and the reinforced midfields: Italy, with six players from Juventus, and West Germany, who had knocked out the more aesthetic Brazilians and French. There was much talk of efficiency in football as if a team was like a machine or a business. Both in 1982 and 1986, although it was recognised that international football had become more physically and athletically demanding, the toughness had not eliminated artistry as Maradona, Platini and Zico, among others, showed. There was also tactical innovation in the way that full-backs were beginning to use the space in front of them to turn defences. Optimists also pointed out that defenders were more skilful and this was in turn pushing the development of the highly skilled individualist to combat them. Teams were working hard-

er off the ball both in attack and defence, running into space when in possession and pressing opponents when they had the ball, trying to provoke a mistake or intercept a flawed pass. In 1966 players and coaches had doubted that footballers could get any fitter or faster. They had been wrong. The optimists thought they had clinched their argument by pointing to the fact there were still great players and great matches and the World Cup attracted a large worldwide television audience.

However, Italia 90 severely damaged the position of those who thought there was little wrong with modern football. Most teams took few risks. Astonishingly, only three teams won after going behind. Only 2.21 goals were scored per game, an all-time low for any FIFA competition. Cynicism and foul play disfigured many games with referees apparently unable or unwilling to do much about it. Many games were very unattractive to watch and in the knockout phase it was clear that most teams were playing for a goalless draw in the hope of winning in extratime or in the penalty shoot-out. The final itself was a tedious non-event, littered with petty fouls and appropriately decided by a

30 Klinsmann celebrates after he opens the scoring against the Netherlands in the 'Round of 16', 1990 World Cup finals.

31 Maradona trapped by the German defence during the World Cup final 1990.

32 The Brazilian Romario attempts a shot on goal despite being marked by the Italian Maldini. World Cup Final 1994.

33 Under Thuram's nose, Barthez gets past Ronaldo. World Cup final 1998.

penalty kick. Had it been a boxing match it would have been stopped before the end and declared no contest. The whole world saw it on television. The media were very critical. Even the general public sent in over a thousand letters to FIFA suggesting ways of improving the state of the game. The defensive mentality and its no risk policy had triumphed and in the most disreputable fashion.

Of course, referees and linesmen came in for a very large portion of criticism. FIFA noted that they were the only 'non-professional' element in the whole structure of the World Cup tournament. Serious thinking about professionalising the refereeing elite began here. Linesmen too should be specialists. Most FIFA referees had no recent experience of running the line. It was claimed that two-thirds of the appointed referees failed to follow FIFA instructions and it was the General Secretary's view that strict application of FIFA guidelines was designed to protect the attacker. The Referees' Committee were given the job of creating a set of instructions to help National Associations further improve refereeing standards. An Executive Committee working party was also set up to look at short, medium and long-term strategies for making football more attractive. After Italia '90 it was realised that the cost of 'fair play' was eternal vigilance.

Three major changes were eventually introduced. As part of the reform package after Italia 90, the offside law was amended in favour of the attacking player. Previously, a forward level with the last defender when the ball was played to him was offside; now he would be onside. From 1992, in an attempt to speed up the game and eradicate time-wasting, goalkeepers were no longer able to handle intentional back passes from their own players. For the 1994 World Cup, the tackle from behind was effectively outlawed. Referees were also urged to issue more cautions and dismissals for serious or persistent foul play. These changes do seem to have been beneficial. In the 1994 tournament, for example, forwards scored 66 per cent of all the goals and the average of 2.71 per match was second only to the 2.8 of 1982. Thankfully, none of the tournaments since 1990 have produced the same level of public and media criticism.

In 2004 does it make much sense to talk about national styles? There seems to have been little tactical innovation of late. What there appears to be is a kind of football globalisation. Most teams now play to a similar standard so that only small details decide who wins or who loses.

NATIONAL STYLES, TECHNIQUE AND TACTICS

Indeed, although the modern footballer is expected to have both defensive and attacking duties as well as be part of the collective team effort, it is individual brilliance that often decides the outcome of games. One such example was the long diagonal pass of Frank de Boer to Dennis Bergkamp in the Holland-Argentina quarter-final in 1998. This should not surprise us. In the two most recent World Cups, most teams had players who played in the leading European leagues and had adopted the systems and tactics of those leagues. All but five of the thirty-two teams in France '98, for example, had either European or South American coaches and the other five had worked in European leagues. Today, most teams want to play a counter-attacking game to exploit those fleeting moments when the opposition is disorganised and has allowed space to appear between and behind their midfield or defence. Twenty per cent of all goals in the 2002 World Cup came from counter-attacks, another twenty per cent from particular pieces of individual skill – a long-range shot, a free kick, a quick dribble and shot – and thirty per cent from set pieces. The collective pressing of ball and ball carrier is now almost universal and all teams demand versatility from their players and particularly those players who can play in several positions with no loss of effectiveness. Everyone needs to be able to attack and defend and, as with the basic WM, it is the spine or the axis of the team which remains important from goalkeeper to central defence to midfield to a reliable goalscorer. Each coach has to be flexible in changing and reforming his basic formation, be it 4-3-3, 3-5-2, 4-4-2 or 4-5-1.

It seems doubtful that there are any national styles left and yet there are still temptations to see the short passing preferences of Argentina and Brazil, for example, as being very different to the more varied game of some European and African countries. Footballing times have changed and footballers no longer need to be in thrall to circumstances and local conditions. In the past, a plausible argument could be constructed that, although football was a game everyone could play, different nations played it differently. But in the modern football world these differences have been ironed out as football styles have converged in the search for more efficiency. Organisation, the avoidance of mistakes, the ability to take chances and the reduction of risk seem to be the aim of all teams in major championships. Football has become a mental game and a running game and to stop thinking and running usually leads to defeat.

In the first sixty years of the twentieth century football was often called a universal language. It was a simple and attractive game that everyone could play and understand. The next chapter will explore both the history of the phrase and attempt to describe and analyse how the words we use to talk about football have changed.

35 >

34

34 Harry Cavan, FIFA Vice-President, sets out the 'Guts and Spirit' of football during a Futuro Academy session in Peking, May 1982.

35 Ronaldinho in action with Neuville in the World Cup final 2002. Roberto Schmidt received a World Press photo of the year prize in the sport category.

Manos (Hands)

THE UNIVERSAL
LANGUAGE OF FOOTBALL

Speaking a different language has never stopped people from playing football together. Teams from different countries can communicate on the pitch through the game, despite not speaking each other's language. Yet, ever since its inception, FIFA has had to contend with a world where communication is not so simple...

Fig. 16. — LE COUP DE TÊTE. — L'utilisation du front pour le renvoi de la balle en avant. (Voir ci-contre.)

Phot. G. Riebicke, Charlottenburg.
Abb. 10. Kopfball nach vorn.

2

Anglophilia, Nationalism and Universalism

As we have seen, football was initially an English game. This was borne out not only by the rules and style of the game, but also the language used by the players on the pitch. Outside of Great Britain, players were eager to use English when naming their clubs, not only by using 'Sporting Club', 'Football Club' and 'Racing Club', but also by sometimes using more obscure English words. One of the teams that dominated Swiss football at the start of the twentieth century was made up of 'Grasshoppers'. This team played against old boys' teams: 'Young Fellows', 'Old Boys' and 'Young Boys'. In Holland some club names referred in English to the qualities which they hoped their players would display. The team from Groningen were 'Be Quick', and the team from Deventer were 'Go Ahead'. In Bolivia, one of the clubs in La Paz was simply called 'The Strongest'. In many cases clubs chose to use the English translation of their town (Antwerp, Milan, Genoa) or their region (River

Plate). More often than not, the early players, who came from different countries, spoke English among themselves. At their AGM in Paris, in 1891, the White Rovers declared that English should be the language spoken between the players on the pitch. This led to the Italian national gymnastics federation mocking young trainee footballers that 'play, dress and swear in the English way'.

The newly formed national football associations were often divided on the issue of language because of its cultural importance and symbolic power. Nationalisation of football terms happened in many countries. In 1908 the Federazione Italiana di Foot-Ball was renamed the Federazione Italiana Giuoco Calcio, 'calcio' being the name of a traditional Italian ball game. This nationalization was an attempt to distance the organisation from the English roots of the modern game. Shortly before the First World War, most of the national football associations had translated the word 'football' into their own language. In some cases it was a phonetic translation as is the case in Spanish where the game was christened 'Fútbol', and in Portuguese where the word 'Futebol' was chosen. In other languages

3

1 The rules of football with comments by Pedro Escartín, international referee and member of the FIFA Commission for the laws of the game and refereeing (Madrid 1943).

2 An Anglo-Swiss event, the match between Polytechnicum Football Club and Grasshopper Club Zurich (November 1888).

3 The early days of Mohun Bagan, one of the best Indian clubs, and the first Hindu team to win the IFA-Shield, the oldest football tournament in Calcutta, 1911.

4 The Uruguayan version of *Laws governing football and the way it is played*. Montevideo, 1911.

5 *The rules of football, referees' guide*. Published by the Italian FA (Rome 1940).

6 In contrast to their European neighbours, the French kept a large number of English football terms. *Association Football* (Paris 1922), by former international player, journalist and future creator of the European Cup competition, Gabriel Hanot, was an introduction to the game.

Fig. 6.

a literal translation was made, '*Fußball*' in German, '*Nogomet*' in Croatian, and '*Labdarugas*' in Hungarian. Only the French and the Russians continued to use the English term. The nationalization of the football terms was part of a larger movement of 'nation building' in which translations of foreign words were imposed and national symbols were chosen as replacements for those of the colonial or dominant powers. In Germany, following the First World War, English seems to have disappeared from the German football lexicon. In the official DFB yearbook of 1920, German club names now made reference to the national gymnastic movement, such as 'Jahn Regensburg' or the Luebecker 'Turnerschaft' or bore patriotic identifiers such as 'Germania' or 'Teutonia'. Old terms such as 'Union' or 'Sports Association' were translated to 'Eintracht' and SpVgg (Sportverieningung) respectively. In Italy the clubs which formed from the

Italian gymnastic movement preferred to use Latin in their names, for example 'Pro Patria', 'Ars et labor' and 'Juventus'. In France most clubs incorporated 'Football Club' and 'Sporting Club' in their names and there were also references to national symbols such as 'Jeanne d'Arc', 'Patriotes' and 'Enfants de France'. During the development of national football associations the question of language made the issue of nationalism ever present. Central European countries and the Balkans, where conflict between different national groups was particularly bitter, were the main problem areas. In Split, Dalmatia, the most successful team was named 'Hajduk', the name of a band of locals who fought Turkish and Venetian invaders in the fifteenth and eighteenth centuries. In Prague, 'Slavia' and 'Sparta' were linked to the independence movement. At the same time there was also the 'Deutscher Fussball Club' and other clubs such as the 'Bohemians'

4

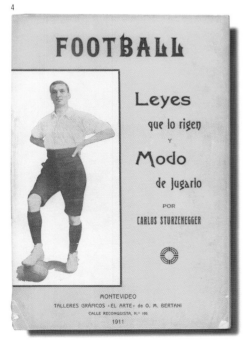

5

6

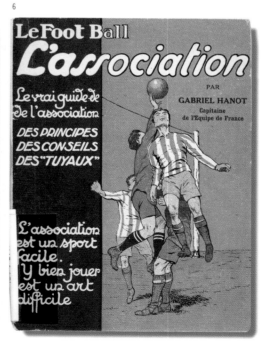

who chose to retain their English roots. Nationalist naming conventions existed beyond Europe. In Santiago, Chile, a club was called 'Colo Colo' in honour of an Indian chief who had fought Spanish invaders.

If club names were often English the terms used to describe the game and phases of play were exclusively English. In the early days, whether it was describing the position of the players on the pitch, or the various phases of play involved in a game, British references were always used. The words 'back', 'half', 'keeper', 'forward' and 'referee' were used by all languages to define the player's positions. 'free kick', 'penalty', 'off side' and 'corner' were all part of the jargon used by the first players who were proud of being able to display such an exotic vocabulary. In 1909, this lead to one commentator writing that: 'an elegant account of a match, written by a journalist with good taste, must be completely unintelligible to French-speaking readers. This sits oddly with the concept of this sport being democratic.' With nationalisation, however, English terms gradually disappeared until only two truly English terms remained: 'fair play' and 'Gentleman'. In this period borrowing terms from languages other than English was rare, but in Bulgaria a penalty was called '*onze pas*', a reminder of the French players who first played football in that country.

FIFA was confronted by linguistic issues from the start. The question of which language should be used was raised at the first meeting in Paris. In fact, none of the participants was a native English speaker, but some of those present, such as Hirschmann from Holland, and the Scandinavian representatives, spoke the language of Shakespeare perfectly. No documentation exists to prove if the two Frenchmen, Espir and Guérin, spoke English. The first account leads us to believe that the early meetings took place in French, with some periods of German and English. The delegates chose to give the organisation a French name, which did not please the English. The official monthly publication launched the following year was written in French with certain pieces written in German. English was curiously absent.

Congress, the Secretariat and Documentation

Within FIFA English, which gradually imposed itself as the universal language, and French, which at the start of the century was the language of the social elite and diplomacy, influenced each stage of the evolution of the organisation. It was strange that the legitimacy and use of German was never brought to the debate. The

THOMAZ MAZZONI

· FUTEBOL ·
Regras Ilustradas
Arbitragem e Códigos
Aprovadas pela Confederação Brasileira de Desportos

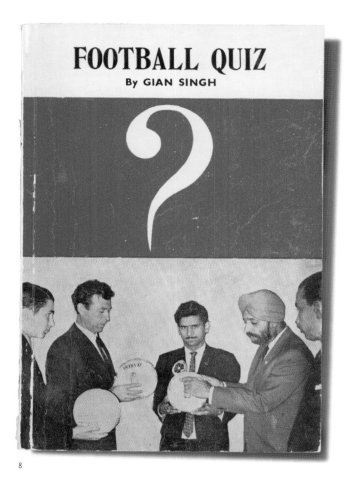

7 Laws and rules for refereeing explained by the Brazilian journalist Thomaz Mazzoni called 'Olimpicus' (São Paulo 1964).

8 A didactic approach to football for 'referees, players, trainers and organisers', (New Delhi, 1968).

9 3rd edition of *Reglamento de Futbol Asociacion* suggested for 'general use' by the Spanish FA (Barcelona, 1934).

Congress that met in June 1906 in Berne adopted a resolution making French the official FIFA language. However, when Daniel Woolfall took over the presidency in 1906, English immediately became the official language and was used in FIFA's reports. The choice of English was important for Woolfall as he had to deal with all the correspondence. Until this point, debates at Congress, which were the main activity of FIFA, were held in both French and English. At the Vienna Congress the following year, the English President proposed to make English the sole official language of the Federation. In opposition, the Italian representatives requested that French should be the official language. The English proposition was put to the vote and was rejected. For the British and European members of FIFA this was an important issue. As it stood, the British felt that football was a British game which foreign countries wanted to play and, if they wanted to play, they should all speak English. It is clear that British domination of the game was never questioned, because everyone wanted them to be part of FIFA.

Various signs indicated that world football was entering a period of nationalisation, of the game, the terms, the club names and the practice of using languages other than English. FIFA was swimming against the tide. All around the world anglophiles began to lose ground to nationalists. In 1913 in Montevideo the Central Uruguay Railway Cricket Club became CA Peñarol. Alumni of Buenos Aires, a team made up of mostly British players, gave up playing, leaving the ground to teams with much clearer Argentinian roots. The nationalisation of football terms in German and Italian has frequently been attributed to Hitler and Mussolini. However, this process started before the First World War. The totalitarian regimes only completed a process that was already running. Despite all this, the English tradition had not completely disappeared. In 1930, in the introduction of a football manual, two well-known Italian coaches excused themselves for having to use non-Italian terms but they had found that players and coaches were still in the habit of using them. Even though the official terms for player's positions had been translated it was not unheard of to speak of a 'half' or 'back' in the 1950s in both Italy and France.

When Jules Rimet became President in 1921, the situation had changed a great deal. The membership of the new South American football associations encouraged the Spanish Royal football association to ask for Spanish to be recognised as an official language and to be used for correspondence and documentation. Met with a refusal due to technical problems (the Honorary Secretary

پـاـفــن زدن
(ديربلينگ)

10

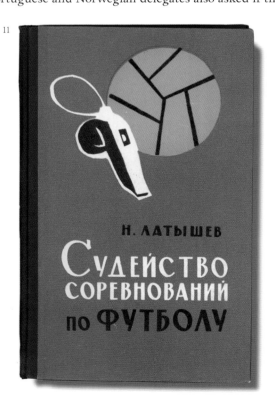

11

Н. ЛАТЫШЕВ

Судейство
соревнований
по Футболу

Hirschmann did not speak Spanish) the request was abandoned. Four years later the same request was made by six Latin American countries, and was again refused. However, a concession was made, as the minutes record: 'les délégués pourront parler leur langue au congrès s'ils transmettent une traduction dans l'une des trois langues officielles'. (Representatives may speak their language at Congress if they provide a translation in one of the three official languages.) The South Americans, who dominated the competitions held by FIFA, were particularly hurt by this refusal. With no permanent representatives on the Executive, they had difficulty making their voices heard. During these discussions the Italian, Portuguese and Norwegian delegates also asked if their languages could be admitted as official languages. In contrast the Dutch representative thought that French, the language of diplomacy, should remain the language of discussion. The reorganisation of FIFA in 1931, the decision to relocate to Zurich and the employment of a salaried General Secretary relieved these tensions. It was mainly thanks to the linguistic skills of Ivo Schricker, a German speaker born in Strasbourg who spoke perfect French and English and also wrote Spanish, that the considerable correspondence of the General Secretary was able to appease the different factions. French was always used for his, sometimes daily, correspondence with the President. He also wrote in French to Seeldrayers, Dupuis from Uruguay and Barassi and Mauro from Italy, the latter two often replying in Italian. In Northern Europe, German and English were the most widely used languages. Von Frenkel from Finland and Lotsy the Dutchman wrote in German or in English while the South Americans were soon only using Spanish even though it was not yet an official language. The Berlin Congress in May 1931 authorised both the publication of official communications in Spanish, and the use of the language during Congress. Despite this concession, Spanish was still not officially recognized in the FIFA statutes. There is no doubt that the flexibility Schricker showed led towards an improvement in the relations with the South American associations who were astounded at what they perceived as a lack of recognition from Congress.

After the Second World War the return of the British and the arrival of the Russians as members of FIFA further complicated the language issue. The Luxembourg Congress in 1946 was the first example of the growing problem. Until this point the organising football association had always undertaken to cover the costs of conference interpreting. However, in Luxembourg, for the

10 How to dribble past a goalkeeper. Illustration from the Iranian manual *What is football* by Dr Abbas Ekrami (Teheran, 1983).

11 *Refereeing football competitions,* Russian guide based on N.Latyshev's experience as an international referee *(Moscow 1965).*

12 UA sought after member. The Russian FA agrees to join FIFA (letter dated 15th November 1946).

13 Kurt Gassmann, FIFA General Secretary was at the centre of international communications from 1951 to 1960.

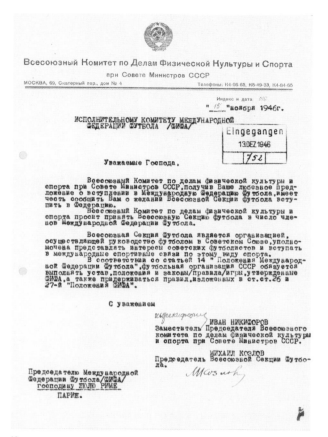

12

13

first time, the organisers asked FIFA if they would pay for the translation costs because they could not be met by such a small association. Spanish-speaking countries requested a Vice President position for one of their representatives to bring them into line with the positions that had been accorded to the recently rejoined English and the newly joined Russians. They also repeated their request that Spanish be officially recognised. FIFA was reluctant, conscious that the translation costs for all the official documents and minutes from the different committees would be high. In a gesture of Real Politik, FIFA finally agreed to support the request, which passed Congress unanimously. With the Spanish dispute having been resolved, Russia was the next football association to raise the issue of language. At the London Congress in 1948, the Russian representatives demanded that Russian be added to the list of official languages, but no decision was made. The Executive did however authorise the translation of official documents into Russian. The Russian football association refused to adhere to the FIFA rules about correspondence and wrote all their letters in Russian, a language that Schricker did not speak. This forced the

secretariat to have the correspondence translated by the Russian legation in Berne. Schricker's retirement in 1951 revealed the true extent of the difficulties managing this tower of Babel posed FIFA. Although Gassmann, the new Secretary, spoke both French and English, in 1952 he requested a thorough reorganisation of the secretariat, including an increase in the personnel which was necessary for a 'grande et puissante, possédant une fortune appreciable' (large, powerful and wealthy) organisation. From this point onwards an assistant helped the General Secretary with his correspondence and in the 1970s a team took over this task. The archives show the extent to which a polyglot General Secretary was essential to a successful Presidency. President Jules Rimet and Ivo Schricker shared tasks and were crucial in the consolidation and development of FIFA. Later, when Sir Stanley Rous became President, his understanding with Dr Kaeser was equally excellent, but neither were accustomed to the language, writing style and customs of South America. While Kaeser understood English mannersims, he often found himself infuriated by the South Americans whom he failed to understand properly. The

THE UNIVERSAL
LANGUAGE OF FOOTBALL

14 In 1975 the administrative team was still quite small. Helmut Käser (middle), General Secretary from 1961 to 1982. Joseph S. Blatter, director of development (in the foreground holding a ball).

14

archives show that some of the main crises between FIFA and the South American Confederation were, without doubt, due to linguistic differences. Rous and Käser were uncomfortable when faced with Spanish speakers, which often made dialogue difficult. When João Havelange, who spoke perfect French and excellent Spanish became President in 1974, it was the turn of the Anglophones to feel marginalised. Over twenty-four years, the diplomatic and linguistic skills of General Secretary Joseph S. Blatter allowed Havelange, who was particularly aware of the linguistic balance required within FIFA, to create a model of secretariat management where each of the four official languages was equally represented. The working language of the President and General Secretary is French, but all the development programmes are issued in all the different languages, and official publications are published in each of the four official languages. With considerable growth in the number of member associations, commissions and members of the Executive Committee,

FIFA developed an internal translation service. During Congress and meetings simultaneous interpreting is available. Although the official languages have remained the same since 1946, the position of German and French on the international stage has deteriorated whereas English has moved towards a world language. There are many members of the Executive who do not speak English, but, in the near future, it is reasonable to expect that, as is the case for all other international organisations, multilingualism is unlikely to continue. On the other hand, non-European languages such as Arabic and Chinese have already requested official status more than once. The cost of translation and interpretation makes the addition of new languages to the official list difficult, but thanks to external funding, Arabic is now spoken by Arab delegates during Congress.

15 Helmut Käser, FIFA General Secretary in the 1960s faced an ever increasing pile of correspondance.

16 Translation was one of the main tasks of the FIFA offices in the 1950s.

17 At a time when the *Azzurri* dominated international football, an Italian publication on football techniques (Milan, 1936).

15

16

ITALO DEFENDI

TECNICA CALCISTICA

"LA PRORA"

18 *Laws of the Game* booklet by
FIFA, an annual publication.

19 Variations on Football. *Laws
of the Game 2003*, published by
FIFA.

20 How to judge when a goal is
scored. *Spielregeln 2003* booklet
published by FIFA.

21 From yellow to red. The scale
of punishments as set out in
Reglas de juego 2003, booklet
published by FIFA.

Interpretation and contributions from other languages

The rules of the game apply all over world, and their
translation from English into other languages brought
about interesting differences in interpretation. In the
area of refereeing, the domination of English was never
challenged. Because the International Board used only
English when setting the rules, FIFA's standardisation
of the translations and interpretations of the rules was
limited. During the creation of the consulting committee for rules and refereeing, one of the questions
on the agenda of the first meeting concerned the translation of the rules. Taking into account the complexi-
ties of interpretation, the issue of translation was a
problem which occupied much of the time of the FIFA
officials. Stanley Rous, who had been a referee, thought
it was essential that the rules were interpreted in the
same way all over the globe. There is no doubt that he
did not realise what this would mean with regard to
language. Pablo Escartin and Henri Delaunay, who were
both members of the Referees' Committee, were responsible for checking the translations of the rules.
Strangely, the book published by FIFA to celebrate the
centenary of the International Board remained entirely silent on the subject of translation and other linguistic problems.

Another potential communication problem facing
FIFA was the languages spoken – or not spoken –
by their international referees. Of the twenty-nine
referees chosen to officiate during the World Cup
of 1958, eighteen spoke English, fourteen spoke
German, twelve French and only six spoke Spanish.
International referees were required to speak one of the

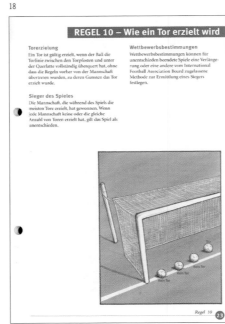

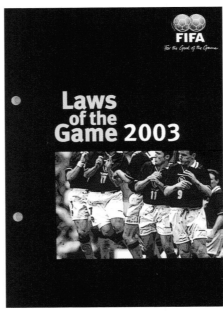

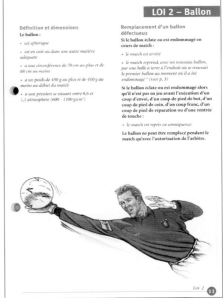

18

19

20

21

22

official languages, but speaking more than one language was not enforced and no language was obligatory.

The quarter final between England and Argentina in 1966 highlighted the importance of this issue. Following his sending off, the Argentinian captain Rattin asked the German referee, who only spoke German and English, for the mediation of an interpreter: 'Pedi que veniera un intérprete para aclarar las cosas. El referi considero mi actitud como un desacato a su autoridad. Yo le mostré la banda de capitan … Cuando ingreso el interprete, fue para decime que estaba expulsado. El problema del idioma fue decisivo.' (The referee thought my attitude questioned his authority. I showed him clearly my captain's armband, and, when the interpreter came onto the pitch, it was to inform me that I had been sent off. The language barrier was a decisive factor.)

Once again the South American associations felt they had been systematically penalised, and that double standards were in operation. Since then, things have improved, nothing more so than the linguistic skills of the referees. Oral communication on the pitch has become one of the most important functions of international referees. During the World Cup in South Korea and Japan, all the referees had to have a good grasp of English to be able to communicate with the players. The phenomenon of globalisation, with English becoming a more generally used language, seems to have provided a solution to the thorny issue of communication. Following an increase in international transfers and the number of continental club competitions, language skills among players have increased, and there is greater understanding of the different interpretations of the game, which is without doubt the best remedy for mis-

understandings between players and between the players and the referee.

Football is now a global phenomenon, but the terms used to describe it have changed little over the last century. It is true that the big national schools have introduced some rare terms recognised the world over but the international language of football has changed very little. The Italian language has contributed *'libero'*, a central defender with no specific position, *'catenaccio'* a completely defensive style of play, and the *'tifosi'*, or Italian supporters. The Spanish language has provided the term *'oriundi'* which classifies players of one nationality, born to parents of another and the most widely known of the recent linguistic development, *'ola'* or Mexican Wave), first performed during the World Cup of 1986.

23

2

WOMEN, YOUTH
AND FIFA

Women playing football in any numbers
was one of the unforeseen consequences
of the First World War. It was played by
young French female munitions workers
in the Paris region but it was even more
widespread in Great Britain.

3

< 1

4

An early history of women's football

Well before 1914, football had established itself as a recreation for young men and as a commercial spectacle had become one of the most visible features of British popular culture. But until the war it was not for women. Its association with working-class aggression and competitiveness meant that many deemed it unsuitable for 'ladies' and influential doctors pronounced it harmful to the female body. Meanwhile working-class girls who must have seen and heard the interest in football shown by their brothers and fathers had too little leisure time to think seriously of playing themselves even if they had been prepared to stand up to the cultural disapproval it would undoubtedly have provoked.

The war changed all that. By 1915–16 many young women – fourteen-and fifteen-year-old girls – had left their homes, towns and villages for jobs in the munitions industries. They left a life of parental and communal control for a new world that promised hard work and harsh

discipline but also high wages and new opportunities for leisure. In order to look after these workers the Ministry of Munitions set up a Health and Welfare section. Workers' recreation represented a large part of its activities. Astonishingly, football, the quintessential man's game, took its place alongside dancing and swimming as the three most popular forms of leisure for the 'munitionettes.' From Portsmouth to Carlisle, Preston to Southend, Newcastle to Bolton and even in the engineering factories of London, teams of girls and young women exploded onto the football fields of Britain.

Soon they were not only playing in factory knock-out competitions between different departments but were setting up representative teams in the towns and cities and playing matches on the grounds of professional clubs. Spectators were charged admission and the proceeds went to war charities. No one could have predicted how well supported these events would become during 1917-18. When two factory teams from Preston in Lancashire played a match on Christmas Day 1917 at Preston North End's ground 10,000 spectators turned up and £600 was raised.

1 Before a crowd of predominantly male officials, Linda Medalen, captain of Norway, holds the World Cup aloft after victory over Germany 4-2 (Stockholm 6 June 1995).

2 Beyond the iron curtain. Hungarian youth team participating in a FIFA tournament organised in Germany, April 1954.

3 The first Russian women's team. Players from Pouchkine near to Moscow (1911).

4 Wallsend's women's team and their male coach, 1917.

5 Women's Football or football played by women? The first match of the British Ladies' Football Club, *The Graphic* (March 1895).

6 In the era of suffragettes. Miss Nettie Honeyball, captain of the British Ladies' Football Club, declared women's right to play football (1895).

7 Sport and charity. Dick Kerr's Ladies' Football Team formed in Preston in 1917 to collect donations for a military hospital.

5

The game was refereed by the sixty-two-year-old John Lewis from Blackburn whom we met earlier officiating at the final of the 1920 Olympic Games football tournament. One of the teams, from Dick, Kerr's engineering factory, were so successful that, helped by their employer and by a local man, they continued to play against all comers, including what could be claimed to be the first women's international against Femina (Paris) in 1920. Femina was organised by Madame Milliat, a French pioneer of sport for women. A return visit was arranged later in the same year and the French came again in 1922.

Women's football was not just a phenomenon of the war. It clearly continued into the immediate post-war years. During the coal miners' strike of 1921, for example, young women footballers in the coalfields of northern England began forming teams and playing matches to raise money for the strike fund. But what is really interesting is that within a short space of time in Northumberland a competitive structure had emerged and the games were being taken increasingly seriously both on and off the field. Women's teams were beginning to be seen as representative of their communities.

For a time, a small league of women's teams flourished, mainly in the north of England but as many as 150 clubs may have existed in the United Kingdom as a whole. There was an attempt to set up an 'English Women's Football Association.' But it did not last and one of the reasons was the opposition of the English Football Association. On 6 December 1921 they issued a notorious edict which deserves full quotation.

6

MISS NETTIE HONEYBALL, CAPTAIN OF THE BRITISH LADIES' FOOTBALL CLUB.

FROM A PHOTOGRAPH BY MESSRS. RUSSELL AND SONS, BAKER STREET, W.

7

DICK, KERR'S LADIES' FOOTBALL TEAM.

8a Jüngfrauenspielvereinigung Altwien gegen F.C. Die Herzkäferl.

Complaints have been made as to football being played by women, the Council feel impelled to express their strong opinion that the game of football is quite unsuitable for females and ought not to be encouraged ...

Complaints have been made as to the conditions under which some of these matches have been arranged and the appropriation of the receipts to other than charitable objects. The Council are further of the opinion that an excessive proportion of the receipts were absorbed in expenses and an inadequate percentage devoted to charitable objects.

For these reasons the Council requests the clubs belonging to the Association to refuse the use of their grounds for such matches.

This need not have been the end for some teams. Although many men and women agreed with the FAs by no means everyone did. Even some conservative newspapers felt that football was a pleasure which should not and could not be denied to women. A prominent Scottish football administrator came out in anonymous support and strictly speaking, if young women wanted to play football, there was nothing the FA could do to stop them. But the attempts to organise the women's game faded away although several clubs, Dick, Kerr's most notably, had a more or less continuous existence over the next thirty years.

Post-war developments

Certainly when the end of the next war arrived in 1945, it ushered in another era when attempts would be made to extend the cultural, economic and social opportunities for women. The desire of some young women to play organised recreational football was part of this, although what later became known as the women's movement took little interest in sport and none in football. But the urge to participate was not only a European phenomenon. In 1951, for example, T. Cranshaw of the Nicaraguan football association wrote to the FIFA Secretary about the Pan-American Games in Buenos Aires which he had recently attended. There were five women's football teams in Costa Rica and

8a / 8b Curves and coquetry. Female football as seen by *Fussball* (1924).

9 In front of 26,000 spectators in Turin, the Danish team won the first unofficial Women's World Cup (1970). According to *Football Magazine*, 'The joy of the Danish women, world champions, was a pleasure to see'.

10 Wil Michels (right) and Danny Cruyff (left) the wives of Rinus Michels (coach) and Johan Cruyff (player), watching the match between Netherlands and Bulgaria at the 1974 World Cup.

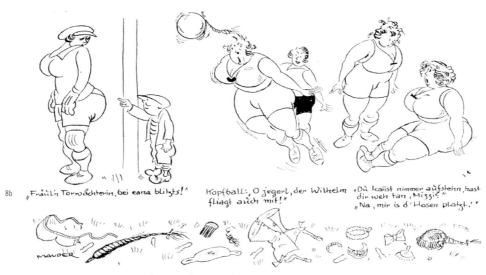

8b "Fräul'n Tornwächterin, bei eana blitzts!"

Kopfball: O jegerl, der Wilhelm fliagt auch mit!"

"Du kañst nimmer aufstehn, hast dir weh tan, Missie" "Na, mir is d'Hosen platzt!"

Das Spielfeld nach dem schweren Kampf.

9

the opportunity of the games were used by the Costa Ricans to present a case for women's football to be part of them. Argentinian doctors turned it down on the usual grounds that it was too dangerous for women. Cranshaw was not surprised by this but nevertheless disappointed and he told Gassmann that perhaps as many as 19,000 girls were playing 'what they call soccer' at high schools in the United States. What was FIFA doing about it? The answer was nothing. 'FIFA has never concerned itself with women's football. It has no jurisdiction and in consequence does not give any advice to affiliated national associations.' For FIFA women's football was a question of biology and education best left to doctors and teachers. In 1952 the future was not feminine.

Nevertheless, there were also signs in Europe that young women were taking up the game, forming clubs and setting up competitive structures. In West Germany in 1955, for example, the Deutsche Fussball Bund (DFB) discussed whether to include women but decided against it. Kicking was masculine and not feminine. By 1957 there was a body called the International Ladies' Football Association which was sufficiently established to organise the first European club championship. Teams from England, Austria, Luxembourg, the Netherlands and West Germany took part and a team from England, Manchester Corinthians, won. In the next decade a new generation of women would vigorously pursue equal opportunities in a range of fields and contexts. In Denmark, West Germany, the Netherlands, Czechoslovakia, Finland, Norway, Sweden and Scotland young women and girls were now playing football and forming teams. In November 1969 the first attempt was made to co-ordinate these activities through the Fédération Internationale et Européenne de Football Féminin (FIEFF). This organisation with the support of the drinks company Martini and Rossi, presented what it called a women's world

championship in Italy in 1970 and a second in Mexico the following year. Neither received very much media coverage. A Munich journalist who followed the German team to Italy wrote after their defeat to England that the prettier team lost! By the early 1970s there was also a professional league in Italy that was attracting women from other countries.

These promotions stirred interest in some national associations. Several – France and West Germany in 1970, the English in 1971 – at least lifted their bans on the women's game, perhaps because they did not want to see independent bodies set up to run it. UEFA agreed that national associations should take control of women's football in 1971. Although this was mainly a European and North American phenomenon, an Asian Ladies' Football Association had also been founded in Hong Kong in 1968 with the host, Chinese Taipei (Taiwan), Malaysia and Singapore as members. More about them later.

10

FIFA and women's football

FIFA played a waiting game with women's football. Here was a grass-roots movement that men's football did not necessarily welcome. When FIFA conducted a survey in 1970 to discover how many of their affiliated national associations were in favour of officially endorsing the women's game only 90 out of 139 replied and of those who responded only twelve were in favour. One Asian association allegedly replied 'God save us from women's football.' The DFB, for example, allowed its sixteen regional associations to organize championships for women in 1972–73 but watched a private initiative set up an unofficial national championship before taking it over in the following season. It was not until 1982 that an official West German national team for women was established after a club side from Bergisch Gladbach had returned victorious from an unofficial women's world cup in Taiwan in 1981. By this date there were nearly 3000 women's football teams in West Germany. In Switzerland an unofficial championship of 1969–70

became an official one in 1970-71 but the women's teams had to affiliate to men's clubs who were themselves members of the Swiss football association. This meant that Swiss women had their own football league a year before they had the right to vote. Things were even more advanced in Scandinavia. Finland had played Sweden in an international match in 1973 and by the mid-seventies there were 95 women's teams playing football. By the mid-eighties it would be 2000. Sweden had a regional championship by 1970 and a first national one by 1973. The first European Championship would be held there in 1984. Norway and Denmark also had a flourishing women's game with national leagues and in Norway the sport was taught to girls at school.

FIFA was quite uncertain about how it should respond to these developments. As we have seen, many national associations were not interested in women playing 'their' game and some were positively hostile for cultural reasons. Even FIFA's own bureaucracy was sceptical. When the Secretary of the Finnish football association drew the attention of FIFA Secretary Helmut Kaser to his correspondence with a

11 Players of IFK Hässleholm, the first female Champions of Sweden with their coach Borje Nartinsson (1973).

12 Gunn Nyborg (Norway) playing against Finland (1986).

13 A strong hold on women's football. Scandinavia's Nordic Women's Football Championships. Match between Norway and Denmark (July 1979).

11

12

13

14

UEFA official on women's football, Käser replied that he had seen women's football and noticed with 'astonishment' how some female players were physically, technically and tactically impressive. Nevertheless, he was 'personally of the opinion that football is not fundamentally a women's sport.' However, FIFA had always been clear that it could not countenance competing organisations in any section of the sport. But it needed all its resolve to cope with the Asian Ladies' Football Confederation (ALFC).

Their Secretary wrote to Käser in September 1975 to inform him that the first Asian Cup Ladies' Football Tournament in Hong Kong had recently taken place. Teams from Australia, Malaysia, New Zealand, Singapore, Thailand and Hong Kong had taken part. New Zealand beat Thailand in the final. The ALFC was now looking to the future. 24 players had been selected for special training in Hong Kong in July 1976 preparatory to choosing the best 18 to represent the Asian All-Stars team for a European tour to France, Switzerland, West Germany and probably Great Britain the

15

14 The women's team Stade de Reims during the 1972-73 season. The players from Reims were the start of the rebirth of women's football in France, and won the first French Women's Championship in 1975.

15 When Charles D. Pereira, Secretary of the Asian Ladies Football Confederation, informed Helmut Käser that they planned to organise a Women's World Cup 1977, FIFA was forced to react.

16

following month. What women's 'soccer' needed was a world body to control it and they were proposing to set up a 'Female (sic) Internationale de Football Federation', or 'FIFF', – a FIFA for women in fact. Once this had been done, a world cup tournament for women would be organised. Would FIFA give its blessing? The answer was a haughty negative!

Two years went by during which time a second Asian ladies' championship was held and 40,000 saw the final in which Thailand lost again, this time to Taiwan. Pereira then wrote again asking if the ALFC could affiliate directly to FIFA. Käser repeated that women's football had to be organised through the affiliated national associations. It was not possible for FIFA to affiliate or recognise independent organisations dealing with women's football. FIFA then told Holland that it should not accept the ALFC's invitation

1st FIFA World Championship for Women's Football

China 1991

17

to participate in the 'Women's World Cup' in 1978 as it was not promoted by FIFA or an affiliate.

But the ALFC persisted, even though it seems that by 1981 only in Hong Kong, India, Malaysia, Singapore and Thailand was women's football not under the jurisdiction of the appropriate national association. The ALFC was inviting national associations to send representatives to a meeting in Hong Kong in order to form a World Women's Football Confederation. This may have encouraged FIFA into approving a Women's Football Invitation Tournament in Taipei (Taiwan) in October 1981. By November 1983 the AFC was confident that it had 'been able to reduce the resistance' of the ALFC 'through several informal discussions. In the Asian culture, there is a saying that they must be given 'face' meaning that the parties concerned must recognise their past contributions and discuss amicably their integration with the national associations and the confederations.' This seems to have worked as the ALFC was taken into the AFC's committee structure.

By the early 1980s opinion was building within FIFA's membership that more should be done to develop international football for women. First, the Executive Committee underlined the need for FIFA to take responsibility for an international tournament if only to show that it was, with its members, the controlling body for all football. Then the 1986 Congress instructed the Executive Committee to do more for women's football. The Norwegian delegate claimed that FIFA had not devoted enough attention to what was a very popular sport in his country. Norway's women's team had just won the first European Championship in 1984. Of course, FIFA had been doing its research – though the results were not all good news. Women were playing in large numbers in Europe, the USA, Canada, Oceania, Asia, even in North and West Africa. But in Latin America

18

19

the men were, as FIFA diplomatically put it, 'still a little reserved.' Nonetheless, in 1986 a Committee for Women's Football was established although for several years there was only one woman on it. Two international tournaments were then quickly organised. The first was held in Chinese Taipei (Taiwan) in 1987 and although it showed a great variation in standards between the teams 'for the most part, the football played was attractive and professional enough'. The 'A' team from the host nation beat a Californian Selection from the USA in the final. But it was the first FIFA international women's tournament, held in the Republic of China in 1988, that finally persuaded the bulk of the doubters in the world's governing body that the future might just be feminine. Played over eleven days in June it was an invitation tournament with twelve teams from six continents. 360,000 attended the twenty-four matches of which eight were shown live on Chinese television. The President of the Swiss football association was so overcome he wanted to nominate FIFA President Havelange for the Nobel Peace Prize.

China was also the venue for the first Women's World Cup held in 1991. Twelve teams competed: five from Europe, three from Asia, and one each from North America, Africa, Oceania and South America. The United States beat Norway in the final. In Sweden in 1995 Norway beat Germany and in the United States in 1999 the USA beat China. It cannot be denied that these tournaments were excitingly dramatic spectacles with big crowds in the stadiums and many watching on television but there were two minor clouds on this otherwise perfect picture – one easier to solve than the other.

When the first European Championship for women had been held in 1984 there had been no women referees. This was partly because it was difficult for them to get the kind of big match experience required but it was also because football refereeing was a male world and wanted to stay that way. Initially, male referees had better training and more experience than their female counterparts, and in this difficult transitional stage some women preferred male referees because they were better than the available women. Again, the Scandinavian countries and the United States led the field in addressing this problem. In America it probably helped that male football structures were relatively weak. In Scandinavia, Norway, Sweden and Denmark had played a lot of matches against each other in the 1980s – the women of Norway and Denmark actually met for the one hundredth time during the 1991 World Cup (Norwegian Gunn Nyborg played in all 100 games) – and

20

21

had gone out of their way to appoint female officials. The Norwegian football association and FIFA organised an instruction course for female referees in 1989 and six women oversaw matches in the 1991 World Cup. But it was 1999 before all the World Cup matches were refereed by women following two decisions of the FIFA Referees' Committee. The first, in 1994, set up an official FIFA list of female referees, and the second, in November in 1998 put into practice a long-held aim that female referees should be chosen for women's matches.

The more difficult problem facing organised women's football is that except, for the major international tournaments, no one wants to watch it. This has meant that the media, both newspapers and television, offer it very little space or airtime. This may change as professional leagues develop but there must be a limit to the size of the market for football and perhaps in Europe and the United States at least, that limit will be gender-based.

18 Nicole Mouidi-Petignat (Switzerland), a top European female referee, takes charge of the Women's World Cup final 1999.

19 A victory for women's football. The first Olympic Games final between the United States and China in Atlanta, 1996.

20 Disappointment on the face of Elane, a Brazilian player, after defeat at the hands of the Chinese team in the semi-final of the Olympic Games football tournament in Atlanta, 1996.

21 A tough game. China v. Australia during the second FIFA Women's World Cup in Sweden, 1995.

Finally, do women play football in the same way as men? The pitch, the equipment and the ball are the same although the International Board has allowed some flexibility over the length of the game and the size of the ball. In the early seventies there was some suggestion that Law 12 as it applied to handball might be amended to allow women to protect their breasts with their hands but it was felt at the time that it was premature to make such a change and the passage of time has shown that to have been the right decision. Many women players have also complained about the difficulty of getting good boots in small sizes.

After the tedium and cynicism of Italia '90 the Women's World Cups of 1991 and 1995 came as a breath of fresh air. The women played attacking football but were less physically aggressive than the men. Moreover, they apparently embraced the ethic of fair play in a most idealistic way, not only committing few serious fouls but also never arguing with the referee. In addition, opponents were treated with more respect than in the men's game. Paul Hyldgaard the Danish head of the FIFA Committee for Women's Football is given the credit for summing up in a memorable phrase, the difference between the men's and women's games: 'Women want to win a game, men don't want to lose.' There was also a certain amount of careless talk in which value loaded words such as beauty, grace and elegance were bandied about. In fact, most of the teams were coached by men and over the decade, as players became fitter and trained harder there were signs of change, such as the emergence of a more phyiscal game. Norway, who appeared in the first two World Cup Finals and won the Olympic tournament of 2000 in Sydney have a very similar style to their men's team. It is based on teamwork, and a mental and physical strength which is reflected in a vigorous, fast game with a judicious use of the long pass. Even in 1995, in Sweden, it was noticed that teams had become more organised in defence and were also more competitive and aggressive. Some critics have said that teams often play like that to conceal technical, athletic or tactical deficiencies – so it is possibly not an accident that the first two goalless draws in three Women's World Cups were in the final and third place matches of 1999. This might also suggest a narrowing of the gap between the leading teams and the rest but it does not necessarily mean a rise in the standard of play. We do know that the average number of goals per game is also falling. China were said to have played a 6-2-2 formation in some matches in 1999. What 1999 and 2000 seem to show

is that in order to win you have first not to lose so, as in the men's game, the women go for defensive organisation and increase both the speed and strength of the players. Most teams prefer a careful approach based on the lightning counterattack, only switching to a more attacking mode when they go behind or play the much weaker teams. This is very like the men's game and helps to explain the large number of tournament victories of one or two goals to nil. So perhaps the women's game is more like the men's than it was but their respect of fair play, the referee, and the opposition still give it a character closer to the ideals of FIFA's founding fathers

FIFA and youth

Women's football was a self-starting movement that the founders of FIFA could hardly have imagined and which the modern officials took some time to accept but both old FIFA and new FIFA recognised the importance of youth. 'Youth' has, of course, in football terms gradually taken on the meaning of those years between the end of childhood and becoming an adult. In those countries with national systems of education this often meant the period between leaving school and being eligible for organised senior football. In England, on the other hand, youth meant, before 1945, boys aged between fourteen and eighteen. The FA was aware in the 1920s that many boys lost the opportunity to play football during these transitional years and never regained it. In some anxiety over the growth in popularity of rugby in grammar and public schools the FA set up a committee in 1926 to promote youth football, drawing up model rules and urging all the county football associations to focus on this important group. Professional clubs

22

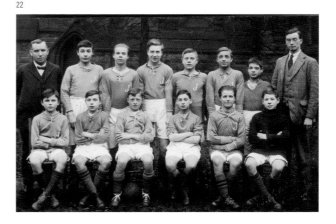

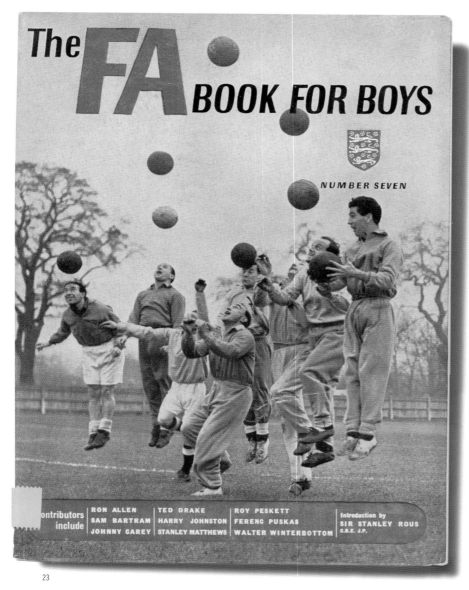

in England did not run their own youth teams before 1945 but they had already developed the bad habit of poaching promising schoolboys and by 1950 they were allowed to sign seventeen-year-olds on licence. By this time there was an FA County Youth Cup for which representative teams from county football associations consisting of amateur players under the age of eighteen competed.

The FA's desire to modernise youth football led them to introduce coaching schemes and produce periodicals such as the *FA News* and the annual *FA Book for Boys,* which was published every year from 1948 to 1973. The same impulse founded the FA Youth Cup in 1952 for the youth teams of professional clubs, which the so-called 'Busby Babes' of Manchester United won in each of its first five years. A part of the same process was the organisation of coaching weeks, usually during the Easter holidays when teams from secondary schools would compete and practice together. Youth leagues became part of the fabric of the English game. The FA thought that football was of great benefit to the

nation's young men, that it could help to improve their lives and provide a pathway to a better society. It should be no surprise then that an international organisation such as FIFA should also see the potential of football as a game without frontiers and focus particularly on the rising new generation. Indeed, the Executive Committee meeting in Rome in March 1952 suggested that an international youth tournament should be organised in each continent.

Secretary Gassmann's report in 1952 emphasized the duty of FIFA to stress 'the moral and physical value of the sport that it controls and promotes so that the youth of every country throughout the world may profit from it.' In spite of the difference in character and outlook of the affiliated national associations, now up to eighty, this was a goal towards which all could strive. One of the ways of doing it was through the international youth tournament. The first of these had already taken place in London in 1948 and was followed in successive years by tournaments in Holland, Austria, France, Spain and Belgium. It had become a hard-fought competition. But for the leaders of FIFA that was not its main purpose. As Gassmann wrote, it was important:

to bring together young people of different countries, different and opposed ideologies, ideas and languages. It is a means for these young people to get to know one another and to find out by personal experience that, in spite of all real or imaginary differences, it is possible to understand and respect each other. Sport should form the basis for open and sincere comradeship.

One should not forget the context in which these ideals were expressed. Europe had only recently emerged from six years of armed struggle and had already plunged into the potentially disastrous hostilities of the so-called 'Cold War.' Perhaps a sport like football, that had an appeal which transcended different countries and cultures, could be

24 Programme from the African Youth Championships in Ethiopia, 2001.

reshaped in such a way as to make some contribution to international understanding. It is interesting nearly half a century later to see how far the FIFA executive was prepared to go in pursuit of their attempt to use football to influence the way young men thought about the world.

Between 10-19 April 1954 the youth tournament was held in West Germany. That in itself was symbolic, signifying one more, albeit small, step towards the hosts' reintegration into the community of civilised nations. Players from East Germany and the Saar, both disputed territories, also took part and Argentina sent a team, providing a real flavour of internationalism. A long-serving FIFA Vice-President, Karl Lotsy from Holland, thought the organisation was first class but that the tournament had not met the exacting standards with which FIFA wished to invest it. For one thing it was too big. Eighteen teams took part and the matches were gratifyingly but also ludicrously popular. A crowd of 70,000 saw the final. Lotsy was convinced that this was wrong and contradicted the idea behind the international youth tournament structure: 'In my opinion these tournaments should take place in a simple and modest way and the participants should be accommodated in a school if possible, so that they can meet and get to know each other and enjoy themselves.' Lotsy also felt there were too many gifts and receptions, which could make these junior players too conscious of their own importance. He was very impressed by the standard of play, especially by the top three countries, Spain, West Germany and Argentina, but suspicious that some teams were not as amateur as they were supposed to be. He noted that all the matches were broadcast on the radio and that often the players were interviewed at the microphone, an Argentinian practice of which he disapproved. Such tournaments were to be organised in all the confederation areas but Lotsy

was opposed to any notion of a Youth World Championship – though the South American association wished to organise one. He also thought that anyone sent off in a match should be suspended for the duration of the tournament. After West Germany in 1954 the Executive Committee decided to make changes:

The Competition itself must not be the main aim. The tendency to seek victory at any costs, to take the results of the matches a as matter of prestige, rivalry or even nationalism, is not comparable with the first aim of the tournament. The gathering of young football players of different countries to get to know each other in spite of the difficulties of language (and) differences of political opinion must be the main goal ... This does not exclude playing the matches in a competitive but friendly or chivalrous spirit.

The changes suggested were dramatic. In future, the teams would be divided into groups but there would be no classification and no winner! The games would be restricted to two halves of forty minutes, the age of the players would be strictly controlled and there would be no substitution of uninjured players. Was this brave or quixotic, or even both? For two seasons, what was in effect the European Youth Championship had no champion. Inside football there was disagreement. East Germany and Yugoslavia, for example, supported the idea that young footballers should get to know each other better. England, on the other hand, said that many of their best youngsters were already professionals and therefore not eligible. Arguments over the definition of who was, and who was not, an amateur had not gone away. Was this a realistic way to control the excesses of competitive

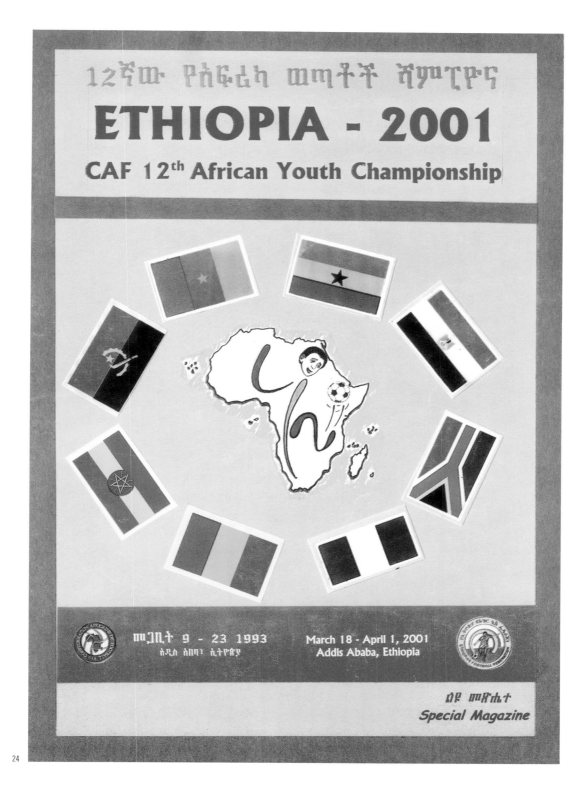

spirit that could disfigure the football field? Moreover, the real world beyond the pitch was never far away. The East German team could not obtain visas in 1955, and in 1956 Greece refused to play against Turkey.

A tournament without a champion did not have much of a future, but international youth tournaments did. The continued expansion of international football and in particular the profits from the quadrennial World Cups meant that by the 1960s FIFA had some real money to spend and some of it went to support confederation youth tournaments. It was not always necessary – the South American tournament, which had begun in Brazil in 1955, made US$92,000 in profit when it was staged in Barranquilla,

Colombia, in 1964. In Asia and Africa it was different. The huge distances involved in Asia, where the host nation had to meet fifty per cent of the travelling expenses, meant that none of the early tournaments such as Bangkok in 1962, Penang 1963, Saigon 1964 nor Tokyo 1965 paid for themselves. Even in Europe the championship in Holland lost 22,000 Swiss Francs in 1964. However, providing FIFA received a full report and a set of detailed costs from the organisers then a contribution was made. Africa's problems were more deep rooted. Although some African governments were keen to provide financial help, this usually came at the price of political control, which FIFA refused to countenance. FIFA ran its own aid and development scheme for Africa but it was 1966 before the African Football Confederation decided to organise a youth tournament and 1979 before they actually did so. Since then, the African Youth tournament has been held twelve times.

International Youth tournaments, of course, were only for the young elite of the sport. It was the coaching of young footballers and, perhaps more importantly, the education of native-born coaches that did most to improve playing standards and further the reach of the gospel according to football. In 1967 FIFA appointed a German, Dettmar Cramer, as their peripatetic trainer. Over the next five years, he visited all the world's continents and a large number of its countries. Cramer went to national associations in Asia, Australia, Africa and Central and North America, usually spending a month in each country where he taught sixteen to eighteen national players, sixteen to eighteen youth players, and a number of selected coaches and referees. In Asia he emphasised the value of coaching school boys and youths and ran two coaching schools of three months' duration each, the first in Japan and the second in Malaysia. As well as football skills, tactics and techniques, students were also

taught first-aid, psychology and physiology before returning to coach in their individual countries. FIFA subsidised these schools but the host countries also had to put hands in their pockets.

Cramer found Africa much harder work but stressed that it was by no means a continent whose national associations all shared the same problems. In North Africa, for example, the standard of football organisation lagged little behind Europe. Football was well-organised in Tunisia, with the government working closely with the national football association. There were football schools for boys under twelve funded by the government. There were also many French, Hungarian and Yugoslavian trainers there doing good work as well as very competent Tunisians. Cramer recomended that Tunisian youth football would benefit from the national team being admitted to the UEFA tournament. On the other hand, he found the first week in Gambia much more difficult! Gambia had never had an experienced coach.

The players were neither used to punctuality nor hard training. They arrived late, and liked to finish when they were tired. To convince them of the necessity of training-discipline required several days But it was wonderful after

25

25 Representing a famous African footballing nation from the 1960s. Guinea was unsuccessful in the 2nd FIFA World Youth Championship, 1979.

26 The match between Burkina Faso v. Qatar at the U-17 World Championship in New Zealand, 1999.

27 Port-Saïd stadium. The U-17 World Championship in Egypt, 1997.

28 Football Mangas. Stickers sold for the FIFA World Junior Championship, the Coca Cola Cup in Japan, 1979.

that and he was sad to leave!

Cramer was convinced of the importance a strong national team could have on the development of football in a country as they set an example to all the others. So for him it was not enough only to coach the junior players he ought to give some of his time to the elite. Cramer was also optimistic about progress in another of the world's relatively underdeveloped football regions. He admitted that 'coaching in the USA was a challenge' but he noted, in 1970, that:

'the progress made in the youth sector over the last two years is gratifying. Football is now being played by many thousands more youths than was the case two years ago, and football has made its entrance into many High Schools and Colleges. The strongest and most important factor is that the American youth is now playing the game and their parents are interested in it.'

Cramer thought the USSFA should set up a national coaching system and further develop the youth programme. By the mid-1970s, of course, FIFA was on the brink of its first agreement with the Coca-Cola company to spon-

sor a FIFA World Youth Championship to be contested every two years by players under twenty years of age. These Championships were designed in part to further encourage the development of youth football in areas of the world where it remained poorly developed. It also provided opportunities for FIFA members, such as Malaysia and Qatar who would probably never be able to host the World Cup, to stage a major football tournament. Not surprisingly, the finalists tended to be drawn from the strongest footballing nations like Argentina, Brazil and Germany. But some national associations were tempted to try to deceive the authorities and improve their chances of success by fielding over-age players. Costa Rica, Iraq, Mexico and Nigeria were suspended from all international competitions for two years after being found guilty of breaking the rules.

FIFA celebrated its golden jubilee on 20 June 1954, declaring the day in honour of the young footballers. The following morning President Jules Rimet addressed Congress for the last time. Having spoken about the growth of football throughout the world he warned that 'the satisfaction we may take from this success must not make us forget the principal aims of our task: developing the

practice of the game, and increasing the number of its players. We must put the game at the disposal of the youth, for the moral and physical education of the youth of the world.'

Of course it was not only FIFA who organised youth tournaments. Many national associations also established their own. Norway, for example, initiated its Norway Cup in 1972. Held in and around Oslo during the summer holidays it attracted 10,000 participants, boys aged between twelve and eighteen, and girls over eighteen, from all over Europe. Sixteen years later in 1988, it was still prospering with 20,000 young people from all parts of the world in 1000 teams playing 2500 matches in the friendliest spirit. In a football world dominated by the commercialised spectacle it is perhaps worth reminding ourselves that this is perhaps as important an event as the Under 17 and Under 20 World Youth Championships.

Perspectives

According to FIFA's *Big Count*, a statistical survey carried out by FIFA in 2000, 240 million people had played some form of football in that year; one in twenty-five of the world's population. About thirty million played with organised clubs and associations: the rest were casual or occasional players who participated in the game largely outside its formal structures. They ranged in age from the over-forties to university students and quite young children but included about twenty-seven million male youth of whom only twelve million were attached to registered clubs. These are impressive figures but they don't provide any indication of movement up or down. There is some suggestion that in Europe and North America, for example, and in parts of Asia, the numbers of male youths playing football may be declining. In a world in which the focus is increasingly on the individual, collective team sports like football may be threatened by the legion of other sports now competing for the attention of male youth. In a city such as Hamburg in Germany, for example, it has been estimated that there are 240 different sports from which the young may choose: from skate boarding to mountain biking to BMX racing. Then there are other competitors, old and new, for the money and leisure time of the young like partying, the internet and computer games.

If male participation is beginning to decline it is not certain that female footballers can take up the slack. Football remains a largely male domain. 12.5 million adult men played organised football in 2000 but only 500,000 adult women. The *Big Count* suggested that the overall proportion of female football players was nine per cent of the total. On the other hand the women's game seems to be much more for the young. In the male game, fifty-five per cent who were registered with a club or association were under thirty-years-old. In the women's game, the figure was eighty per cent. But the development of women's football in the world remains very uneven. Asia, Africa and South America have low proportions of women involved compared to Europe and North America. A survey among Brazilian girls and young women in the mid-nineties showed that football and weightlifting were considered the least appropriate sports for women. The vast majority of female players are of school age or at college. In many parts of Africa, for example, it remains difficult for girls to get an education. Many spend fifty hours a week on domestic work and subsistence food production. They have little leisure time, usually less than the men. Fifty per cent of young women will be married by the age of eighteen and many will be heavily involved in caring for the young, the sick and the old. Even where there are opportunities for leisure, sport, or

even football, women players find themselves competing with the men for scarce resources. Women's teams, for example, have been withdrawn from international tournaments at the last minute due to lack of money. So far, FIFA has been unable to stipulate how the aid they send to individual football associations should be spent. Perhaps a proportion ought to be allocated to the women's game.

There are also cultural issues that have inhibited the development of women's football. Nigeria won the CAF tournament in 2000 but in the north-west province of Zamfara, women's football has been outlawed as un-Islamic. Yet there was a national championship for women footballers in Algeria in 2000. Moreover, in Egypt, Sahar El-Hawary developed an indoor league in which the players covered their legs to avoid criticism. Out of this came an Egyptian national team and the spread of the game to some schools. El-Hawary has become the first African Arabic woman of the FIFA Women's Football Committee. There are now fourteen members of that committee of whom half are women but there are few women occupying influential positions in FIFA or in many national associations or the confederations. It is in China and the USA that women's football seems to be most firmly established outside western Europe. In the USA it continues to grow faster then any other collegiate sport, emphasising the importance of educational institutions in its continued development. Certainly, football now captures the imagination of boys and girls and men and women from all cultures in a way that would have seemed unlikely half a century ago and has become a part of global popular culture. The questions is whether it is art? The next chapter will explore some of the many ways in which football has influenced and been represented in painting, sculpture, film and literature in the football century.

FOOTBALL, ART, LITERATURE AND CINEMA

Pierre de Coubertin, the founder of the modern Olympic Games, thought that great sport and great art should be closely linked. Both artists and writers would flock to these modern festivals of bodily competition and exuberance and produce a spectacular amalgam of the creative, both mental as well as physical.

1 *Any Wintry Afternoon in England* by C. Richard Wynne Nevinson (1930), oil on canvas, Manchester Art Gallery.

2 *The injured footballer* by Douglas Tilden, bronze statue. Reproduced in *La Vie au Grand Air*, 1900.

3 Cover of the Romanian children's book *Unsprezece* (Eleven) by Eugen Barbu, 1961.

LA VIE AU GRAND AIR

LE SPORT DANS L'ART A L'EXPOSITION

4

Sport and the arts

The first Olympic arts' contest was held at the Stockholm games in 1912 with medals awarded for sculpture, architecture, poetry, music and literature. This was a pentathlon of the Muses, as in the ancient games. By the time the games arrived at Los Angeles in 1932 the cultural event was almost as big as the athletic; 1100 works of art were displayed in fifteen Los Angeles galleries and 400,000 people eventually saw them. Similarly, in Berlin in 1936, the art contest was a formidable part of the celebrations. The austerity games in bomb-damaged London in 1948 also featured an exhibition but few remember many of the works on show. In fact, the day of the sponsored festival of Olympic art was almost over. The new President of the IOC, Avery Brundage, did not like the way in which the arts contest had become contaminated by professionals so the IOC-sponsored contest was discontinued. In future, host cities would be encouraged to embellish the games with cultural events of their own. In 1992, Barcelona, for example, staged a grand and expensive arts festival with prizes of £20,000 for those judged best in Architecture, Music, Media and the Plastic Arts. The IOC even presented an Olympic prize to an artist, Harry Evans, who had worked on sporting themes all his life. There remained a powerful belief that high sport and high culture should be linked.

5

6

FIFA did not have the standing nor the resources of the IOC and it would be several decades before the World Cup would rival the Olympic Games as an international mega-event. By the 1920s, though, football was drawing bigger crowds than any other Olympic sport. Art exhibitions became an accompaniment to World Cups, most notably in Italy in 1934. Although FIFA did not go out of its way to promote football through art, many young artists were drawn to it as a subject. In the early twentieth century, football was the epitome of modern sport, spreading to many countries and cutting across class lines. It was a fashionable craze, a prime example of modernity. It was up-to-date, and even futuristic – especially when played in front of huge crowds in the massive urban stadiums. Moreover, it was yet another example of the human figure in action. How could the painter or the sculptor ignore it? It was almost as much a part of the modern world as film or flight.

Football and art

Representations of athletes and gymnasts had tended to hark back to the days of ancient Greece and imperial Rome. They were neo-classical, muscular figures but footballers were never shown in this way. They represented a new kind of bodily movement which particularly appealed to the Italian Futurists who were promoters of action in all its forms and wanted to rehabilitate the physical. As Filippo Marinetti said, 'sport should be considered an essential component of art. Futurism finds, in football, a means of exalting movement, speed, confrontation and nationalism.' Another member of the avant-garde, Umberto Boccioni, painted *The Dynamism of Football Players*. It is a colourful abstract picture clearly inspired by the shapes, speed, colour and movement that for

Boccioni summed up the power of the game. It marked the beginning of a shift away from a realist representation of football which is seen in the work of artists such as Georges Braque, Robert Delaunay, Fernand Leger and Pablo Picasso. Picasso, for example, showed a good deal of freedom in the way he portrayed the footballers playing on a beach in what looks like Brazil in 1928. Around the same time, the German artist, Willy Baumeister, exploring the relationship between sport and the machine, portrayed the footballer as a 'smoothly running mechanical contrivance, anonymous, expressionless, geometrical but powerful.' He also experimented with photomontage including action shots of players and actual stadiums. In Britain, the modernist Christopher Nevinson produced a Cubist-influenced representation of a football match in which stylised though well-turned out footballers confronted each other before a 'typical' urban industrial landscape. He called the picture 'Any Wintry Afternoon in England', a strange title in that it leaves out the word 'Saturday' before afternoon – the day when most English football matches were played in the 1930s.

By the 1930s painters of the Surrealist school and the Dadaists were suggesting that footballers were no better than anyone else and indeed were inconsequential and inarticulate, part of the muddle that modernity had become. An example of this would be John Heartfield's

9>

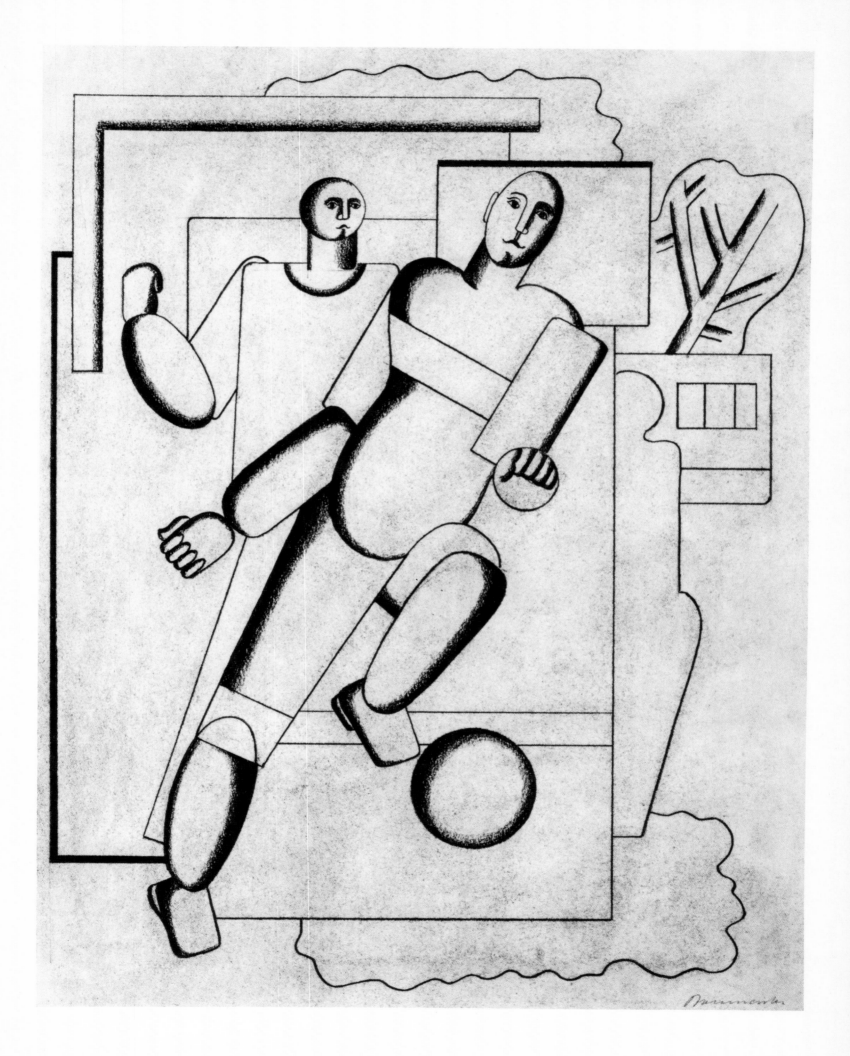

FOOTBALL, ART, LITERATURE AND CINEMA

10 *Corner* by Jean Jacoby (1924), oil on canvas, Olympic Museum, Lausanne.

11 *Association Football* by Benito. Cover of *La Vie au Grand Air* (1921).

10

11

photograph of a footballer with his head replaced by a massively swollen football.

Of course, more orthodox artists were still trying to capture the thrill of the spectacle, as in the French painter Jean Jacoby's *Corner*. It was inspired by the football at the Paris Olympics in 1924 and focuses on an incident at the goalmouth. Five players make up the composition, the central figure being the goalkeeper leaping to take the ball before it can reach the head of two equally airborne opponents. It was the kind of picture that might appeal more to the public than the art critic. Capturing the essence of such a dynamic spectacle is very difficult but many have tried and many continue to do so.

In 1953 the English FA and the Arts Council staged an exhibition of paintings to mark the ninetieth anniversary of the first football association. Of the 106 oil paintings, drawings and water colours that made up the bulk of the exhibition, at least fifty-four confronted some aspect of football as spectacle. Contemporary critics thought that the best ones were those which did not focus on the play but on its setting. It was football in the context of the industrial world of post-war Britain that produced the most emotionally powerful pictures.

… the hurry of figures converging on the turnstiles, the thousands of faces stretching away on every side with a

blue mist of tobacco smoke rising into the fog of the late afternoon, the surging currents of a mass of heads blindly pushing and surging towards the exits. The poignant empty terraces littered with papers when all but the last stragglers have filtered away, the curious architecture of the stadium itself – the steep vertiginous terraces of the Valley, the great flat sweeping bowl of Stamford Bridge with its scattered irregular stands looking as if they had been improvised overnight …

The best were pictures of stadiums and crowds both inside and outside them. Arthur Hackney entered *Spectators Returning Home after Port Vale v Accrington Stanley* with an anonymous crowd walking home under a threatening late-afternoon sky. The best of all, and one of four to share the painting prize, was L.S. Lowry's *Going to the Match*. It is a Lancashire townscape with typical matchstick figures hurrying not to miss the kick-off outside the former Burden Park ground of Bolton Wanderers. The painting was recently bought for £2 million by the English Professional Footballers' Association.

Interestingly, at the same time Lowry was at work in Bolton, Nicolas de Stael was also having his creative impulse vigorously stirred by a football match. On 26 March 1952 de Stael went with his wife to the floodlit international between France and Sweden at the Parc

12 An Argentinian artist working in the River Plate stadium, Buenos Aires 1963.

13 *Just Another Bloody Saturday* by Peter Howson (1987), Scottish National Gallery of Modern Art, Edinburgh.

14 Former footballer Jack Charlton in front of the painting by L.S. Lowry, *Going to the match* (1953). Photograph by Ben Blackall, The Lowry, Manchester.

12

13

des Princes in Paris. He was entranced by the fervour, colours, action and acrobatics of the bodies displayed on the bright green turf marked out, as he put it, 'like graph paper.' Returning to his studio after the match he set to work immediately and in a night of inspiration organized his incandescent impressions on a gigantic white canvas called *Footballeurs* (1952). Full of life, movement and colour, it impressed many with its energy and power, although some contemporary critics damned it as a return to impressionism. Over the following few days he painted another twenty-four canvases. The work has remained popular and was put on show again at the Pompidou Centre in Paris in 2003.

14

The expression of football in art has always mirrored the fortunes of the game itself. These have fluctuated from the peak of popularity in the decade following the Second World War to the depths reached in the hooligan-infested and disaster-prone 1970s and 1980s. In the last ten years enhanced television coverage and the large sums of money which accompanied it have created a booming football business in many countries. It is not surprising that all kinds of artists have taken advantage of this, from satirical conceptual artists such as Mark Wallinger, who exhibited an outsize Manchester United scarf in the form of a DNA spiral, to an outbreak of statues of famous players appearing in public places as diverse as Lisbon (Eusebio) and Hanley (Stanley Matthews). When the European Football Championships were held in England in 1996 exhibitions of football-related art were staged by Gallery 27 in London and the Manchester Art Gallery. In 1998 the Scottish painter, Peter Howson, had a one-man show of football paintings, his 'energetic muscular footballers … enunciated in bold strokes of raw colour.'

Posters could bring the work of serious artists to a wider audience. In Britain, for example, the modernist painter Paul Nash, produced one for the Shell Oil Company in 1933 entitled 'Footballers Prefer Shell'. Nash employed an 'informal cubic style depicting a

deserted goalmouth and grandstand with a football hovering over the goal line.' London Transport commissioned several prominent contemporary artists in the years between the wars to persuade football fans to use their buses and underground trains on match days. One by Sybil Andrews and Cyril Power created a striking football motif of the London Underground. Similar posters were produced each year to coincide with the FA Cup Final which was held at Wembley from 1923.

The first three World Football Championships organised by FIFA were distinguished by the production of spectacular posters much influenced by the Art Deco school. They were produced by the host country and the first, advertising the World Cup in Uruguay in 1930, was particularly sumptuous. The top half contained the

15 *Football* by Sybil Andrews and Cyril Power (1933), lithograph, London Transport Museum.

16 Poster for World Cup Finals in France 1938 by Desmé.

upper torso of an elastically sinuous goalkeeper in bright blue, stretching to catch a light brown ball before it passed between an orange right angle made by crossbar and post. The lettering is stylishly decorative and sans serif with *Campeanato Mundial de Football* in black above Uruguay in white capitals. Below that, Montevideo is in dark brown with the year 1930 embossed in white over its central four letters. The final line, also in white, gives the date and duration of the event, 15 Julio, Agosto 15. Guillermo Laborde was the artist who created this delicious piece of modern graphic art. Neither Italy 1934 nor France 1938 could quite match this but their posters were both very eye-catching. Gino Boccasile's design in 1934 showed a footballer imposed upon a diagonal line of the flags of some of the finalists while Desmé for France in 1938 filled half of his poster with a globe, above which a football rested under a rather militaristic leg plus football boot. Interestingly, the Uruguayans left FIFA off their wonderful poster but the famous initials appeared on the other two above those of the Italian and French football associations. As far as the attractiveness of World Cup posters went this was as good as it got, although in 1982, when the tournament was held in Spain, Joan Miró produced a typical piece of brilliantly coloured invention which adorned the walls of many households long afterwards.

17

18

19

Literature

Some people think that football is a perfect subject for serious fiction. Every match brings a plethora of human interaction both on and off the field. Moreover, football is a central life interest for many people – it matters. Again if you happen to be good at it – or even good at writing about it – it can be a pathway to social advancement. Few would dispute football's capacity for drama and excitement. Moreover, a frustrating but also attractive characteristic of the game is that the best side does not always win. The struggle of the underdog against the top team rarely fails to capture the imagination, as

20

17 Poster advertising the first World Cup Finals in Uruguay 1930 by Guillermo Laborde.

18 Poster for World Cup Finals in Italy 1934 by Gino Boccasile.

19 Poster for World Cup Finals in Spain 1982 by Joan Miro.

20 Cover of *Contos de Futebol* by Aldyr Garcia Schlee (Brazil 1997).

was shown in the World Cup Finals of 2002 when not many people outside Germany wanted them to beat South Korea in the semi-final.

Yet the fact is that serious, creative fiction about football is rare in every culture. It is not clear how far this is due to football's relatively low cultural status. FIFA may have had this in mind when the Executive Committee agreed in 1957 to give a prize for the best essay about football. Committee members were clearly keen to get writers interested and a literary prize was the temptress. But the idea was dropped after two years of argument due to 'great difficulties realising such plans in the international field'. Even in Argentina, where football was and is an interest shared by intellectuals and populace alike, Jorge Luis Borges, one of their greatest writers, was not a fan and famously remarked before the 1978 World Cup, which was held there, that he was going to leave the country until the tempest passed over. On the other hand, Aldyo Garcia Schlee, a Brazilian living on the border with Uruguay, published *Contos de Futebol*, ('Football Tales') (1995) which was a finalist for the Jabuti prize, and Mario Vargas Lhosa has often used football in his novels about modern Peru. Indeed, football is often alluded to in the novel, but rarely its focus.

In the United Kingdom, for example, Arnold Bennett's *The Card* (1911) amusingly shows the part played by football in the local politics of an industrial town when one of the candidates for Mayor shrewdly signs a goalscorer for the local team. J.B. Priestley, in his novel *The Good Companion* (1929), hardly mentions the game but briefly underlines its attraction for working class communities in an often quoted paragraph. Similarly, Henry Green's *Living* (1929) included a Saturday afternoon trip to Villa Park as part of his evocation of the life of Birmingham workers in the 1920s. Barry Hines' *Kestrel*

FOOTBALL, ART, LITERATURE AND CINEMA

for a Knave (1968) also includes a memorable football scene. It is set during a games period in a northern secondary school. A bully of a P.E. teacher not only pretends that he is Bobby Charlton but insists on his side winning. During this performance the schoolboy central character is humiliated in his role as an unwilling and, it must be said, incompetent goalkeeper. The darker side of the game was occasionally featured in short stories, a particularly good example being Alan Sillitoe's *The Match* in which the aftermath of a defeat for Notts. County leads to domestic violence when the fan returns home. More recently, Nick Hornby used football to explore issues of identity and obsession. His book *Fever Pitch* became a bestseller just at the moment in 1992 when, after England's relatively successful World Cup in Italia '90, the inception of the Premiership and an injection of money from satellite television projected English football into the marketing stratosphere. Other high-profile British novelists such as Martin Amis, Julian Barnes, Irvine Welsh, all mentioned it in major works, and D.J. Taylor – now outed as a supporter of Norwich City – published *The English Settlement* (1996) about a hard-up Fourth Division club and what happens when they ask an American business consultant to help them out.

However, there are two novels in English that are exclusively about football. One is by a Scot, Robin Jenkins. Called *The Thistle and the Grail* (1954), it is set in the economically depressed 1930s. The thistle is Drumsagart Thistle and the grail is their pursuit of the Scottish Junior Cup. It is not a book which focuses on a star player, someone whose footballing skills are going to allow him to challenge his ordained place in society. Instead, its main focus is on those who run the team and those who follow it. It is the local community whose passion and commitment

make even their run-down little ground 'a stage which can evoke all the emotions once associated with the highest art forms'. There is a funny but also touching scene which illustrates this well. When the team travels north to play in the semi-final, most of the supporters cannot afford to go. They hold a meeting and decide that everyone should make a small contribution so that one of them can travel to watch the match and report back on its progress to the public phone box in the centre of town. There, they all gather in a downpour of Scottish rain waiting for the news …

In *The Thistle and the Grail* football symbolises mutal dependence. As outstanding players still depend on their team, so in society no one can shoulder all responsibil-

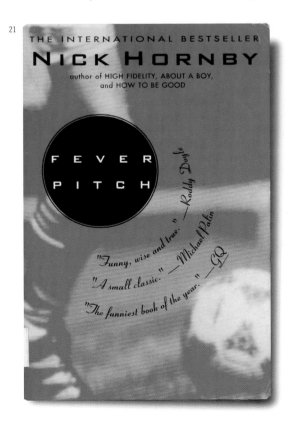

21

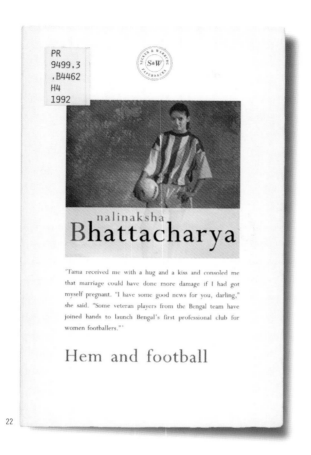

nalinaksha
Bhattacharya

'Tama received me with a hug and a kiss and consoled me that marriage could have done more damage if I had got myself pregnant. "I have some good news for you, darling," she said. "Some veteran players from the Bengal team have joined hands to launch Bengal's first professional club for women footballers."'

Hem and football

22

ities – even the rich depend on the poor. The book is about a search for community in which both football and religion are ultimately found wanting, but communal participation in both helps people cope with the dehumanising forces of the industrial world.

Drumsagart lose their semi-final but they escape the consequences of defeat by challenging the registration of one of their opponent's players. They win the challenge and go on to win the cup, but find that, even though their challenge was legally justified, it has somehow compromised their victory. To quote Cairns Craig:

The storybook success of Drumsagart Thistle becomes the symbol in Jenkins's novel for a grail which cannot be held in human hand without being soiled by the means used to achieve it. And like all sporting climaxes it becomes instant nostalgia, no sooner achieved than a mere memory which is no bulwark against the reality of tomorrow.

If Robin Jenkins treats football as a serious subject, J.L. Carr went to the other extreme with his attempt, as he described it, to attract the vast non-novel reading public with a story that had football at its core. *How Steeple Sinderby Wanderers won the FA Cup* (1975) is the story of how an English village football team makes it to Wembley and actually wins the trophy. The aim was partly to see if such an unbelievable feat could be made to sound

believable. His cast of characters included an exiled Hungarian intellectual who applied himself to devising seven basic principles for producing winning football, two excellent former professional players with good reasons for having given up top-class football and a chairman of Napoleonic ability. It is a splendid comic novel which offers a range of insights into England in the early 1970s, parodies football match reports in newspapers and meditates, as Jenkins did, on the difficulty of 'catching at happiness' before it disappears. Life is a matter of making the best of the chances available to you before they vanish. But it is also a book about loss as the final half a dozen lines suggest. Victory has been won, the team dispersed and Joe Gidner, the narrator of the story, is standing alone in the dusk when he is joined by his Chairman. 'Mr Gidner,' says the Chairman, 'I know what you're looking for. But it's gone and it'll never come back.'

Not everybody liked this book, including Brian Glanville, a well-known football writer and novelist of the game with five books on football themes, including *The Rise of Gerry Logan* (1963). It is true that Carr took a few liberties, omitting the second, third and sixth rounds of the FA Cup and sidestepping the thorny issue of ticket allocations. The book was an anti-modern fantasy, but a very entertaining one that also appealed to England's love of the underdog. If J.L. Carr was ultimately a pessimist then his pessimism was 'continually redeemed by sheer high spirits'.

A final novel which ought to be mentioned not only features football but also women playing it. *Hem and Football* by Nalinaksha Bhattacharya is about a thirteen-year-old Calcutta schoolgirl Hempzova Mintra. She is growing up and trying to be herself in the face of the expectations of a traditional family when she is chosen for the Champaboti Girls' High School football

team. Later, she is good enough to have a trial with the first women's professional club in Bengal. Again, this is a book speckled with humour. The team's coach is a Marxist called Miss Nag who uses the Communist Manifesto to shape the team's game. A teammate tells Hem that 'the whole thing only makes sense if we consider ourselves as proletarians and our opponents as the bourgeoisie.' Interestingly, the novel came out in the same year as *Fever Pitch* and both share the notion of football as 'refuge, palliative and escape route.' Ultimately, any novel ostensibly about football is, of course, about much more than just the sport.

Theatre

If football has rarely been a major inspiration for novelists it has not tempted many dramatists either. The first serious drama in English that centred on football was probably Harold Brighouse's, *The Game* (1913), which suggested that, even when tempted by money to lose a match, top professionals remained basically honest. Like his much more famous play *Hobson's Choice*, his real intent was to explore inter-generational conflict.

Interestingly, serious plays were no more supposed to be about football in Brazil than in Britain, even though football appealed to a much broader cross-section of Brazilian society there than it did in the country that invented it. In 1953 Nelson Rodrigues wrote a play called *A Falecida* (The Deceased Woman). It was about a widower who spends the money his wife had been saving up to meet the cost of her funeral on football after he discovers that she had been unfaithful to him. Despite Rodrigues' formidable reputation, the play was not a success.

An important play about football was written by Peter Terson in 1967. *Zigger Zagger* was a topical attempt to dramatise and make sense of the growing problem of football hooliganism in Britain. In particular, it examined the relationship between football hooliganism and youth culture and its first performance was at the National Youth Theatre.

Apart from this tiny handful of plays focusing directly on it, the beautiful game has had to confine its theatrical ambitions to walk-on roles. In *The Dumb Waiter* (1960), for example, Harold Pinter includes an amusing though sinister slice of dialogue about it. A typical piece of public bar football talk that always gets a laugh from the audience was also featured in his *A Night Out* (1960). Tom Stoppard uses the dramatic coincidence of an international football match in Prague between Czechoslovakia and England with a conference of academic philosophers on ethics to pose a few ethical problems for his main character, Professor Anderson in *Professional Foul* (1970). Anderson even-

tually agrees to smuggle out a paper written by a Czech scholar criticising the Communist regime, but does it by secreting it in the luggage of a colleague.

Otherwise in recent years there has only been a comedy by Arthur Smith and Chris England, *An Evening with Gary Lineker* (1992) which deals with some of the responses to the elimination of England at the semi-final stage of the 1990 World Cup. It was a West End hit that reflects the revival of top professional football in England which was, as we have already seen, one of the features of the 1990s.

Of course, football is often talked about in theatrical terms and it is true that both football and theatre involve the presentation of a dramatic spectacle. However, theatrical performances are usually scripted and carefully

CHORUS [*sing*]:
> There'll always be a City
> While there's a football fan,
> We're standing right behind you,
> We'll back you to a man.
>
> Red, white for you, what does it mean to you?
> Surely you're proud,
> Shouting aloud,
> City's away.
> We look to you,
> We can depend on you,
> Shouting aloud,
> Singing aloud,
> City's away.
>
> There'll always be a City
> While there's a football fan,
> We're standing right behind you,
> We'll back you to a man.

rehearsed while plays deal with ideas and relationships. A football match may be a narrative text but it is not scripted. It is inherently unpredictable and the details rarely fail to surprise. Moreover, despite the tense atmosphere of the game, dramatic outcomes cannot be assured. Therefore it should not astonish us that, although the theatrical output of football-related plays probably depends on the national standing of the game to some extent, the real problem is that football is too self-contained. It is just not a universal enough subject.

Cinema

The difficulties of making good sporting films are well known. Only boxing has been convincingly depicted at the cinema. In 1998 the American Film Institute listed the top 100 films of the previous century. Only two films with sport as the central theme were included and both were about boxing: *Raging Bull* and *Rocky*. It is easy to see why. The boxing ring is small and the action is focused on two men. The fight is not complicated and the primitive struggle has an immediately communicable emotional power.

Why are there so few half-decent football films? Most are what the Germans call *trash-aesthetique* and *Kassengift* – poison at the box office. It is difficult to capture the tension and excitement of football in the cinema. You cannot reproduce the emotion of a real match. *How Steeple Sinderby Wanderers Won the FA Cup* was bought for filming but the idea was given up because no one could think of an effective way of showing the football scenes. Football films have either been full of footballers who can't act or actors who can't play

FOOTBALL, ART, LITERATURE AND CINEMA

26 Poster for the film *The Cup (Phorpa)* by Khyentse Norbu (1999).

27 Poster for the Israeli film *Gmar gaviya (Cup Final)* (1991).

28 Poster for the French film *Les Rois du Sport (Kings of Sport)* by Pierre Colombier (1937).

football. Or real footage of old matches are used which often distorts the magic of the film for an audience who recognise the German Cup Final of 1986!

As an example of an excruciatingly bad film about football, *Escape to Victory* (1981) is hard to beat. There were some notable footballers in this film but it did not help. The film is about a football match between a group of prisoners of war (POWs) and their German captors. At half-time the Germans are leading 4-1 having had some help from the referee. At this point the French Resistance turns up to help this strange group of Americans, British, Brazilians and Argentinians to escape. But the French rescuers have failed to appreciate the irresistible magnetism of football. Pele scores with an overhead kick despite having a broken shoulder, and Sylvester Stallone saves a penalty which earns the POWs a draw. In the end the French crowd storm the pitch and rescue the POWs. There's little more to be said except that a British film about the rise and fall of a modern professional footballer, *Yesterday's Hero* (1979), was just as bad with the hero brought down by drink and a bad script.

But some good films have used the power and popularity of football to underline their message. Several have used the World Cup Final, stressing the historical importance of the moment. Fassbinder's *Die Ehe der Maria Braun,* ('The Marriage of Maria Braun') (1978) is a story about the misadventures of a woman trying to find her way out of the ruins of post-war Germany. In the last scene, as a fresh relationship finally brings hope, Herbert Zimmermann's famous radio commentary on the final moments of the 1954 World Cup Final between Germany and Hungary can be heard in the

background. This moment was symbolic of German revival and, perhaps, a milestone on the road to acceptance back into the community of nations and a sign that self-confidence was returning.

Werner Herzog also uses World Cup commentary in his film *Wo die grunen Ameisen traumen,* ('Where the Green Ants Dream') (1984). This time the radio commentary is Argentinian, perhaps from their final qualifying match against Peru in the 1978 World Cup. The film is about a struggle between Australian aboriginals and a large mining company that wants to prospect for uranium on sacred aboriginal land, and how a geologist employed by the company becomes more and more sympathetic to their view. No one seems interested in football, but the two short bits of commentary in the film help illustrate the isolation of the Australian out-

26

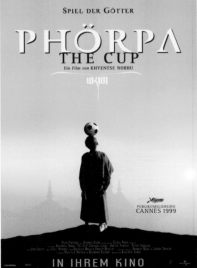

27

216

28

back from the rest of the world and the rest of the world's concerns.

In *Gmar gaviya,* ('Cup Final'), the two central characters also have one eye on the World Cup Finals, this time those of 1982. *Gmar gaviya* is an Israeli film which concentrates on the relationship between an Israeli prisoner and his PLO captor. Both share a love of things Italian and they are trying to keep in touch with the matches. There are few shots of the games: Rossi's goals against Brazil in the quarter final and the last Italian goal in the final is seen on TV through binoculars. A powerful and persistent image is that the Israeli has a ticket for that match in his pocket which he fingers throughout the ordeal. There is no happy ending.

The World Cup is much more important in Khyentse Norbu's film *Phorpa* ('The Cup') (1999). It is apparently based on a true story of young Tibetan boys who have been sent to India by their parents at great expense, and risk, in order to receive the 'dharma', a formal religious education in a monastery at Chokling in the foothills of the Himalayas. But religion is not the only thing on their minds. They are forbidden to go to the local village to watch the 1998 World Cup Final, so

they must bring the World Cup to the monastery. But to obtain a television set and a satellite dish they need money ... The director of this film used non-actors and members of the monastic community and employs a light touch in his exploration of the nostalgia felt by Tibetans living in exile.

There are many other films that have used football in interesting ways. Wim Wenders' *Die Angst des Tormanns Bein Elfmeter* ('The Goalkeeper's Fear of the Penalty') of 1972, based on a P. Handlke story of a man moving towards collapse, had a cult following for a time in the 1970s. Bill Forsyth's *Gregory's Girl* (1980) could not have been more different, focusing on teenage fantasy in a Scottish secondary school where the football team not only included an attractive female player but one who was much better than the scrawny lads who made up the rest of the side. Finally, *Bend it Like Beckham* (2002) by Gurinder Chadu, is a positive attempt to explore the issue of cultural diversity in Britain. The teenage daughter of Indian immigrants becomes one of the star players in a woman's team, eventually winning her parents round before she has to move to the United States on a college football schol-

29

30

arship to further her professional ambitions. These are all worthy films, but we are still waiting for the footballing masterpiece. Perhaps Quentin Tarantino will provide it. He has promised to make a football film to equal *Rocky*. It is to be a trilogy set in a Premiership club in northern England. A young latino from south Los Angeles will be the central character, and the famous director has declared he will use real stars. The final instalment of the trilogy is scheduled to coincide with the 2006 World Cup in Germany. And the title? *Goal!!!*

29 Poster for the French film *Coup de tête (Header)* by Jean-Jacques Annaud (1978).

30 Poster for the East German film *Der neue Fimmel (The New Craze)* by Friedel Hart (1959).

31 *Tumulto no campo* by Ozias (2000), Oil on wood, MIAN, Rio de Janeiro.

32 Hannes H. Wagner, *Fans* (1979), mixed media on canvas, Land Sachsen-Anhalt, Halle.

Conclusion

During the first half of the twentieth century, in Europe and in South America, many painters and sculptors – often from the avant garde – seem to have been more inspired by football than novelists, playwrights or film makers. Artists could fashion their own interpretation of both the bodily movements associated with football and the spectacle in front of a tense and excited crowd. Writers and film-makers never quite discovered a way of convincingly describing the game. It may also be true that few intellectuals liked football before 1950. Jean Cocteau included it among his false gods: the others were machines and New York.

After 1945 circumstances changed. The war was a democratising experience for many people. A football subculture was rampant in the armed services, and the sport became part of the sentimental education of intellectuals, a way of integrating them into the wider world of popular culture. Television may also have played some part in this as football extended its empire across the world. Jean-Paul Sartre even used the example of the football team to illustrate his theory about the fusion of the group in his *Critique of Dialectical Reason*. By 1970 football had become 'the beautiful game' – the World Cup dominance of Brazil clearly had a lot to do with this.

A football match has aesthetic qualities, like a work of art. It possesses some of the qualities of art – beauty, grace of movement, fantasy – and some players are described as artists. Many people thought that teams like Real Madrid of the 1950s and Brazil in 1970 played artistic football. But football is also physical confrontation, a game of journeymen and cloggers. Certainly, people don't experience football as the beautiful game all the time – it is also about winning and losing, and losing is not easy. Often it is not beauty or even pleasure that is the most common experience of football, but disappointment, and the emotion which is often associated with it – anger. The 'beautiful game' is a cliché which it is perhaps time to abandon.

THE MAKING OF THE WORLD GAME

Football is now the world's most popular sport and, with 204 countries, FIFA's membership is greater than that of the United Nations. However, this process has not been without its problems ... This chapter looks at FIFA's efforts to tailor its development programmes to each of the world's five continents.

< 1

THE MAKING
OF THE WORLD GAME

Under the presidencies of Joseph S. Blatter, Dr. João Havelange (1974–98) and Sir Stanley Rous (1961–74), one of FIFA's main interests has been the development of world football. Over the last forty years this has led to FIFA broadening its areas of expertise. The growing popularity of football throughout the world, while enabling FIFA to assert its position as sole representative of the game, also led to medium and long-term development programmes in response to varied needs. To replace the European–South American bipolarity with a fairer system, FIFA had to be innovative in its organisation, approach to investment and its representation in different areas of the world. In 1977 the President of the Cameroon association wrote in a letter to Dr Havelange that they should have a system that would make it possible, *'d'instaurer dans le domaine sportif et du football en particulier un nouvel ordre international où l'écart entre les pays hautement developpés et le reste doit être de plus en plus réduit pour un meilleur équilibre des forces, facteur de paix et de comprehension mutuelle'.* (To establish in the world of sport, and of football in particular, a new international order where the gap between well-developed countries and others must be further and further reduced in order to achieve a better balance of strength, peace and mutual understanding.)

In the 1960s Stanley Rous had already initiated the first cycle of co-operation with developing countries by organising training courses for referees and coaches in Africa, Asia and Central America, aimed at improving the standard of officials in the various associations. A former referee and teacher himself, Rous believed that the development of football in the 'young' associations came from the training of referees and coaches. At times the referees' courses met little success, as in Puerto Rico in 1966: 'Bearing in mind that Puerto Ricans have other favourite sports… it was not surprising that the course did not have as great a response as we might have wished for.' Former international referee Ken Aston was responsible for organising conferences, in English, for referees from these associations. When interviewed on Jamaican television, and several days later on Curaçao television, Aston pointed out that 'FIFA spent its time and money promoting and helping the game all over the world and it was as interested in the smaller countries as the large'. Rous himself had presided over conferences on refereeing in all four corners of the world. For Rous it was important to standardise the interpretation of rules and to share scientific train-

1 After his election as President in 1974, Havelange starts his globalisation project.

2 Stanley Rous, recently elected FIFA President, takes control of the future of world football (28 September 1961).

3 A book about the trio essential to all football teams (the manager, coach and the referee), Tunis 1996.

4 Starting the second phase of the FIFA/Coca Cola education project. Futuro II (1996-2000).

5 Players training in Egypt in 1929. One year earlier, the national team came fourth in the Olympic Football tournament in Amsterdam.

6 Well before the Iranian national team was successful, the team of the Persian army are pictured with a trophy won in 1929.

7 Colonial football. The *Lune* (Moon) and *Lions* teams in French Africa in the mid-1930s.

8 A poster for the Georgian film *First Swallow* by Nana Mchedlidze (1975) on the subject of how football arrived in the Caucasus.

9 FIFA Refereeing Conference. Another way of renewing ties after the war. London 1948.

10 National meets International. Passing on the FIFA flag during the match between Ivory Coast and Ghana in the African Nations Cup (Abidjan 1965).

5

6

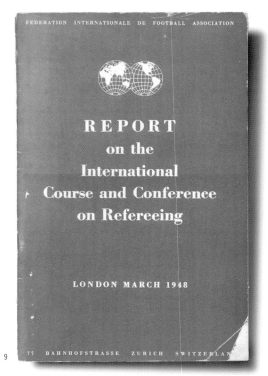

ing methods and techniques rather than just fund haphazard initiatives. In his eyes, the role of FIFA was to promote knowledge of football. In 1963 in Cairo, the Executive Committee decided to institute a Technical Development Committee, with the responsibility to 'improve coaching, refereeing, youth football and football administration throughout the world'. To finance this development policy, FIFA launched the Grant Aid project to fund the production of films and the organisation of courses. Sometimes FIFA even went so far as to contribute to other costs. In Mauritius, FIFA paid part of the salary of the national coach, a former Scottish professional, Sandy McLennan. But at this point investment by FIFA was still small. For example, when in 1967 the confederation of Oceania

requested the appointment of a coach-instructor to teach in Australia, Papua New Guinea and Fiji for eight months, FIFA refused, stating that it could only cover the travel costs. It is true that FIFA's development budget was still small – 1.4 million Swiss francs for the period from 1970 to 1974, of which more than half was committed to itinerant courses for coaches and referees, and a quarter to the production of films on modern refereeing and coaching methods. In addition to contributing one-third of the salaries of the African and Asian Confederation secretaries, FIFA's co-operation consisted of three things: providing a salary for a full-time itinerant coach (initially the German Dettmar Cramer who subsequently carried off the European Champion Clubs' Cup with Bayern Munich);

11

12

sporadically sending referees and coaches to non-European countries; and finally making a contribution to the support of amateur and youth tournaments.

Within FIFA, concerns were being raised about the numerous African initiatives. So much so that the President of the African Confederation, Yidnekatchew Tessema, felt obliged to respond. 'The basic concept within FIFA is that each continent contributes to FIFA's finances according to its abilities… Consequently we feel that we have a right to obtain higher financial assistance corresponding to the real needs of our continent.'

Following his election, João Havelange made concrete moves towards globalisation by holding the Executive Committee meeting of 30 April 1975 in Dakar, in Central Africa. In the same year Havelange created a new post by recruiting Joseph S. Blatter, a Swiss businessman, as Director of Technical Development Programmes. Blatter was responsible for finding funding for organising and co-ordinating initiatives for the promotion of football throughout the world.

In the eyes of the new President, funding development programmes should not be the responsibility of FIFA alone.

11 Even Pharaohs play football! Opening Ceremony for the U17 World Championships. (Egypt 1997).

12 Principles of refereeing explained before being put into practice. Futuro II Seminar (Haiti 1998).

13 Sponsors sign on the dotted line (13 May 1976). Signing of the contract between FIFA and Coca Cola in London. From left to right: Käser (General Secretary), Blatter (Director of Development), Havelange (FIFA President), Graul (International programme coordinator) and Killeen (Executive Vice-President of Coca Cola).

With support from Coca-Cola, a sponsored development programme was set up. From 1976 to 1979, a total of 3.5 million Swiss francs were spent organising seventy-four courses around the world, of which four-fifths were paid for by Coca-Cola. Under Havelange there was a perceptible diversification of FIFA's development projects and an evolution of its various programmes, tailoring them according to need. In his initial proposal of 1975, the concept of co-operation was born of a genuine desire for fair play, willingness to promote the development of football and a respect for the individual circumstances of each country. For FIFA, it was important that this co-operation should not mean the imposition of European standards throughout the world. In the proposal FIFA asked its instructors to gain an in-depth and thorough understanding of the countries they visited.

The Futuro I project, launched in the early 1990s, followed the framework of Sir Stanley Rous's training policy but proposed a four-point strategy to improve football the world over. Firstly, it aimed to establish a well-directed and efficient football administration, secondly to train coaches according to the level required, thirdly to provide an introduction to first-aid and an improvement in medical care and finally to adapt the laws of the game and refereeing standards to contemporary requirements. As financial sponsors of this development policy, Coca-Cola were to be FIFA's principal partner for a quarter of a century.

In its first year (1991) the programme concentrated on football associations which were relatively marginal in terms of their sporting results and very peripheral to the centres of world and European football power. Twelve courses were run during the latter half of 1991: four in Asia (Macão, Vietnam, India and Nepal), four in Africa

TABLE: FIFA'S DEVELOPMENT PROGRAMMES

1975-1978	**World Development Programme.** Administration, coaching, sports' medicine and refereeing (74 programmes)
1980-1982	**International Academy (I).** Courses for national coaches. Five participants per course: the host country and four neighbouring countries. (16 programmes)
1984-1986	**International Academy (II).** Improvement and specialisation courses for the participants of the first courses. (16 programmes)
1987-1990	**World Youth Academy.** Courses for youth team coaches. (87 programmes)
1991-1997	**Futuro I.** Week-long courses in administration, coaching, sports' medicine and refereeing. (136 programmes)
1997-2000	**Futuro II.** Education programme. A continuation of the Futuro programme. (109 programmes)
2000	**Goal.** A programme financing development of association infrastructures: headquarters, stadiums, competitions to help promote participation.

13

14

15

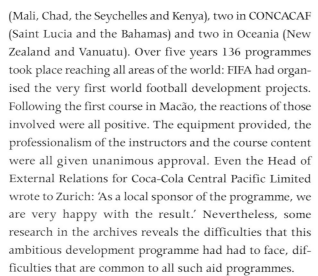

(Mali, Chad, the Seychelles and Kenya), two in CONCACAF (Saint Lucia and the Bahamas) and two in Oceania (New Zealand and Vanuatu). Over five years 136 programmes took place reaching all areas of the world: FIFA had organised the very first world football development projects. Following the first course in Macão, the reactions of those involved were all positive. The equipment provided, the professionalism of the instructors and the course content were all given unanimous approval. Even the Head of External Relations for Coca-Cola Central Pacific Limited wrote to Zurich: 'As a local sponsor of the programme, we are very happy with the result.' Nevertheless, some research in the archives reveals the difficulties that this ambitious development programme had had to face, difficulties that are common to all such aid programmes.

What happened in Nepal, where such a course took place in September 1991, is very revealing. Twenty participants from the country's clubs were invited to follow an intensive six-day course. In his report, one of the Asian instructors commented on the specific limitations of the programme: 'The structures chosen are unsuitable for developing nations ... Club structures like the ones found in Asia and Africa should be included in the manual.' He had highlighted the problem of applying European issues on a world scale. One of the participants added in his end-of-course questionnaire: 'We learned about the professional clubs of Great Britain and Germany but our country is economically too poor and underdeveloped to apply the same system as Germany or Great Britain. It is my request that in the future, if you conduct this type of course in the Third World countries please, please, add a module relating to financial problems and how to overcome them.' The same opinion was expressed in

Mozambique where the participants stressed the need to adapt the course to the development level of each country. Overall, though, the project was working. In the Dominican Republic, students described their instructor as an *'excelente entrenador, humilde caballero y un maravilloso diminador de la didactica y sublime comprensión de nuestras limitaciones'*. (An excellent coach, a modest man and a marvellous teacher who understood our limits perfect.) With very few exceptions, the instructors and participants were united in emphasising the keenness of the students who 'were hungry for such lessons'. During a course in Benin the German instructor Peter Schnittger, a great expert on African football, observed that 'the content of the programme was able to be understood and then put into practice on the pitch'.

In collaboration with Adidas and Coca-Cola, FIFA took care to offer participants everything they could possibly need, from teaching manuals and medical guides to FIFA's Statutes and technical reports from the major competitions. Refreshments were provided by Coca-Cola and sporting

16

17

14 The virtues of football democracy set out on the board. Futuro administration course (Sierra Leone 1994).

15 Presentation of the basics of sports health at a Futuro Seminar (Congo 1992).

16 A serious moment during a Futuro course. Presentation of Certificates in Mauritania 1993.

17 Practical Refereeing on the pitch. Futuro course (Ivory Coast 1995).

18 Sports medicine. Teaching First Aid at a Futuro Seminar (Kuwait 1993).

19 The Futuro programme was also aimed at new players. Marie-Thérèse Mouhanou, President of the African Women's Football Association at the administration course (Congo 1992).

18

19

equipment by Adidas. There were a few teething problems regarding the sporting equipment. During the course run in Guam, the participants protested because, as the General Secretary of the Guam football association emphasised, 'One of the difficulties was that, although Guam is part of Asia, the inhabitants here are generally larger than the Asians, and we had difficulty fitting everyone with the right-sized equipment'. In general, as was expressed in Togo, 'the distribution of the sporting equipment to the trainees was particularly appreciated'. These generous gestures helped FIFA to extend its authority over coaches, referees and administrators who were far removed from football's nerve centres. Unaccustomed to such consideration, they were to become ardent missionaries for the promotion of world football.

From the mid-1990s a new type of development policy evolved. Until this point everything had been managed from the Zurich office with the logistic support of the various FAs and all the courses had been run by FIFA's in-house staff. Two major initiatives were going to form the

axis of this new policy. Firstly, President Havelange signed an agreement with the University of Neuchâtel in Switzerland to create the Centre International d'Etudes du Sport or International Centre for Sports Studies (CIES) which would act as the link between the academic world and FIFA. From this point onwards university lecturers ran the courses for administrators and from the year 2000 an International Master's in the Management, Law and Humanities of Sport was offered jointly by the Bocconi (Milan), Neuchâtel, and De Montfort (Leicester) universities. The course trains professional managers responsible for running football associations, which are destined to become complex businesses in the future.

The GOAL project of 2000 granted, for the first time, development funds directly to football associations. Every association that applied could receive up to one million dollars over a three-year period. These funds are to facilitate the improvement of organisation and infrastructure, to help women's football and to help the less well-off associations participate in all FIFA competitions. Joseph

20

20 A promising youngster. Maradona and an Indonesian player at the FIFA/Coca Cola World Youth Championship, Japan 1979.

21 The Saudi Arabian team winning the FIFA U-16 tournament, Scotland 1989.

22 The Russian team, winners of the inaugural FIFA World Youth Championship (Tunisia 1977) with the Coca Cola Cup and the Habib Bourguiba trophy.

23 Football, a chance for cultures to meet. Opening ceremony of the 8th FIFA/Coca Cola World Youth Championship, Qatar 1995.

S. Blatter took this gamble to demonstrate that money poured directly into the football associations could be used in a useful and lasting way and that, far from creating a new form of corruption, this direct aid would lead national associations to become more aware of their responsibilities. At the moment the results of this new policy of redistributing FIFA's revenue appear to be positive.

The direct funding also allowed FIFA, if necessary, to monitor the autonomy and good working practice of national associations. With this in mind, a National Associations Committee was created in 1999, whose role 'was not merely to intervene in disputes but also to preserve and defend the rights of national associations.' Equally, FIFA modified its strategy and sent its representatives out to settle conflicts with political authorities, or to verify the validity of membership requests. A joint inspection report by the AFC and FIFA about the affiliation of the football association of Bhutan noted that football, along with archery, was the most popular national sport – even the royal family was passionate about it. But the desire to ensure that national associations were autonomous sometimes led to complications as was the case when the president of one national association was accused of misappropriating funds. 'FIFA is in a delicate situation, because although it opposes any government interference it cannot support the association president if he is dishonest ...' The case was in the Sudan and the president was subsequently cleared of any accusations.

Alongside this development policy a wide-ranging programme of competitions began in 1977 when the first World Youth Championship was organised with Coca-Cola in Tunisia. Won by the USSR, the new competition did not initially generate much enthusiasm in Europe but it was a different story in Africa and Central and Southern America where this opportunity to showcase world youth talent had been impatiently awaited. Appropriately, the first two Youth Championships were held in Africa and Asia; the second took place in Japan in 1979. This tournament saw the appearance of a talented young footballer called Diego Maradona, the captain of the victorious Argentinian team. The Youth Championship quickly became a clear demonstration of the globalisation of FIFA. In 1981 the third tournament was held in Australia, a member of Oceania, the youngest confederation, which until then had not hosted a FIFA championship. This competition provided opportunities for the emergence of new nations, as seen by Qatar's victory over England in the semi-final. Following this, three other Asian countries, Saudi Arabia in 1989, Qatar in 1995 and Malaysia in 1997 hosted the competition. Another symbol of globalisation was the 1991 inauguration of the FIFA Women's World Cup in China, which included the participation of a team from Taiwan. The last competition to be established, the FIFA Under 19 Women's World Championship, took place in Canada in 2002 where two North American teams met in the final, with a victory for the United States over Canada.

21

THE MAKING
OF THE WORLD GAME

Alongside these developments, one of the most palpable changes for the general public regarded the representation of different continents in the World Cup. At the 1982 Finals in Spain, the number of teams was increased from sixteen to twenty-four, with those from the four 'small' confederations increased from four to eight (two from Africa, one from Oceania, one from Asia and two from CONCACAF). The Cameroon and Algerian teams both did well in 1982 and new countries also took part in the competition: New Zealand, Kuwait and Honduras participated in 1982, Iraq and Canada in 1986, Costa Rica, Ireland and the United Arab Emirates in 1990, and Saudi Arabia, Nigeria and Greece in 1994. The World Cup broke new ground in 1998 when the number of participants in the final stages rose from twenty-four to thirty-two. On this occasion South Africa, Japan and Jamaica made their first appearances. In 2002, China, Ecuador, Senegal, Slovenia took part for the first time. Since 1982 FIFA's policy of opening the major competitions up to small associations has

been justified by the results of the African countries, of whom at least one has reached the second stage. This improvement in African football also saw teams from Nigeria and Cameroon achieve Olympic victories in 1996 and 2000.

Despite FIFA's efforts over the last few years, enormous differences in the standard of results and infrastructures between confederations remain apparent. Asia and Africa have succeeded in integrating themselves at the highest level, but Oceania is still on the sidelines, as the President of the OFC explains: 'Oceania, as you are aware, is a little different from any other confederation within FIFA in as much as, not only is it a region heavily influenced by a colonial past, but that the various colonies, dependencies and states are geographically widely scattered, of small population by any standard, and of extremely limited financial resources.' The integration of outlying areas remains one of the essential tasks of FIFA's development policy for the future.

24

25

26

24 A great athletic effort resulted in a victory for the African team over the winners of the previous World Cup. Goal scored by Omam-Biyick for Cameroon against Argentina, World Cup Finals 1990.

25 An acrobatic duel between Ma'ad (Iraq) on the left and the Mexican Cruz, World Cup Finals, 1986.

26 Bartlet (South Africa) performs a scissor kick during the match between South Africa and Saudi Arabia, World Cup Finals, 1998.

From sporting association to Non-Governmental Organisation

FIFA was originally an international sports organisation which administered rules and regulated competitive matches, as similar organisations did for other sports. As we have seen, it only began to extend its duties in the 1970s when officials from the new member nations, particularly in Africa, extended the interpretation of Article 2 of the FIFA Statutes 'to promote the game of association football in every way it deems fit'. These men insisted on improving football in the so-called Third World countries. From this time on FIFA began to engage increasing numbers of professional staff and grew to become a business on a global scale with a vastly expanded financial basis: at first via sponsorship from Coca Cola, Adidas and other firms, and later with the help of its own marketing branch. From the 1980s onwards FIFA enjoyed an unexpectedly high level of income from TV rights for the World Cup,

which in turn was directly responsible for an extraordinarily dynamic upturn in its activities.

From the start FIFA conducted these business activities in order to make profits. This approach aroused criticism from opponents who accused the organisation of operating as a capitalist entertainment business. They believed FIFA's commercial operations had turned football into a 'millionaire's gambling casino' and that FIFA were using the game as a licence to print money. These and similar allegations were put forward by commentators and academics who used investigative journalism to 'uncover' sizeable financial transactions. These often included 'discoveries' freely available to the general public as they had already been published in FIFA's annual

27 Horst Hrubesch frustrated by the Algerian defence. The North African players beat Germany, the double World Champions, in Spain 1982.

28 The draw of six groups for the first round of the World Cup Finals in Spain 1982.

29 Bobby Charlton, World Cup winner in 1966, visiting an SOS Children's Village in Cairo, 1999.

30 Referees at the African Nations Cup (Mali 2002) show 'Red Cards to Child Labour'.

31 Nelson Mandela takes part in the official opening of an SOS Children's Village in Cape Town, 1996.

reports. Is FIFA now run as a capitalist business as the critics allege?

At first sight this description might appear to be accurate. FIFA's business activities have expanded dramatically to take advantage of the commercialisation of football (*see* chap. 12). But on closer inspection there are interesting deviations from this alleged mode of operation. True, FIFA's approach to business has been thoroughly capitalistic, in that it has accumulated income for internal uses. Nevertheless its principles of profit distribution have been (and remain) unorthodox. By contrast with joint stock companies, surpluses are not distributed according to the size of the initial capital investment. FIFA's beneficiaries are the member associations who are treated equally or according to their needs. Thus FIFA conducts its dealings more like a co-operative where dividends are not a reward for the capital invested but are used to benefit all members and their activities. But even this comparison is unsatisfactory. Going beyond the co-operative principle, even non-members benefit from surplus profits. This is the declared aim of the football development aid programme based on Article 2 of the FIFA statutes 'to promote the game of association football in every way it deems fit'.

This programme, agreed on by the member nations, simultaneously enables FIFA, whose headquarters are in Zurich, to profit from Swiss laws exempting 'public benefit' businesses from taxation.

On the strength of this particular feature it seems reasonable to describe FIFA as a Non-Governmental Organisation (NGO). The NGO concept was 'invented' by the United Nations. The UN so defined all types of voluntary co-operative bodies (associations, societies, foundations, unions, committees, clubs, leagues, conferences, groups, federations, conventions, etc.), which, independent of governments, pursue cultural, humanitarian and developmental aims and try to implement universal standard values, principles and activities with the help of an official elite. When NGOs operate at an international level and take up specific issues, we can also speak of International Non-Governmental Organisations (INGOs). Prominent examples would include the International Red Cross, Greenpeace, Amnesty International or global organisations covering specific professions, technical questions, industries, hobbies or sports. All these organisations co-operate with national and local social pressure groups, not to speak of other NGOs and INGOs with whom they are networked for mutual benefit. Furthermore, the United Nations and its subsidiaries UNESCO and UNICEF are important partners for INGOs. For its part the UN is also interested in a political dialogue with the INGOs, which explains why some of them are invited to participate in international negotiations and conferences. FIFA has enjoyed such privileges since the 1990s. It maintains licence agreements with the UN and runs sponsorships and project partner-

ships. These include initiatives against racism and child labour in the production of footballs ('Red Card to Child Labour') and, in co-operation with the African Football Confederation (CAF) and the World Health Organisation (WHO), a campaign entitled 'Kick Polio Out of Africa'. Furthermore FIFA finances SOS children's villages and supports them with sporting equipment.

In the world of INGOs, entrepreneurial dealings are seen as a legitimate means of raising the level of an organisation's material resources, its ability to solve problems and achieve political aims. The fact that this is sometimes detrimental to its prestige and moral authority among the general public is accepted as the price to be paid. In this respect FIFA is not a special case amongst INGOs. That said, it does differ from other INGOs in that it has

remained a membership-based organisation despite its entrepreneurial side. Most other INGOs are, by contrast, purely executive organs. This particular feature has now become a problem for FIFA. Income from entrepreneurial activities has reached such a size that membership fees have been reduced to a purely symbolic level. A comparison between the incomes of the UN and FIFA underlines this only too clearly. Both organisations have a similar number of members, around 200, but forty-seven members of the UN contribute around ninety-nine per cent of the regular budget. By contrast FIFA's membership subscriptions and levies for international matches amount to less than one per cent of its income. Even wealthy member associations receive more money from FIFA than they contribute to it. As a result, and because there is no major association with a power of veto amongst the 204 FIFA members (a further difference with the UN), the Zurich headquarters and its professional staff have an extraordinary amount of power concentrated in their hands, a fact which erodes the association's democratic basis. We shall return to this in chapter 14.

On the other hand one of the salient features of INGOs in general is that they operate more from the 'top down' than from the 'bottom up' Otherwise, they would be unable to achieve their universal values and uniform standards. In FIFA's case the huge amount of power enjoyed by Zurich is an important precondition for the productive use of another structural feature: its capability to focus its funding. By contrast with the similarly wealthy IOC, which has to serve a great many different forms of sport, FIFA only needs to promote football. And by contrast with UEFA (the Union of European Football Associations) which

32

is compelled to take account of the interests of the major clubs, FIFA is able to devote its funds exclusively to national associations. When business is good this can mean cash injections to the order of millions which can drive enormous development when purposefully applied to specific local projects.

Without a doubt FIFA is today one of the world's most financially powerful INGOs but it clearly conforms with contemporary trends. All the NGOs and INGOs together can mobilise more money for their projects than the whole of the United Nations' system. The increase in the number of INGOs alone confirms what a model of success these organisations have proved to be in the late twentieth century. Around 1900, when FIFA came into being, there were only 200 INGOs. In 1930 this had risen to 800, and by 1960 to 2000. After this, the rate of growth was enormous. During the following twenty years the total doubled to 4000. Between 1980 and 1990 the speed of growth was even higher and by the early 1990s there were between 5000 and 6000 INGOs. FIFA was a part of this growth. It developed as an INGO in the midst of a global associational revolution that, as recent international relations research has emphasised, may prove to be as significant to the later twentieth century as the rise of the nation state was to the later nineteenth.

The associational revolution had many causes. At first it was a reaction to the increased need for private aid that arose as a result of cutbacks in state funding all over the world. The global recession and financial crises of the 1980s led to a reduction in public expenditure in many countries. In some extremely poor regions of Africa, like Somalia, Rwanda and Sierra Leone, the state apparatus and infrastructure actually collapsed. Other countries like Tanzania, Burundi and Zaire were dragged into poverty by an overwhelming influx of refugees. In the 1990s the collapse of the Soviet Union and its satellite states had conspicuous consequences. Many INGOs were now confronted with a huge challenge resulting from the breakdown of the political systems in Yugoslavia, Bosnia, Kosovo and elsewhere, not to speak of armed conflicts, appalling refugee problems and other emergencies. In this situation FIFA regarded its football development aid as a flanking contribution to re-establishing social life. At the same time it reacted to the vacuum which had been left at the end of the Cold War by the general withdrawal of state funding to sport. Whereas the Soviet Union had promoted a deliberate policy of sending trainers and other helpers to Africa and Asia in the early 1970s in order to win over newly founded states in the wake of de-colonisation, this development aid had been reduced even before the final

32 George Weah from Liberia, the FIFA Player of the Year 1995, visits an SOS Children's Village in South Africa, 1999.

33 Abedi Pelé (left, Ghana), Ike Shorunmu (centre, Nigeria) and Frank Verlaat (right, Netherlands) meet Bosnian children from an SOS Children's Village, at a match for peace between FIFA All Stars and Bosnia-Herzegovina in Sarajevo, April 2000.

collapse of the Soviet Union, at which point it ceased completely.

The associational revolution has not only reacted to massive global emergencies, it has also mirrored the INGOs' extended sphere of influence. Between 1973 and 1989 a considerable number of states in the particularly poor regions of the world, especially Latin America, moved from dictatorships to reasonably democratic forms of government. This opened up new areas of action and provided better working conditions for aid organisations. They were now able to freely exchange information and co-ordinate their activities for better results, results that were further enhanced by the more recent global revolution in communications. Satellite telephone connec-

tions, the invention of fax machines, and most recently e-mail and the internet have enormously helped the activities of NGOs and INGOs – especially when these technical innovations have been used alongside improved educational opportunities. Between 1970 and 1985 the proportion of adults in Third World countries unable to read and write sank from fifty-seven to forty per cent, down to twenty-nine per cent among men, and an urban middle class sprang up for the first time in certain Latin-American, African and Asian countries. With the help of their committed co-operation the aid organisations have been able to reach populations in surrounding areas much better than before, and build permanent links with scattered activists.

33

THE ECONOMY OF
FOOTBALL

Until 1930, FIFA's income came from membership fees and a share of the revenue from ticket sales at international games. Early World Cup competitions generated a war chest which allowed FIFA continuity and funding for audacious medium- and long-term policies. Over the past fifty years the arrival of television and lucrative advertising deals has altered FIFA's finances dramatically. In the long term, this money has also re-shaped the Federation's objectives on an international level.

1 For more than 25 years,
people sent post for FIFA
to an address in the
Netherlands.

2 In 1931 FIFA used
Ivo Schricker's address in
Karlsruhe (Germany) as
a temporary address.

3 FIFA moves to Zurich,
1932.

FIFA's finances
before television

At the Congress in 1928, during the annual budget
presentation to the delegates, Hirschmann, FIFA's honorary Treasurer and Secretary, announced that there
would be a deficit of 6000 florin, which represented a
third of the annual budget. The highest authority of
world football had never demonstrated financial astute-
ness. Housed in Hirschmann's office, FIFA's only
employee was a part-time secretary. Although the
organisation managed the relations between national
associations and managed the Olympic football tournament, it could only rely on the membership fees
from its thirty members, and one per cent of gate
receipts from international matches for income. In addition to this, the matches between the British international teams were exempt from paying FIFA any
dues. FIFA's spending was in line with its standing,
consisting of general running costs and postal expenses, and the cost of hospitality for delegates during the
annual Congress. The annual budget shared the characteristics of many a European bourgeois family of the
era: forced to enter into debt in order to keep up
appearances.

Following Hirschmann's departure and the headquarters' move to Zurich, FIFA's budget doubled in three
years. The cost of the administrative staff and rent for
the offices on the central Bahnhofstrasse in Zurich made
up more than a third of the entire budget, even though
the organisation's administration was still in an embry-
onic state and the only employees were the Secretary
and his assistant. Income was still low. Schricker spent
the majority of his time reminding the national associations to pay their annual membership fees and FIFA's

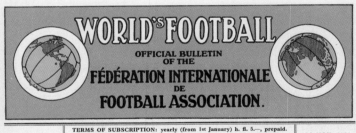

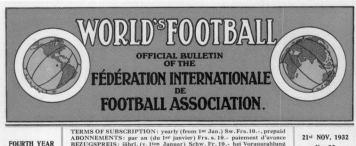

4 After Hirschmann's bankruptcy, the Dutch and Belgian FAs organised a friendly match and the gate receipts were given to FIFA. In this picture, the Belgian players are running onto the pitch before the game, February 1932.

5 In aid of FIFA and for the good of the game, the Dutch forwards lay siege at the Belgian goalmouth, February 1932.

6 The Duke of Kent shakes hands with the Italian centre forward Silvio Piola in front of Vittorio Pozzo, the coach of the Azzurri. The second match between a FIFA XI and England, London 1938.

share of gate receipts from international matches. The Federation was eventually able to consolidate its situation in 1934 when the World Cup in Italy generated 60,000 FRS, two percent of FIFA's total revenue. As supporters of amateurism, the FIFA chiefs could not see any other way of financing their operation. Their only other source of revenue was from the rare matches played between the Central European and the West European representative teams, or matches between national teams. FIFA's Statutes stated a desire to govern world football, but at first the organisation had to be lenient towards the many members who frequently forgot to pay their fees, or to declare their match takings. Costs were limited to infrequent publications and growing post and telephone bills. But despite the precariousness of FIFA's finances they were just about tolerable. The Second World War increased the financial difficulties of the Federation. Many football associations were unable to pay the membership fees and in Europe the number of international matches fell dramatically. In addition to this, Switzerland put in place strict financial exchange restrictions which slowed the movement of money.

The financial situation of FIFA suffered renewed criticism after the war, but the popularity of international football matches and the arrival of new members soon enabled the organisation to put its finances in order. To help the process of consolidation, Congress in London in 1948 took the decision to double the percentage FIFA should be paid from international matches. The results of this were immediate and the following year revenue from this source was 100,000 FRS whereas the budget had predicted only 35,000 FRS. The profits from the World Cup in Brazil the following year surpassed all expectations and the day after his return

7 FIFA moves up in the world in Zurich. In 1954, FIFA purchased this upmarket bourgeois villa on the hillside above Sonnenberg. This was the first FIFA House, and was replaced in 1979 by a more functional headquarters built of reinforced concrete.

8 The interior of FIFA House in 1955, cross between a *salon anglais* and a country retreat.

from Rio, Schricker wrote to Rimet *'Nous sommes riches!'* (We are rich!)

Now in possession of both capital and cash, FIFA considered buying a headquarters more befitting a global organisation. In 1948, the Executive planned to spend 250,000 FRS on the construction of a new building project in Basle. An Emergency Committee considered the idea, but opinions differed. Arthur Drewry thought it would be better to rent rather than buy a building. He considered that the smaller football associations would be against the purchase of a property and would demand a reduction in the percentage of the gate receipts paid to FIFA. Thommen thought that, without a home of its own, FIFA lacked a sound base on which to found a tradition. Seeldrayers was in favour of the purchase of offices and reminded those present that 'until now, FIFA has had no money and little more than a PO Box. However, today we need to do more and organise and house ourselves accordingly'. Those present were not swayed from their opinions, but the idea of a purchase eventually gained ground and it was decided to look at properties in Geneva and Zurich.

The Committee chose 11 Hitziweg, Zurich, a large house above the lake in a residential area. This property was a large bourgeois building of 2500 square metres comprising fourteen rooms over three floors. There were two meeting rooms and offices for the President, the General Secretary and his Assistant. The third floor was used as an apartment for the Assistant General Secretary. The move took place in early 1955. In his report to Congress, Gassmann wrote that 'after fifty years in existence, FIFA is finally housed in a property which befits its growing importance and actual needs'. The new headquarters was named FIFA House.

Meticulous management by Rimet and tireless efforts of the secretaries minimised expenditure and succeeded in collecting all the membership fees over the next few years. In conjunction with the revenue from the World Cup in Brazil, this boosted FIFA's capital to two million FRS by the end of 1955. Despite all this, FIFA was still a relatively small organisation with an annual budget of less than one million Swiss francs. FIFA was, like many other international sports associations of that time, resistant to all marketing contracts. The Federation did not seek to develop new areas of expertise, earnings, personnel or its global development policy. Financial Committee meetings and the Executive limited them-

As regards expenditure, the cost of various meetings and Congress was more than the salaries of the staff whose number remained fixed for over thirty years. The entries on the revenue side of the balance still consisted of only two things: the World Cup and a share of revenue from international matches. No special effort was taken with official FIFA publications as the organisation was still lacking in staff. When the World Cup was recognized as the goose that laid the golden egg, an egg capable of guaranteeing the financial stability of the organisation, the directors of FIFA were content to manage their revenue safely without taking into account changes that were occurring and requests for help that were arriving from the distant and poor associations which by the 1960s had begun to join the Federation in droves.

So, during the 1950s FIFA's coffers continued to swell, but these resources were not made available to member associations. It is important to remember that the

selves to making decisions about the investment of the organisation's assets. Large-scale projects requiring an equally large expenditure were never considered.

Until the middle of the 1950s, the Executive Committee consisted of the same men who had dealt with the crisis that threatened to end the organisation a quarter of a century before when Hirschmann failed to diversify FIFA's investments. Following FIFA's first prosperous years, cautious investment was made in low risk and low earning Swiss, French and American treasury bonds, and gold. Unsurprisingly, for more than twenty years this was accompanied by an almost total lack of spending either on advertising or the development of football.

9 Lighting for the biggest stadium in the world. A powerful advertising image in 1950. Official World Cup Programme, Brazil.

10 The 'Federale' ball in a league of its own. Advert in the official World Cup Programme, Italy 1934.

11 The Allen ball was the first to be the official football of the World Cup, France 1938. Official World Cup Programme.

12 Cinzano, the aperitif for sportsmen. Official World Cup Programme, 1938.

directors of the Federation had been educated at the start of the century and had very limited ideas on the international role of the organisation: basically to run Congress and the World Cups. From FIFA's early days, the Statutes included the goal of developing world football, although in the eyes of the FIFA leadership this did not involve financial investment. The only concession made to the poorer members was to allow late payment of their fees, or in some exceptional cases an exemption from paying them at all. Direct financial aid was considered as interfering in the affairs of the national associations and was therefore rejected on principle. It was also principle that prompted FIFA to reject all advertising contracts as it was thought that they might compromise its independence. The chiefs watched the arrival of television and other new technologies with fear. TV was seen as competition that was likely to empty stadiums during the World Cup and cause a reduction in FIFA's revenue.

In 1958 television money was mentioned in the General Secretary's report: 'Gate receipts, indemnities for television film and percentage of the friendly matches'. FIFA reiterated that it was against broadcasting live matches without authorisation from the participating football associations and a protest from the Danish to that effect was recorded by Zurich.

13

13 Stanley Rous watches the success of his policy of referee training on the pitch in Coverciano, Italy, 1961.

First partnerships

After Stanley Rous became the head of the Federation, the first moves were made to sell the television rights for the World Cup, revenue began to be redistributed, more personnel were employed and a search for business partners began. The World Cup in England in 1966 demonstrated that, far from distancing spectators from the game, television actually generated new interest in the competition. The Executive was forced to decide if it should remain true to its principles of amateurism and refuse the large amount of money that could be earned from the sale of television rights. Stanley Rous was without doubt better acquainted with the media than his predecessors had been. As a member of the BBC's Consultation Committee, Rous was well aware of the necessity to work with television and the media in general. One of the first steps he took was to employ René Courte from Luxembourg as Communications

14

15

Officer. Rous saw that television could finance his grand project of training referees throughout the world and help develop aid schemes. 'We are increasingly involved in complex commercial negotiations, and we need help from people in this difficult task, to win the best return from merchandising and franchising operations, so that we generate the income to carry out these new tasks.'

However, the success of the televised World Cup and the publicity that the event generated caused new problems for FIFA. As we have seen, until this time FIFA had been against all forms of advertising. Rous felt that FIFA could no longer ignore the offers it received, but should nevertheless maintain their total independence. Faced with this dilemma, Rous chose to break with the intransigence of his predecessors and follow a policy of short-term investment. He entrusted the sale of television rights and advertising to the World Cup

Organising Committee while retaining the right to inspect their decisions. Although obviously interested, Rous did not wish to become involved in the bitter battle for television rights which took place between seven commercial television stations in Mexico in 1970. The broadcasting of European Cup matches in the 1960s also posed a problem for FIFA when it came to redistribution of the revenue between the associations, confederations and FIFA.

There was an increase in the volume of articles written about sport, examining the large impact advertising had on football and the World Cup. The President seemed disturbed by the intrusion of the merchants in the temple, even though he knew that the arrival of new members and growing expectations obliged the Federation to look for new sources of revenue. In his letter to Käser regarding an exclusive contract with

16

14 The early days of merchandising. The ideal fan wearing his kit, England, 1966.

15 Africa represented a new horizon for referee training. Professeur Andrejevic, a member of the FIFA Executive, leads a training session in Addis Ababa, Ethiopia 1964.

16 Minimum comfort for maximun concentration. African referees on a FIFA course in Tunis, Tunisia 1963.

Adidas to supply the referees of the Mexican World Cup, Rous asked that *FIFA News* announce that 'FIFA have accepted an offer from Adidas to provide the referees who were selected to officiate in the World Cup Tournament in Mexico with a track-suit and shoes', and he repeated his insistence that this should not be presented as a commercial partnership. At times, Rous could be considered a reformer compared to his predecessors, but he was also conservative in his desire to maintain a distance from the commercial world. He suggested that the confederations should employ full-time secretaries, but refused to increase FIFA's own personnel. The number of permanent staff could still be counted on the fingers of one hand, as the people recruited to give refereeing courses and training were under temporary contract. Television and advertising contracts were still rare, and the revenue was small (402,605 FRS for the four years 1962–65) compared to the increasing demands of the new member associations. It was symptomatic that, even though 'sponsorship' featured in the Rous presidential electoral programme of 1974, it was at the very end of the document. External investment could be 'a large source of money for football, however, the committee needs to maintain a tight control so as not to risk the independence of the elected officials'. A former teacher, and Secretary of the English FA, Rous seemed ill at ease with marketing discussions and preferred to occupy himself with the courses for referees and officials. He set up six commissions during his fourteen years of office, none of which was concerned with commercial activities and at no point did he create any posts responsible for pursuing contacts with businesses.

João Havelange, Rous' successor, was well used to Boards of Directors, and business meetings. As Chairman and Managing Director of Cometa SA, the main Brazilian bus company, and a board member for other companies, Havelange considered commercial partners a necessity if he was to improve the structure of the Federation and to pursue a development policy without increasing membership fees.

17 An American-style campaign. Brochure for J. Havelange's campaign for presidency in 1974.

18 Socialist or Coca-Cola Red? The Hungarian team at the second FIFA/Coca-Cola World Youth Cup, Japan, 1979.

19 Global sport and drink. Coca-Cola advertising (FIFA Magazine, July 1985).

20 Adidas goes to Japan for the FIFA/Coca-Cola World Youth Cup, 1979

21 FIFA and Coca-Cola travel to the USSR. Programme of the World Youth Cup, 1985.

17

18

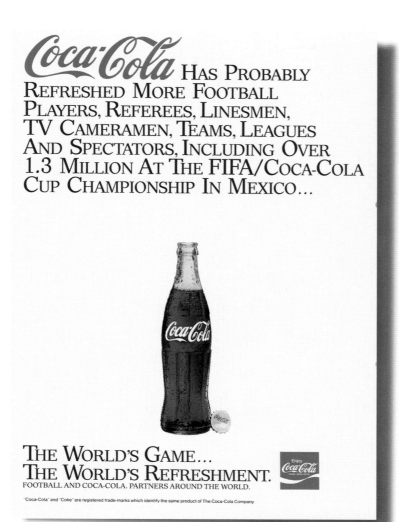

19

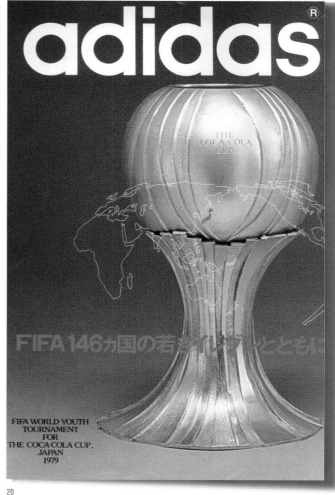

20

21

A new style of partnership

Even before his election, Havelange proposed that, if he was to succeed, a reliable commercial partner would be found who would finance his modernisation and global development programmes. The agreement between FIFA and Coca-Cola was made two years later on the 13th May 1976 in London. In the joint press release it was described as 'a first between a global distribution company and an international sporting association, and without doubt the biggest sport sponsorship contract in the world at this time'. The initial agreement was for a payment of $5 million, of which the larger part would be used to fund a global development project and the creation of the Coca-Cola Youth World Cup. This agreement enabled FIFA to establish its development strategy and opened up new markets that were still closed to American consumer products, such the Middle East and Eastern Europe, for Coca-Cola. The President also cemented the relationship with Adidas by signing a long-term agreement that would not only supply kit for referees and balls for the World Cup, but also for the FIFA development programmes.

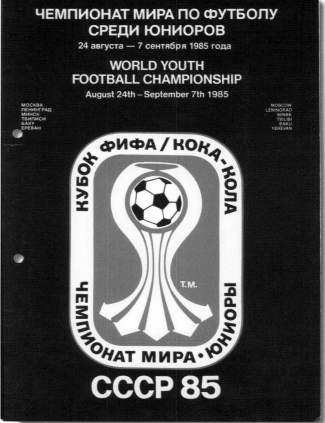

22

FIFA officials picked up modern marketing techniques from Coca-Cola. Correspondence between the two parties shows that working with Coca-Cola allowed FIFA to discover public relations, mass communication and event management techniques. In 1980, during the early years of the agreement, at a meeting between the two partners, the Vice President of Coca-Cola remarked that FIFA's public relations work was still insufficient although both sides recognised the benefits the contract had brought.

From the moment he was elected as President, Havelange strove to improve the Federation's image. Firstly, in a gesture symbolic of his modern vision, he undertook major building work at the headquarters. After finding a separate residence for the General Secretary, the third floor of the building was vacated and has since been used as offices and meeting rooms. Recruitment of reception personnel and new secretaries gave FIFA House the appearance of a modern international organisation. Although it has always been located at Hitziweg, FIFA House has changed a great deal over the past twenty-five years. In line with FIFA's new image, the building has been enlarged, modernised, and opened to the world. In 1983 FIFA started to computerise its operations at a cost of 250,000 FRS. Currently FIFA employs 150 staff, and has many collaborators around the world. At Aurorastrasse 100, purchased in 1992, a new modern annexe of 3000 square metres has been built and more recently another property has been bought within a few hundred metres of FIFA House. These new buildings house FIFA's translation and legal departments.

22 Horst Dassler presents official Tango (Adidas) ball to President Havelange, World Cup 1978.

23 Many duties to perform. Havelange, FIFA President and Blatter, General Secretary, at the sponsors' hall during the FIFA/Coca-Cola World Youth Cup, Qatar 1995.

24 FIFA also travelled to China, but this time accompanied by Kodak. World U-16 Cup/Kodak Cup, 1985.

23

25

26

Thanks to the World Cup, FIFA's revenue has continued to grow. The Federation receives television broadcast rights, rights for the use of the World Cup logo and derived products, as well as money from sponsorship and advertising agreements. In 1982 the Spanish World Cup organising committee recouped 6 million FRS from marketing rights. Four years later the World Cup earned FIFA almost 50 million FRS. Both increased demand for football by television companies and their advertisers, and the arrival of competition in the television market of Western Europe helped to raise the price. The EBU (European Broadcasting Union), which had bought the European television rights for 10.9 million FRS in 1982, had to spend five times that sum for the rights in 1998. This breathtaking rise in television revenue affected not only FIFA but also the entire European elite sport economy. Until the 1960s, revenue from ticket sales was the only source of income for clubs. However, following the start of a more open television market, and the development of advertising opportunities, club revenue began to be derived from three equal sources: the turnstiles, television rights and various advertising contracts, and the same was true of FIFA's revenue. Following the Italian World Cup in 1990, ISL (International Sport and Leisure) – the company which had been in charge of television rights since 1982 – paid FIFA 100 million francs, of which thirty per cent was from ticket sales, forty-five per cent from the sale of television rights, and twenty-five per cent from advertising deals.

During his presidency, Havelange worked closely with his General Secretary Joseph S. Blatter, a former student at the Ecole de Commerce (business school) of Lausanne and employee of a company specialising in sports sponsorship. Both men sought to continue the partnerships with Adidas and Coca-Cola which had lasted for more than twenty-five years, and to follow a unique model for the redistribution of profit – both of which provoked criticism from European associations in the media. The European associations did not appreciate the large sums of money being passed on to the

27

Third World associations, even though the majority of FIFA members had received support and financial help from Zurich to increase participation and to cover team transport and other costs incurred at various FIFA competitions. One of the main assets of the Federation was its truly global impact and solid presence. This was not immediately accepted by the European associations, who struggled to come to terms with the new order that involved financial generosity towards the poorer members.

After his election as President in 1998, and aware of the cost of a large-scale interventionist policy, Joseph Blatter decided that, for the first time in its history, FIFA should give to its members directly from its own account. Conscious of the commercial value of the World Cup, FIFA became more assertive with its business partners, while at the same time showing a greater generosity towards the member associations. A programme of direct financial assistance for football associations was launched in 1999, disposing of one million dollars in four years. The GOAL project has assisted the improvement of the infrastructure of many national associations but it was a policy that increased the workload of the Financial Committee. During their first meeting together the new President requested that the committee meet more often in order to address the many issues it now faced, in particular the administration, distribution and supervision of the large sums of money arising from television and advertising contracts for the World Cups of 2002 and 2006. Following his suggestion, the committee increased the annual number of meetings from two to four.

Blatter's first period of office was marked by a major financial crisis. In May 2001, ISL, the company responsible for the sale of television rights, was declared bankrupt. In April the following year, Kirch, the German media group who had bought the television rights for the period of 1999-2006, suspended payments to FIFA. On the eve of the presidential election, alarmist rumours

28

28 Pelé and the new MasterCard, 1999.

29 Football in orbit. Korea Telecom was behind the World Cup in 2002.

regarding FIFA's financial predicament were rife. A financial report of more than 100 pages was presented to the representatives at the Seoul Congress, and the President announced that all agreements would be met and that the organisation's finances were, in the words of Julio Grondona, FIFA Vice-president and Chairman of the Financial Commission, 'healthier than they have ever been'. The financial report explained that, thanks to the creation of FIFA Marketing AG before ISL's bankruptcy and a policy of selling rights in advance, FIFA would be able to honour all its agreements without requiring external funds. The positive resolution of this crisis and the financial skills shown by the President and his finance team made a huge impact on Blatter's re-election at the Seoul Congress. The crisis had highlighted that financial experts, experienced in international finance and as capable of directing sports associations as an international company, were crucial to large international sports federations who handled a lot of money. With the creation of FIFA Marketing, FIFA took a large step in this direction and was committed to taking direct control of managing its image.

Over the last twenty-five years, FIFA has sought, often very successfully, to reconcile two apparently contrasting aims of economic policy: the financial notion of 'profit maximisation' and the ethical consideration of fair distribution of profits to all members. Although the idea of seeking profit from a sport that had traditionally been founded on voluntary efforts and amateurism shocked some, it has to be considered that these profits were used to promote football in the developing world, (where television and sponsorship revenues are meagre) and that this was an integral part of FIFA's founding principles of a century ago. FIFA's marketing was unique in that the generation of profit was never an end in itself. The money generated by World Cups and lucrative contracts with Coca-Cola, Adidas and MasterCard is used to enable the most disadvantaged to play football in improved conditions, and to reduce the inequality between rich, self-supporting associations and confederations and football associations from countries where the game could not be played without such aid.

Without accepting money as its ruler, FIFA chiefs have shown that money is the means of spreading football worldwide. It is important to seek out external income, but at the same time it is more important to spend it wisely 'for the good of the game'.

Exciting FIFA World Cup™!

The information and telecommunication technology
which enables you to feel as if you're watching the FIFA World Cup™
at the spot - Korea Telecom makes it happen.

2002 FIFA World Cup Korea/Japan™ Official Partner - Korea Telecom

Korea Telecom
www.koreatelecom.com

2002
FIFA WORLD CUP
KOREA JAPAN

1

FOOTBALL
AND THE MEDIA

The World Cup has been described as a 'general assembly of mankind'. Not simply because FIFA, which promotes the tournament, represents all the states in the world but rather because no other sporting event arouses so much attention: every four years newspapers, radio and television connect billions of people across the planet and allow them to experience this great sporting event.

13. Oktober 1929
Nummer 41
38. Jahrgang

Berliner

Illustrirte Zeitung

Preis
des Heftes
20 Pfennig

Verlag Ullstein Berlin SW 68

Zeitgestalten (V): Der Sportsprecher.
Schilderung eines großen Sportkampfes durch Rundfunk vom Sportplatz aus. (Burghard v. Reznicek.)

Fot. Ullstein.

FOOTBALL
AND THE MEDIA

When the finals of the 1982 World Cup were staged in Spain, statistically speaking each person on earth tuned into live match transmissions at least twice, which meant that the final number of TV spectators amounted to ten billion. At the 2002 World Cup in Japan and Korea the aggregate number of spectators was 28.8 billion which means every person on Earth tuned in 4.6 times on average.

Such figures justify the term 'world football'. The World Cup Final, as such, is a local event but the spectators, of course, come from all over the world. It is the television broadcasts that transform football into an all-embracing culture of the masses because they multiply the number of spectators by several thousands – or by exactly ten thousand at the 2002 finals. Television transcends the architectural confines of the stadium and unites a specific location with as many football regions around the globe as it cares to. More than half the 32 billion viewers who tuned into broadcasts from the 1990 World Cup finals lived in Asia, a continent which had hitherto played only a minor role in international football. TV broadcasts from the 1994 World Cup in the USA went out to 188 countries all over the world, the first ever comprehensive global coverage.

FIFA has always played a mediating role in enabling companies to broadcast international tournaments, especially because a good number of their leading officials and innovators have had some personal experience of journalism. These included the first president, Robert Guérin (1904-06) and legendary sports journalists like Walter Bensemann (Germany), Hugo Meisl (Austria), Herbert Chapman (England), Gabriel Hanot (France), Vittorio Pozzo (Italy) and Ricardo Lorenzo 'Borocoto'

(Argentina), to name but a few. This helps to explain why FIFA has tried to co-operate with the media from the start and to give them the best possible working conditions. The Federation has followed technical developments closely, even at times anticipated them, and has taken care to ensure that the bodies responsible for presenting important tournaments meet the standards demanded by technology. In 1968 a special Committee for Public Relations and the Media was set up under René Courte and since then media relations have been conducted on a serious professional basis. The amount of resources allocated to this service is not simply because FIFA officials are concerned with the welfare of the press, radio and television; their primary aim is to 'make sure that the press serves soccer football'. And the press does serve football: since the 1970s FIFA's finances and the fate of its development policies have increasingly relied on promoting a thriving relationship with the media.

Nonetheless, it would be wrong to say that FIFA has 'made' the World Cup into a global media event or even made televised football. For nobody 'made' this development. It is more the result of a mature and increasingly complex reciprocal relationship between the media and football which developed in the course of the twentieth century and also, it must be admitted, unleashed a few unwelcome surprises. This relationship, between the media, FIFA and football, is the main subject of the current chapter. Since the foundations of co-operation between football and the media were laid down long before the invention of television, print media and radio must also be examined here.

3 Twenty years ago,
typewriters were still
the norm in pressrooms.
(World Cup 1982).

4 Behind closed doors,
technicians working before
the announcement of
which country has been
chosen to organise the 2006
World Cup, Zurich 2000.

The growth of co-operation

A close relationship between football and the press had already grown up by the end of the nineteenth century. This, however, did not apply to all the regions of the world into which British football had been introduced. By and large, contact football was originally only news-worthy in Europe and Latin America. In the USA and Australia 'soccer' was treated as a poor relation by journalists and spectators alike whose attention was absorbed by the overwhelming popularity of American Football, Australian Rules Football and rugby. In Asia and Africa the press was extremely underdeveloped owing to colonialism, poverty, illiteracy and the huge number of different languages, which all contributed to prevent the media from functioning as a link between football and the general public. Such a link would only develop in the 1960s alongside radio and television.

On the European continent and in Latin America three factors contributed to the co-operation between football and the press: both phenomena developed into social institutions at the same time; both sought their market in the rapidly-growing cities; and footballers, like journalists, were recruited from among the ranks of immigrants and the young, ambitious middle-classes who were unprejudiced and open towards all that was new and modern. Many of these young men were active players and football journalists at the same time. For the continent, unlike England, had no tradition of sporting journalism. Who was more competent to report on the new sport than those who were playing it themselves? Who else could provide informed reports? The spectators were not yet in a position to do so because most of them visited games solely out of curiosity. While British football

fans were accustomed to making 'an almost endless row' and to occasionally breaking out 'into a veritable howl', as a close observer reported in 1908, German spectators 'only gave a few weak cheers when the ball found its target. Otherwise they remained silent [...] My personal opinion is that the spectators did not understand the game...'

Given this situation, football reports were urgently necessary to help the general public make sense of the game. It was these football reports that made the game a symbol of ethnic, racial, religious, political and class rivalries. Quite often, they stirred up associations with mythical conflicts which had ceased to play a role in 'real life'. The other function of press reports was to provide current league tables, goal-scorers and attendance figures. All this gave the general public a methodical and systematic introduction to the game and simultaneously provided the material for intermittent poetic tales of the rise and fall of a particular hero or the eternal battles between rival clubs. It was largely the newspapers which helped to make the 'English import' widely known and discussed. They published pre-match reports and summaries, offered critical remarks and unsolicited advice, and disseminated rumours only to refute them almost immediately. In short, they shaped the public image of players, clubs, associations, and leagues – every aspect of the sport. In its early years football did not enjoy widespread social acceptance. Players and clubs, however, were not only in need of social acceptance, they also needed public funds. These needs explain why football officials were so accommodating towards the press.

From the start, co-operation between football and the press was based on the principle of reciprocal advantage: clubs and associations on the one side and the newspaper businesses on the other. The clubs' desire for contacts

5

5 Official FIFA
publications, a continuous
link from 1905 to 2002.

Football's interest in the press was matched by the
press's interest in football. It arose at the same time, the
end of the nineteenth century, and was an integral part
of the commercialisation of the newspaper industry.
During this period, mass dailies were launched onto the
market, some of which published more than one edition
per day. Their editors were thus faced with the challenge
of how to fill the pages. Everywhere the answer was the
same as that given by James Gordon Bennett, the Paris-
based publisher of the *New York Herald* shortly before
1900: 'We need sensations and, if the world doesn't provide us with any, we'll have to make them ourselves'.
Gordon Bennett invented the motor-car race named after
him, Henri Desgranges invented the Tour De France.
Other publishers were committed to football and often
provided active personal assistance with the organisation and presentation of matches and tournaments on
which they wanted to report.

Radio and television started broadcasting in the 1920s
and 1950s respectively, and the problem of finding suit-
able subjects to report on was even more pressing for
their programme planners than it was for the newspaper industry. For the new media had been developed by
civil and military technicians during the First World War
and were ready for use before a single journalist had
even begun to think about exploiting their potential.
Football seemed an obvious solution but programme
planners, both 'serious' and 'popular', had their doubts
at first. Nonetheless, as time went by they became
increasingly keen on exploiting the capacity of the sport
to fill up broadcasting time. However, in the early years,
outside broadcasts had to overcome a number of technical and professional obstacles such as bad sound quality and inexperienced reporters. The upshot was that
football reports and sporting broadcasts in general tend-

with the press grew out of the regional, national and
international features embedded in football. Each home
game automatically incorporated an away game and this
was welcomed by the players as a bonus to their sporting activities. However, most spectators and fans who
helped finance away games with membership fees and
gate money were forced to remain at home for lack of
money. Effective reporting was indispensable to keep
them 'on the hook'. It was regarded as inept simply to
reprint away-game reports in the local paper, notwith-
standing the fact that these might be biased against their
own team. For this reason, club committees and team
managers preferred to take their 'own' reporters to away
matches. The clubs met the cost of travel and accommodation, were generous with expenses and paid newspapers to release staff to report on the matches. It goes without saying that they took care to provide good working
conditions for journalists such as telegraph and telephone facilities, privileged seats in the stands and rooms
for interviews and press conferences.

FOOTBALL AND THE MEDIA

6

ed to sound more like edifying lectures than entertainment. Right into the 1930s, even in countries where technical developments were more advanced, the overwhelming majority of the time devoted to sports' programmes was taken up with this type of 'lecture'.

Broadcasters also valued football because it helped promote the interests of their own particular medium. They underlined the up-to-the-minute nature of radio and, in the context of the age, espoused the virtues of their own media by contrast with the cinema, which was equally popular among contemporaries. They fuelled the interest in up-to-the-minute topicality by stimulating discussions on the unpredictable outcome of football matches or other sporting events, thereby providing a fascinating blend of information and entertainment. They supplied listeners with immediate information on the latest scores and critical developments in a match, even broadcasting 'live' when technical improvements put them in a position to do so. They demanded explanations when results failed to correspond with pre-match predictions and solicited speculations on future chances. In short, they did everything possible to create and maintain a state of tension. From the 1920s onwards there was a seasonal league competition in many countries in Europe and South America, making the sport even more attractive for radio and later for television. Football provided a permanent ongoing sensation. What other subject could achieve this? It was no wonder that in many countries journalists were the prime movers in setting up football leagues.

Lastly, sports reports were comparatively cheap to broadcast. Radio reporters and the print media had the right to report on matches free of charge, a privilege which they generally still enjoy today. Television companies, on the other hand, apart from an initial run-in phase, have had to purchase the rights to matches. The cost of rights has risen steadily from year to year and, in some countries, has now reached astronomical levels. Until the latter half of the 1980s it was worth the outlay, not only because the organisational and logistical expenses involved in outside broadcasts could be kept within limits but also there was next to no risk of failing to attract viewers. But the prime justification for the high price of television rights was that football news and information could be used time and time again in detailed match-day reports, short news clips, football previews, historic appraisals, talk shows and the like. In 1985 the BBC and ITV paid what appeared to be the massive sum of around £19 million for four years' rights to broadcast matches from the English First Division. But seen in terms of an hourly broadcast rate this worked out at a mere £50,000 per hour. The sum was around one-third of what the companies paid to purchase film rights and cover the cost of major drama. It was also generally less expensive than current affairs programmes, documentaries and light entertainment. Commercial companies enjoyed an additional advantage in being able to offset part of the expenses incurred by charging higher prices for commercial spots. For experience has shown that football fans are not only loyal to their own sport but also show high levels of brand-loyalty in other areas of everyday consumption. This makes them a highly attractive target group for companies promoting consumer goods.

6 Eyes are no longer enough. Supporters of Boca Juniors listen to the coverage of a game on the radio 'Spica', Argentina, 1959.

7 The early days of television broadcasts. A BBC camera films the match between England and Scotland at Wembley, 1938.

7

The potential and the limits of media technology

The love affair between football and the media was not equally powerful throughout the twentieth century. Nor was it always balanced with regard to mutual exploitation. Phases in which football clubs and associations deliberately used the media to attract maximum interest in launching a new league or tournament were replaced by others where the media took the initiative because they planned to introduce technical innovations or wanted to maximise their income from major football events. Therefore, it was important that both parties be convinced, in principle, of the benefits to be derived from mutual co-operation, and be prepared to make experiments and risk, occasionally, learning a few expensive lessons. Above all they needed to be convinced of the necessity for patience. Nonetheless, conflicts and concomitant delays in progress were inevitable.

These recurred time and time again when there was a difference of opinion on the value of specific technical innovations. In the 1890s when publishers on the European continent launched the first sporting magazines containing photographs (*Le Sport Universel Illustré*, *La Vie au Grand Air*, *Sport im Bild* etc.), footballers immediately sought publicity in the new medium. But there was no real public interest in football photos because technical limitations made it impossible to take close-ups of individual players in action. This meant that the only photos which could be published were stiffly posed team pictures taken in photographers' studios. It was hardly surprising that footballers were kicked off the glossy pages of the elegantly printed magazines after only a short time. Reactions differed. In England reports were confined once again to the dailies which in any case devoted a set number of pages to football. In other European countries newspapers sprang up which specialised almost exclusively in football (*Sport im Wort*, Berlin; *La Gazzetta dello Sport*, Milan; *El Mundo Deportivo*, Barcelona). By the time press photographers began to take advantage of new technical developments in the 1930s some of these papers had long since become national institutions and football reporting had been raised to the level of an independent literary genre.

Around the end of the 1920s, radio raised the media culture to a new level of loquacity. But now many club and league officials began to put the brakes on any further progress because they feared that such immediate reporting would encourage spectators to stay at home and listen to the radio instead of passing through the turnstiles. Their attitudes towards radio reporters were therefore somewhat unco-operative at first. This largely explains why there were so few football running

8   9   10

commentaries during the period. Around the turn of the 1930s, for example, the Berlin radio station transmitted only between one and eight football reports a year, and from 1931 to 1939 the BBC was forced to dispense with live outside broadcasts completely. In addition it was very difficult for the early reporters to give their audience an adequate impression of a game the listeners were unable to see. At first, many countries tried to find a solution with visual 'translations'. They did this by recommending the listeners to follow the movements on the pitch by means of a chequered graph printed on a piece of paper ('Kick-off on B-C/4-5. Zimmermann takes the ball and sends a long pass from A3 to A4. Sobek's now on the ball and dribbles from A5 via A4 to B1'). The phrase 'back to square one' comes from these years. This procedure, which was claimed to be an English invention, failed to make much impression. It was only when broadcasters started to commentate spontaneously, to include the background roar of the crowd and learned to anticipate events in advance that outside radio commentaries developed into an independent and increasingly popular genre.

Early television outside broadcasts also found it difficult to win over audiences. For a start the pictures on the tiny black-and-white screens of the 1950s tended to wobble and spin. Then it was difficult to conjure up the right atmosphere because the heavy cameras – the early models weighed almost four hundredweight and were crew-operated – were unable to keep up with the tempo of events and cover the movement of the ball over the pitch. Just as television broadcasters were beginning to get this problem under control by using extra cameras and special cameras, football officials once again started worrying about the negative effects on attendances. Many clubs refused outright to co-operate until they were offered financial compensation for the possible loss

in gate money. Further conflicts arose in 1960s when television companies began to include slow-motion replays in their live transmissions. Now FIFA intervened because it feared that the new technology might undermine the authority of the referees. The problem was solved by adding a clause to the rules, which laid down that referees' decisions were final and could not be affected by filmed evidence – which was just as well for England's third goal in the 1966 World Cup.

On the other hand many technical improvements were greeted unanimously as a sign of progress. This applied above all to floodlighting, whose importance in media history has never really been properly acknowledged. The earliest attempts at lighting matches were made at the end of the 1870s but it was not until the 1950s in Great Britain that they were regularly put into practice, thereby enabling midweek evening matches to be played alongside the Saturday afternoon dates. This new pattern of fixtures – known as 'English weeks' on the continent – provided the press with a further supply of stories, gave the clubs an additional source of income and the players a good argument for demanding higher pay and bonuses. Midweek matches were also exempt from the league's ban on live outside broadcasts. The introduction of colour television in the late 1960s led to colourful logos on players' shirts and mass advertising on hoardings around the perimeter of the pitch and a similar range of trickle-down effects.

While these technical improvements helped to improve finances, others increased publicity for football as a whole, which was also in the interests of all those involved. This was particularly the case with the battery-driven portable transistor radio, a humble invention that made a considerable contribution to integrating football broadcasting into leisure culture. For one

11

12

thing it meant that fans in industrialised countries could now follow live commentaries when they were out on a walk, lying on the beach or washing the car. In some developing countries it was now possible, for the first time, to transmit football broadcasts to listeners in rural areas without electricity. In addition, transistor radios raised general levels of excitement and tension because listeners and spectators could now follow a large number of live games almost simultaneously.

Television satellites, a by-product of the arms race and space industry, had an even greater multiplier effect at international level. True, Telstar 1, the first satellite launched by the USA in 1962, proved too weak to be of any real use for radio and television because it could only broadcast signals for eighteen minutes during its two-and-a-half-hour orbit of the Earth. But receiving stations were erected in Great Britain, France, Italy, Brazil and Japan and the International Telecommunications Satellite Organisation (INTELSAT) was set up. Shortly afterwards a new era in international communications began. Sport turned out to be a welcome subject of demonstration. On 25 May 1965 the Early Bird satellite broadcast the legendary revenge match between Cassius Clay and Sonny Liston 'live' from the USA to Europe. Countries as far away as Indonesia were now plugged into international sporting events. The BBC recognised the opportunity to organise live broadcasts of the 1966 World Cup in England and commissioned its Overseas Audience Research department to make a survey of media potential in the rest of the world.

13 / 14 *'Deutschland über alles?'* The two Germanies united through sport and the radio reports by H. Zimmermann (West Germany) and W. Hempel (East Germany) during the World Cup Final 1954.

15 Televisions were not within the scope of all budgets. Germans attempt to watch the live broadcast of the 1954 World Cup Final.

16 Quality transcontinental radio. Coverage of the 1934 World Cup by the Argentinian broadcaster Splendid-Rivadavia.

13

14

The dissemination of radio and television

The BBC's 1964 survey of the current state of radio and television sets has provided market research analysts and historians alike with vital information, corresponding to an important transitional period in the growth of televised football. On the one hand, as we have seen, co-operation between football and the media was now fully established, both technically and institutionally. On the other hand, international programme exchanges had not yet outgrown their teething problems. Accordingly, the BBC survey brought to light the huge discrepancy in media accessibility among countries and continents around the world.

The two most important football continents, Europe and Latin America, were relatively well equipped with radios and television sets. That said, there were enormous regional imbalances. Whereas in Europe the traditional football nations of England, Italy, the Netherlands, Austria, Hungary, Czechoslovakia and the Soviet Union all had a large number of receivers at their disposal, countries like Romania lagged considerably behind and in Turkey television broadcasting had not even been introduced. In Latin America the leading country in the field of electronic media, Argentina, contrasted strongly with countries like Peru and Mexico where even the number of radio sets was below the world average. Even Brazil, the football nation par excellence, failed to meet the 'average' number of 154 radios and 51 television sets per 1,000 inhabitants. Admittedly, data on

15

16

18

19

17 Radio sets the scene for the football at the London Olympics, 1948.

18 The BBC technical centre, an integral part of the nervous system of the 1966 World Cup.

19 The home of the conductor of football match coverage. The BBC producers mixing desk, 1966 World Cup.

ownership do not provide very reliable evidence of the media presence of football. In many countries loud-speakers transmitted commentaries into complete sub-urbs and villages, and television viewers gathered to watch the matches in public squares, bars, bistros and cafés, in front of shop-windows as well as privately at home. Given these circumstances the primary concern of football was simply to ensure that there were enough sets on hand. Both Europe and Latin America had enjoyed radio and television broadcasts since their inception, in the 1920s and 1950s repectively. Thus in the mid-1960s, when the BBC survey was being conducted, the majority of Latin-American countries had sufficient radio and television broadcasting stations (most of them were commercial), to be able to exploit the new technology to the full. In this respect, Brazil was even better supplied than the USA.

The 1964 BBC survey also revealed that radio and television sets were heavily 'disseminated' in precisely those areas with not much real interest in the soccer variation of football: North America and South-East Asia. People in the USA, Canada, Australia and Japan possessed a grand total of 251 million radios and 87 million television sets, that is to say fifty-one per cent and fifty-four per cent respectively of all radio and television receivers in the whole world. As might be expected, the amount of sets in a country was a material reflection of its state of development and general economic health.

Finally, the study showed that in the mid-1960s the majority of people in the world lived in regions where, to all intents and purposes, there was neither football nor media, namely in Africa and Asia. A little more than two billion people, sixty-four per cent of the world's population, were living on these continents at the time,

20

but owned only thirteen per cent of radios and eleven per cent of television sets. If we ignore Japan, which is something of an exception, the above percentage shrinks to only 4.5 per cent of radios and 0.3 per cent of televisions.

Thus in the mid-1960s two-thirds of the world's population were not yet exposed to international media coverage. Looked at from football's point of view, they lacked any chance of getting to know the game at all. It was therefore out of the question to call football a global game. On the other hand, the findings indicated an enormous potential for development in the media sector in general and in televised football in particular. BBC bosses therefore had every reason to look forward to a golden future for the broadcasting business.

In the final third of the twentieth century, especially in the last two decades, the predicted golden future largely became reality. Not only did the population of the world almost double during this period – from 3.3 billion in 1965 to 6.1 billion in 2000, but the average spread in the number of receivers grew even more rapidly. The per capita number of radios grew on average by 270 per cent (from 153 to 416 sets per 1,000 people), and television ownership even grew by 440 per cent (from 51 to 225 sets per 1,000). Even Asia and Africa have now reached the standards enjoyed by European and Latin American countries in the mid-1960s and some countries have surpassed them considerably. Their above-average growth rates do not simply show that they still have a long way to catch up but rather that they are closing the gap on the leading nations. According to a UNESCO study ninety-three per cent of the world's children now have access to a television set, and even in Africa four out of five children are able to watch television occasionally.

The effects of televised football

That said, ownership of receivers was neither a necessary, nor even a sufficient prerequisite for the rise of football to global significance. Demand for live football transmissions had to be created before it could be satisfied. That football proved so extraordinarily successful in global terms depended on many factors, not the least of which was the growing number of international and intercontinental matches, the accompanying developmental measures put in place by FIFA and the spill-over effects of World Cups on the economy of their host countries. The award of the tournament to Latin American countries, in 1970 and 1986 to Mexico, and in 1978 to Argentina, even had a positive effect in other countries on the sub-continent whose media put in as much effort as the host country itself.

The popularisation of football has also left its mark on the traditional football nations of Europe, particularly since the 'push' of radio and television dissemination has in many cases been reinforced by 'pulls' from other social areas. In Great Britain, the cradle of football, which was, and still is, traditionally more interested in domestic than international competitions, the internationalisation of televised football coincided with the gradual dissolution of local football communities. The growth in mobility as a result of urban regeneration, new towns and the general ownership of motor cars helped to prepare many fans for a new and wider orientation. In addition, the collapse of the British Empire, the economic crises of the 1960s and other symptoms of national decline created the necessity of survival on the international stage, at least in football. It is therefore no accident that these were the years in which the image of Manchester United as an

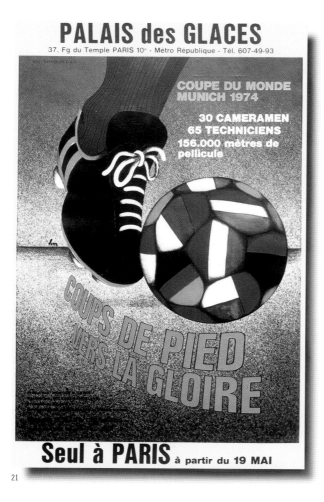

21

20 The Wembley stadium press room during the 1966 World Cup.

21 After the immediate emotion of the small screen, cinema presented a Technicolor version of the exploits of Beckenbauer, Cruyff and other players.

time. Rural inhabitants, too, the old and frail, and above all teenagers and children, who were so important for the future development of the game, were now introduced to football via television.

Televised football also broke through gender barriers and over the course of time the predominance of men and young males in front of the screen was slowly eroded. In this respect the comprehensive coverage of the 1966 World Cup in England had a palpable effect in the home country. The BBC's director of outside broadcasting, Peter Dimmock, remarked with great surprise that: 'Housewives have begun to appreciate that football is not just twenty-two chaps kicking a ball about, but something involving a great deal of skill. A woman in front of me at Wembley on Tuesday was screaming "Hold it! Hold it!" when she thought one of our players was going to pass too early. She told me afterwards she had never been to a match before. She'd learnt it all from the telly.' A survey conducted in Great Britain in 1979 found that sixty-five per cent of the men and thirty-five per cent of the women questioned claimed to be interested in televised football and since the 1982 World Cup in Spain women in England have been tuning into World Cup matches almost as persistently as men. In 2001 seventy-four per cent of men and forty-one of women in England said that football was their favourite form of televised sport. Nowadays, as a rule, the proportion of women and girls among television viewers is directly related to the importance of the match.

The influx of women into the ranks of football fans was not confined to television alone, it also spread to the grounds. Contrary to some assumptions, the boom in women's football during this period was not a crucial factor in this development. For this 'silly spectacle' was ignored by most television stations for as long as it was by

English and European 'super club' was created. Meanwhile in Germany, Willy Brandt's SPD/Liberal coalition promoted peaceful international football contests because they resonated with the government's détente policies. In Austria, on the other hand, televised football via Eurovision compensated for the loss of the once significant central European football network which had been gravely damaged in the Second World War and torn apart for good by the erection of the Iron Curtain. This development went hand-in-hand with Austrian football's shift from central to Western Europe.

On the European continent international radio and television broadcasts also contributed considerably to spreading the popularity of football from the traditional confines of the elite and bourgeois middle classes to a broader, less specific mass of the population. As soon as football could be seen on television it aroused the enthusiasm of all classes and social layers. Market research findings in the 1960s and 1970s from different countries were unanimous in stating that workers were over-represented among fans of televised football. This is truly remarkable when one considers that this particular social group could not be counted as football supporters in many countries in the first half of the 20th century because they lacked the necessary money and leisure

FIFA officials and national associations. The one exception was the USA where women's football was quickly regarded as a perfectly normal activity because men's football was so underdeveloped. It could be argued that feminist ideology played a supporting role in the rise of women's football. In fact, it had very little effect, for football has never counted as one of the more urgent topics on the agenda of the women's movement. Neither did women footballers feature prominently as figureheads of women's liberation during this period. Therefore more weight must be given to television broadcasts when trying to explain why the female half of the population has grown more attracted to football since the 1960s.

In contrast with many men, women's initial contacts with the game had nothing to do with everyday outside activities like kick-abouts on the street, going to a match, playing an active role in a football club or gambling, but were entirely mediated by television. For this reason women can be regarded as archetypically 'modern' football fans. For them televised football means not only virtual reality, that is to say, real experience reflected on the screen, but real virtuality: events on the screen itself were now regarded as 'the real thing'. The broadcasting stations took this new form of perception into account at an early stage. In the 1960s their commentaries began to include information on the personal and private lives of footballers alongside the purely sporting aspects. This was a favourite strategy of tabloid newspapers which were overwhelmingly read by women, and which also discovered the benefits of exploiting the personal lives of football players around this time. By the mid-1980s the primarily 'female' perception of football as real virtuality had become so generalised among men that, even in Great Britain, with its long football traditions, a survey revealed that ninety-eight per cent of people claiming to be personally 'very interested in soccer' based this opinion on the fact that they regularly watched it on television. Only fourteen per cent of them professed to taking part in any additional footballing activities or being members of clubs.

The triumphal march of televised football

In the last few years this tendency has become more entrenched than ever, thanks to two technical innovations in television reception: cable technology and private satellite reception. In many countries these have led to the tearing down of erstwhile almost impossibly high barriers for private companies to enter the national television market. Whereas until around the mid-1980s programmes had always outnumbered broadcasting capacity, around then the reverse began to be the case. More and more bandwiths became available and the programmes to fill them became more and more scarce. In this situation many countries which had hitherto enjoyed a long tradition of public broadcasting were now faced with an influx of new private commercial companies, and within a matter of years this had a powerful impact on the tried and tested programme filler, football. Commercial channels began to compete with public and state-owned companies for

22

23

primary broadcasting rights which in turn enabled clubs, associations and FIFA to exploit their market position as the owners of these rights. The clubs and associations were unable to capitalise on this new state of play. They invested a part of the income from the sale of rights into expanding current leagues and tournaments and set up new competitions like the European Champions League, thereby once again increasing the amount of televised football. Nowadays, European viewers are able to tune into more than 250 television channels, a considerable number of which broadcast football matches at some time in the day. In this way even people who have no real interest in football are getting to know the ins and outs of the game. Anyone zapping through the channels will inevitably come upon a broadcast or summary, a list of the weekend results, a report on a new record transfer or a talk-show with players and trainers.

There are many reasons for the triumphal march of real televised football, most of which have absolutely nothing to do with the sport. First and foremost is the general trend towards individualisation and privacy. Watching television, like listening to the radio and, more recently, surfing the net are among the most popular forms of leisure today. Furthermore, during the last twenty-five years there has been a gradual decline in the amount of free time available to people in the USA, Sweden, Spain, Great Britain, Japan and other industrialised countries with the result that, for many, a visit to the stadium now appears to be a luxury. Finally, there has been an enormous growth in the range of sporting leisure activities available to the general public, and the competition between them all has had an impact on football. The inhabitants of a city like Hamburg, as we have seen, now have a choice of active-

ly participating in over 240 sporting disciplines from BMX biking via Bunjee jumping to free climbing on artificial rock faces.

Simply put, televised football has worked because the public enjoy football and enjoy watching television. Watching a match on television is no longer second best to watching it the stadium – it is almost as if it is an independent and, for many, a better form of entertainment. In many football countries there has been a decline in match attendances, the extent of which – seen over a period of decades – has exceeded even the worst fears of club and association officials, including FIFA. This can be primarily attributed to the extraordinary attraction of televised football. Fans watching television do not have to fear being molested by hooligans, they are not subject to the vagaries of the weather, nor are they likely to miss the winning goal because somebody in front of them is blocking their view. Fans watching at home are offered much more than they would usually get in the stadium including away games and matches from abroad which, for most people, would otherwise be impossible to attend. During the match itself viewers are also offered a continually changing perspective of the game which even a seat in the VIP lounge cannot match. Television companies now use more than two dozen cameras, fixed, moving and flying, to cover important matches. Repeats, close-ups, slow-motion and frame-by-frame replays and, most recently, computerised animations are now standard features. In addition, reporters and studio presenters devote an immense amount of time and effort to pre-match reports and post-match analysis, background information, live interviews from the pitch and interviews with VIPs in the studio or in the stadium. After the match, market researchers analyse viewing figures

24 Emotion of sport...
from a distance.
Young Colombians
follow the match
between Colombia
and Argentina, 2000.

in order to determine viewers' preferences. Viewers are not only demanding, they are much more critical than the fans in the stadium. They do not feel compelled to talk up a match and try to justify the outlay of time and money, but can simply switch channels or turn off the set completely if a match is boring.

Critics of televised football complain that all this has led to a loss of authenticity because viewers at home are neither directly nor wholeheartedly involved in the match and, above all, are excluded from making any form of contribution. They even claim that the general public is being swindled because the match itself is swamped by all the secondary aspects involved in the broadcast. But what does authenticity really mean in a time when fans in the stadium have invented and cultivated a collective form of expression like the 'Mexican wave' precisely for its effect on the viewers back home? Or when hooligans wait until a camera is in the right position before launching their acts of aggression so that they can be seen on the evening news? Or when giant screens in the stadiums show slow-motion replays and close-ups, and even special pre- and post-match television programmes with interviews, competitions and music?

There are other more serious fears. Financially powerful broadcasting stations might be able to force through changes in the rules as well as changes in match dates and times to the detriment of players, clubs and lastly the sporting competition itself. Football might decline in popularity as a result of a tendency, now seen in many countries, towards subscription TV and pay-per-view events. Also, the privileged treatment of the more successful clubs might lead to fans losing interest in the local game, which sooner or later would lead to a dissolution of local supporters' clubs. Such

crisis scenarios have been forecast for developing world countries. Here, broadcasts of European matches predominate because local stations are unable to meet the expenses involved in independent transmissions and are hampered by out-of-date technical equipment.

But when televised football is looked at more carefully many of these fears dissolve into thin air. Experience shows that, when individual broadcasting companies are able to push through changes in rules or kick-off times, the fault lies less with the medium of television and more with local concentrations of commercial power. A company like TV Globo in Brazil, for example, which has a near-monopoly of the market in televised football (not to speak of other areas) can force clubs in the Copa de Libertadores to defer kick-off times to 21.45 so that audiences can watch the daily '*telenovela*' soap beforehand. The result is that the spectators no longer go to the stadium. In many other countries, on the other hand, such a concentration of power in the hands of a single company is unlikely because national monopoly authorities (in the case of Europe, the European Commission) would intervene. In some of these countries even the central marketing of rights by the league is forbidden. Nor is the tendency towards pay TV an inevitable result of cable and satellite technology or any other media innovations. From the spectators' viewpoint subscription TV and pay-per-view are only revolutionary if they disregard the fact that going to the match itself is in essence also a pay-per-view experience. Football became popular on this basis and will not be ruined by it. The risk is even less in Western industrial societies with their ageing populations because pay TV offers viewers a welcome opportunity to 'buy' themselves free of irritating commercial spots aimed at the younger generation.

24

As for the undermining of local supporters' clubs and the loss of football's socialising abilities, something FIFA in particular would regard as a major threat, general experience shows that the more sport can develop into an entertainment business with the help of the media, the more it will be able to fulfil its socialising function. Seen superficially, entertainment, which a keen observer has defined as 'the commercialisation of the pursuit of happiness', contains an individualising component. For, in the last analysis, the viewers themselves become the authors of the stories which are being mediated to them. Paradoxically, this produces quite the reverse social effect. Precisely because televised football entertainment caters to individual perceptions the sport can become the subject of collective sociability. Every man and woman can use the knowledge gathered from television broadcasts to pose as experts, critics and forecasters, and all without having to run the risk of negative consequences if they prove to be

wrong. Thus, televised football helps to strengthen the web of relationships which help bind modern societies together and, seen globally, this simultaneously promotes mutual relationships between individual societies. It not only creates the impression of a global society, it also contributes to making it a reality.

In this respect the younger developing countries are the main beneficiaries. For here, poverty, bad roads and language barriers make it difficult or nigh on impossible for pre-existing societies to support local supporters' clubs and, frequently, football matches themselves. But if football broadcasts from abroad can help these viewers transcend local insularity and open up new areas of experience it is irrelevant whether their 'own' team wins or loses, whether it has a good day or, like all beginners, is taught a lesson by superior opponents. In order for the socialising mechanism to have an effect it is necessary to be 'tuned into' the event.

1904-1945

FIFA AND POLITICAL PROBLEMS

In a piece written towards the end of his life, significantly entitled *Le Football et le rapprochement des peoples* (Football and the Unification of Nations) Jules Rimet describes the ability of football to create mutual understanding and togetherness. This positive judgement on FIFA's first fifty years should be considered alongside the facts.

Tentative steps

Everything connected with the internal politics of member states or the relations between states had the potential to pose difficult problems for the leaders of FIFA. In order to avoid or rise above such entanglements FIFA decided, after a brief period of hesitation, to adopt a position of absolute and intransigent neutrality. In the words of Jules Rimet, they became a sort of mini-League of Nations. FIFA refused to become involved either in the political problems of affiliated countries or with disagreements between European member states. At a time when ideologies were fuelling conflict, FIFA had to maintain a strictly neutral position. It was the only way to ensure the Federation's survival, especially taking into account that some influential people were members of national associations.

FIFA's position was made easier by the fact that it only concerned itself with neutral football associations. Catholic and workers' associations who did not share this neutrality remained outside of FIFA.

For all their ambition to expand the influence of the young institution, FIFA's original membership initially showed little political awareness. There were no statutory measures to safeguard the political independence of national associations. Equally, although the Statutes specified affiliation *'d'une seule fédération par pays'* (of a single association per country) FIFA admitted FC Prague, an association representing the state of Bohemia. At the Vienna Congress of 1909, the Austrian association demanded and succeeded in obtaining Prague's exclusion. In requesting this, the Austrian association conformed to its government's view that Bohemia was no more than a region of the Empire. FIFA had to adapt its rules to conform to the political realities that existed at that time. Interestingly, the Austrian representative did not protest against the presence of a Hungarian association in FIFA even though Hungary was a state within the Austro-Hungarian Empire.

FIFA's leaders were aware of the difficulties that arose from the imprecise and sometimes disputed status of certain territories at a time when there were continual shifts of nationality. Despite the demands of the Swedish association, the FIFA Congress refused to adopt a definition of the word 'country' and therefore to distinguish between a state and a nation. FIFA did not

1 Political prisoners penned into the Santiago Stadium in Chile after the military coup which overthrew Allende's democracy on 11 September 1973.

2 A mass launching of *'papelitos'*. The Argentine supporters celebrate their team's victory in the final against Holland, 25 June 1978.

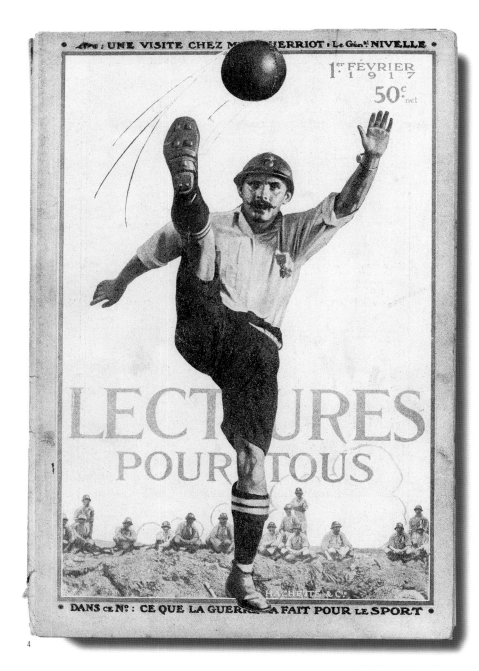

3 The English Army pays respect to a 'football' in 1916. During the Battle of the Somme, Captain Nevill threw this ball towards German lines to motivate his men. Only a handful of soldiers and the ball, as seen in the photo, would have survived this daring venture.

4 What the war did for sport (1917). Wishing to be better recognised by the political and military authorities, sporting bodies promoted the merits of football in the physical and moral preparation of the soldier.

The intrusion of politics after 1919

want to be tied down to a definition and preferred to deal with membership requests case by case, taking into account the international status of the territory from whence they came.

British hegemony effectively forced the entry of the Irish, Scottish and Welsh associations in 1910, despite tenacious opposition from Germany and Austria who also criticised the FA for accepting the membership of the Chilean and Argentinian footballers. Until 1913 two groups within FIFA clashed continually, if restrainedly so. Despite their discussions not being overtly political, the countries of the Entente Cordiale – Great Britain and France – were on one side, and those of the Central Alliance – Austria and Germany – were on the other.

During the Great War FIFA remained silent. But on its return to activity in 1918, politics prevailed and FIFA tried to follow the line of the Olympic movement. The football associations of the Allied countries decided to exclude those of the defeated powers, Germany, Austria and Hungary. Hefner, the German representative, declined to acknowledge the exclusion, denying that his country was responsible for starting the war. Forced by their government, the British then demanded that associations who nevertheless agreed to play teams from former enemy countries should be excluded from FIFA. For its part, FIFA decided the excluded associations should be re-integrated when they were admitted into the League of Nations. The FA finally withdrew from FIFA over this question in April 1920 and ultimately the excluded countries were re-integrated by FIFA before they were admitted to the League of Nations.

The question of nationhood after 1920

The new states built after the dissolution of the Austro-Hungarian Empire, such as Czechoslovakia and Yugoslavia, legitimately knocked at FIFA's door. During the 1920s, the problem of nationality arose again with the formation of the Football Association of the Irish Free State, founded by the footballers of Southern Ireland, a country in the process of establishing its independence. Placed in a very delicate situation and not wishing to anger Great Britain, FIFA nevertheless decided to affiliate the Football Association of the Irish Free State without waiting for the British to recognise it. The resulting dispute endured well into the 1930s. In 1934 the Southern Irish requested that FIFA encourage European teams to come to play in their country to compensate for the politically driven boycott by the British associations. When the FAI decided unilaterally to play under the name Ireland in 1936, it provoked indignation within the Northern Irish Football Association. FIFA decided to remain neutral in this complicated affair, although Schricker offered to contribute.

Another complicated question of nationality for FIFA, and one that would endure throughout the century, was that of Palestine. In 1928 English and Jewish footballers in Palestine founded the Palestinian Football Association which was allowed to join FIFA the following year, even though Palestine was currently under British mandate. By doing this, FIFA was ignoring the broad political consensus – the British mandate was recognised by the League of Nations, but not, apparently, by FIFA. A further difficulty was introduced with the creation of the Arab Sports Club. Its membership were exclusively Arab players, who were eager to play clubs from the neighbouring Arab countries of the Lebanon and Egypt, both already affiliated to FIFA. This desire was behind the Arab Sports Club's 1937 request to join FIFA, stating the impossibility of forming mixed Jewish-Arab teams. FIFA gave a response that allowed no appeal. Its Statutes permitted the recognition of only one association per country and FIFA suggested that the Arab Sports Club should apply to the Palestinian association which was the only authority entitled to sanction international encounters. FIFA's political line was gradually emerging from these encounters. It maintained its neutrality, that is to say, followed the international rules when dealing with post-conflict nations, but showed a tendency to anticipate future developments when territories were in the process of gaining their independence.

Politics played an important part in the first World Cup tournaments. The widespread feel-good factor created by these football events had the potential to become the foundation for a new or reinvigorated national identity. It was with the aim of giving an added, and if possible global dimension, to the celebrations of their country's centennial of independence, that the Uruguayan football association showed it was keen to organise the first World Cup in 1930.

5 The VIP stand at the Fascist Party Stadium, during the singing of the national anthems. According to Rimet (right), Mussolini (centre) followed international matches with interest. Rome, 1935.

5

Leniency towards fascism and patience with the USSR

The objectives of the Italian association were altogether different in 1934. In line with the ruling political power, it wanted to use the second World Cup to improve the international image of the fascist regime and of Il Duce, Benito Mussolini. This was to be achieved by a demonstration of the vitality of the Italian 'race' through efficient organisation and expertise in infrastructure construction. At the end of the final, the winning Italian team turned towards Mussolini and gave the fascist salute; Jules Rimet remained silent in the face of this political demonstration and FIFA accepted this type of regime. Four years later in France, the Italian team was loudly jeered during a game in Marseilles the home of many Italian political refugees. Was the Italian team not acting as the official ambassador of fascism?

The Soviets also used football as an instrument of propaganda outside the USSR. In 1926 Hirschmann noted that a Soviet team was touring abroad in Turkey and in Western Europe. The Soviets played matches against workers' teams as well as others. At that time this con-

cerned FIFA because the USSR was seeking to expand its own organisation, Red Sport International, by uniting workers from all countries at the expense of the tradtional 'neutral' associations. Other associations with known affiliations, Catholic, Jewish or secular, and similar agendas had been deliberately ignored by FIFA.

In 1932 FIFA began a long-running dispute with Turkey over its relations with Red Sport International and the USSR. Matches had been played in Turkey against Russian teams. When questioned, the Turkish association stated that the Turkish teams involved had played under the aegis of the country's only political party rather than that of the association affiliated to FIFA. In fact, the players of the association were unable to refuse the demands of the government. The President of the Turkish football association hoped that FIFA would allow this to continue; he explained that for them it was a question of survival. In return, he undertook to encourage the Soviets to join FIFA. The intrusion of politics at this point put both the Turkish football association and FIFA in an awkward position and FIFA finally gave in to the political imperative. Rimet and Schricker showed their pragmatism, deciding in the case of a deadlock not to insist and instead

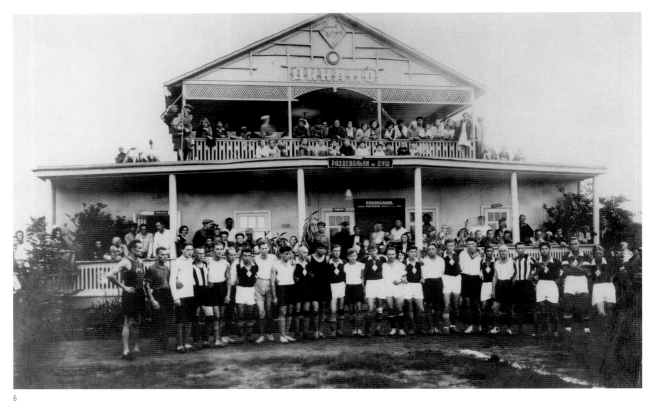

6

Dienamo Moskau. 1926.

7

6 The German workers team on tour with the Caucasian SU, 1932. Despite Rimet and Schricker's insistence, the USSR refused to join FIFA, which they considered 'bourgeois', or to subscribe to its political neutrality.

7 Dynamo Moscow travelling to Dresden, 1926. Under Stalin's dictatorship, compared to other Moscow teams such as Spartak or Lokomotiv, Dynamo appeared to be the product of political power as it was dependent upon the interior minister.

8 A rather disorganised National Socialist salute before the game between Switzerland and Germany, 1937.

to wait for a change in personnel to accomplish their long-term vision.

A similar problem soon arose in Czechoslovakia, who had officially recognised the USSR in May 1934 and wished to develop friendly relations with the Communist state. In response to an invitation from the Czech communist party, the Soviets came to play matches against both Red Sport International and other teams. The president of FIFA wondered whether it was possible to proceed as the Federation had done with the British, tolerating matches against teams who did not belong to the organisation. FIFA hesitated, and eventually turned a blind eye, which encouraged the Czechs to invite the Soviets to join the world organisation.

But by 1935 Schricker was not willing to compromise when the Austrian association wanted to host games with Soviet teams. He now considered that the Soviets would never give up on their workers' organisations and that they were unlikely to become members of FIFA. Nevertheless the Executive Committee gave a temporary authorisation for the matches until May 1936. FIFA had gone to the limit of its concessions in its indirect relations with Soviet football, which it wanted to integrate. At this time Soviet membership seemed no

closer and the USSR remained outside of the Federation.

Nevertheless, these indirect links showed that FIFA had not adopted the IOC's anticommunist policy. FIFA's strategy, that is to say, its ambition to expand globally, always sought to transcend ideological problems. However, the breakdown of international relations and the internal tensions within states continuously put FIFA in a delicate situation. Often, FIFA's strategy was simply to ignore such conflicts, for example Schricker remained both deaf and dumb over the Chaco War between Bolivia and Paraguay (1932–36).

An exception during the Spanish Civil War

At the beginning of the Spanish Civil War in February 1937 the Spanish association was located in Barcelona. In June the Nationalists formed a dissident association in San Sebastián which declared itself the sole legitimate football association for Spain. This was a serious dilemma for FIFA. In practical terms it was immediately confronted with the problem of a Basque team touring Europe and the USSR in aid of Basque refugees. In November 1937 the team went to Mexico where FIFA authorised it to play against Mexican teams, but only after intervention from the Euskadi government. The question arose again in March 1938 when the Basques wanted to play against South American teams. To facilitate this, the Mexican association declared itself ready to affiliate the Basque team. Disorder and insubordination threatened.

The two Spanish associations were asked to meet FIFA's officials. The pro-Franco representative took advantage of the situation to denounce the 'international' employment of the Basque players. FIFA decided not to confirm their suspension, considering that players not wishing to return to a pro-Franco Spain could not be suspended. Only two out of eighteen were to return from South America.

In recognising two Spanish associations at the same time, FIFA was without doubt hedging bets and awaiting the end of the civil war but also seemed to want to defend the principles of freedom. However, at the end of the war, the Italian Mauro, who had always supported the pro-Franco football association, used his influence to gain recognition for it. FIFA's crisis was overcome by returning to its traditional principle regarding the recognition of one association per country.

8

9 Sport did not always follow diplomatic and ideological understandings.
The Italian team trained by Pozzo, made up of young talent and students, won the 1936 Olympic Games football competition…

10 A sporting side to the Anschluss. After the annexation of Austria, the 'Reichssportführer', Hans von Tschammer und Osten visited the Austrian football team, 27 March 1938.

11 Throughout occupied Europe football matches attracted both soldiers and civilians. A German light transport aircraft kicks off a match between Italian and German soldiers in Paris, 1941.

FIFA and the Nazis

With the start of Nazi annexations the Executive Committee, the Emergency Committee and the Board experienced growing difficulties in preserving a neutral line due to the presence of the Italian Mauro and Peco Bauwens, the German. Faced with Fascism and Nazism, it was unclear if a neutral position could be comfortably maintained. On the whole, the long personal friendship that linked FIFA's key leaders meant that an implosion was avoided. However, a flaw appeared at the start of 1939 when a Slovakian association, founded in Czechoslovakia at the invitation of the Nazis, requested membership of FIFA. Schricker denounced their 'political interests' but the affiliation was registered. It was the same for the Croatian football association in 1940 and even for the dissident Nazi Norwegian association. FIFA thus recognised the territorial disruptions caused by the Nazis in Europe and essentially made a compromise with them. After 1945, FIFA was sharply criticised by the Scandinavian football associations for their attitude in the Norwegian affair.

During the conflict, while football thrived in Latin America and found itself exploited by dictatorial regimes, FIFA again distanced itself. The word 'war' was banished from the correspondence, which was never completely broken off, between Schricker in Zurich and Bauwens, Mauro and Seeldrayers. Instead of 'war' it was a question of 'events', 'circumstance', or at best of 'international crisis'. In September and October 1939, Schricker was dealing with the organisation of the next Olympic football tournament, even though the war had already begun. He also circulated the agenda for the Congress scheduled for May 1940. At the end of September 1939, a clear break from this indifference was apparent in a letter from Seeldrayers on the subject of the Olympic Games: 'If Germany joins forces with France, England and Italy to remove the Russian threat and to create a Polish buffer state, there is a possibility of organising the Olympic football tournament.' This slip was the only overt expression of anti-communism made – the principal danger was elsewhere.

In May 1940 Schricker drafted a circular to announce the postponement of the Luxembourg Congress. It included

9

10

FIFA AND POLITICAL PROBLEMS

12

13

reflections on the fact that the merits of sport, such as 'pacifism, solidarity and friendship between nations' had been disregarded. He added: 'FIFA can only express the ardent wish to see the current conflict end as soon as possible'. On 1 June 1940, Mauro disagreed, saying that 'FIFA should refrain from… communications or declarations of a political nature'. He demanded the removal of Schricker's comments, which speaks volumes about Mauro's own political commitment.

At the same time Bauwens repeatedly petitioned Schricker to obtain help bring FIFA into line and under the control of the Nazi sports' authorities. 'If we act carefully, we could place FIFA completely under the influence of the Axis and isolate England even more', he wrote on October 25 1940. Although German, Schricker was evidently hostile to Nazism. Bauwen's petitions were in vain.

The German association and its Brazilian counterpart failed to echo FIFA's apolitical attitude. In 1941 the Brazilian foot-

ball association ordered professional players to refrain from commenting on the political situation in Brazil or expressing 'any opinion against our government'. The players 'should know their national anthem by heart and sing it in unison when required'.

FIFA survived the Second World War almost unscathed. Its prudent policies towards questions regarding nationhood or the USSR had allowed it to prepare for the future. But its fidelity to the principles of neutrality and non-interference had forced it to avoid expressing its beliefs on pacifist ideology and human fraternity. The policy of noninvolvement had led FIFA to tolerate ideologies and politics well beyond the boundaries of humanism. Had there been any other choice? Jules Rimet's optimistic hope had to be put into perspective.

Apart from the worry of managing political problems, FIFA became was becoming increasingly concerned with other preoccupations such as questions linked to the status of players, notably those raised by the growth of professionalism. As we saw earlier, after the war ended FIFA was faced with debts amounting to 100,000 Swiss francs caused by the disruption to international matches and the cancellation of the World Cup in 1942. Nonetheless, it immediately began business as usual and, thanks to two benefit matches, the deficit had been redressed by the spring of 1947. Switzerland's extraordinarily helpful policies towards the international organisations located in that country combined with Schricker's relish for correspondence, had laid the foundations for tried and tested working arrangements to be quickly restarted after the war. The age of the officials also played a factor in maintaining continuity. The vice-presi-

12 A British team sent to support the 'brothers in arms' in front of tomb of the unknown soldier, before a match against mobilised French footballers. Paris, 1940.

13 A tank regiment practice. Before and during the Second World War football was a favorite distraction for British soldiers, including during the desert war in North Africa.

14 A match between a neutral country and a prospective power. The Captain of the Italian team, Rava, introduces his players to the Swiss general Henri Guisan, who symbolised Swiss national unity during the Second World War. Zurich, November 1939.

dents and members of the executive committee were well into old age. For this reason most of them had not been combatants and as a result had survived the war unscathed. A new generation of FIFA officials did not really begin to take over until the mid-1950s following the retirement of General Secretary Ivo Schricker at the end of 1950 and President Jules Rimet in 1954.

This continuity meant that FIFA officials were ready to get back to work as soon as war ended, the more so because the war had left surprisingly few political problems. The 1946 General Assembly ostracised Germany and Japan, banning its members from taking part in any matches against teams or clubs from the two countries. The conflict with the Norwegian Football Association that, with the support of other Scandinavian associations, had objected to the way it had been treated by FIFA during the years of German occupation, was settled when the protest was accepted. In mid-March 1946 Schricker wrote to Rimet: 'a new period in FIFA's history, and in the history of world football in general, is opening up, and a perfect and amicable union of the world's associations seems not only possible but even very probable.'

Things were indeed looking up. Immediately after the armistice, preparations were made to negotiate the re-admittance of the British associations. This was successfully completed at the end of 1946, and the rift which had existed since 1928 was now healed. Around the same time, in November 1946, a letter from the Soviet Union requesting membership fell through the letterbox. The efforts put in by Schricker and Rimet between the two wars to secure the membership of the Soviet Union had finally paid off.

But these successes could not hide the fact that after 1945 FIFA was faced with a radically changed world, a world which was no simpler to deal with than the one which had disappeared in the Second World War. True, there were a number of positive developments. From FIFA's perspective, for example, it was a clear sign of progress that the Red Sport International movement was not revived after 1945. This development was an important precondition for the membership of the Soviet Union. At international level its teams had lost their ideologically acceptable opponents. In other respects, however, sporting politics were more complicated after 1945 than they had been before 1939 and FIFA had to face up to new challenges.

15

16

16 Leading the attack for FIFA's team. Puskas, the Hungarian renegade...

17 ...while Yachine, herald of football and Soviet sport, saves the goals.

15 The FIFA team selected against England for the FA Centenary match in 1963. A line-up that transcended the ideological and political differences of the Cold War. From left to right. Standing: Puskas (Spain), Dos Santos (Brazil), Pluskal (Czechoslovakia), Yachine (USSR), Popluhar (Czechoslovakia), Schnellinger (FRG), Soscic (Yugoslavia), Masoput (Czechoslovakia), Eyzaguirre (Chile), Baxter (Scotland), Seeler (FRG). Seated: Kopa (France), Law (Scotland), Di Stefano (Spain), Eusebio (Portugal), Gento (Spain).

17

18 The elite of world football and the communist bloc pay a visit to the home of true socialism. Action in front of the Soviet goal during a match between USSR and Hungary, Moscow 1954.

19 Two years after the Bandung Conference at which the Third World was first recognised, China hosts India in the return match of the qualifying rounds for the World Cup 1958, with an Indian referee. Peking 1957.

20 A goal to illustrate the sporting separation of the two Germanys. After going past Vogts and Maier (FRG), Sparwasser scores the winning goal for East Germany. World Cup 1974.

The world after 1945

The most significant new challenge facing FIFA was the Cold War, which divided the world into two hostile blocks and resulted in immense humanitarian problems. How, for example, should FIFA deal with Eastern Europe's refugee footballers? This was just one of the questions which confronted the Executive Committee. Should transfers of professional players who had left their countries for political reasons be dealt with differently from those of other players? When Czechoslovakia, Hungary and other Eastern bloc countries declared that they had put an end to professional football were they not also making a political point? In such cases should the playing ban imposed by the relevant association be accepted or should decisions be taken from the 'human point of view'?

Most football refugees were anonymous players whose cases were dealt with internally by the relevant FIFA committees. But the problem really came out into the open in 1956 after the uprising in Hungary when all the regular players of the famous Honved team refused to return home after a South American tour, preferring instead to play for Spanish clubs (see ch. 4). This affair caused the FIFA executive further headaches when the Honved players enlisted in the World League of Hungarian Refugee Sportsmen. FIFA could not acknowl-

FIFA AND POLITICAL PROBLEMS

21 The Budapest Elektromos Sportkör stadium in 1957. It was destroyed by Soviet troops brought in to crush the Hungarian uprising.

22 Recognition of North Korea, a country born out of the Cold War. Although outplayed by the Italian Fogli, the Korean defenders did not concede a goal and maintained their 1-0 lead. World Cup 1966.

edge the legitimacy of this league because this would have undermined their claim to control world football.

The Cold War was the cause of another set of problems: the division of nations into two parts. These notably included the Federal Republic of Germany and the German Democratic Republic, both of which were incorporated into international sporting relations at the start of the 1950s as successors to the defunct German Reich, but also the Republic of South Korea and the Democratic People's Republic of Korea, as well as Taiwan and the People's Republic of China. Each of these states refused to recognise its opposite number and all of them forced their way into FIFA. Worse still, on joining FIFA each association received a monopoly of representation. The problem here was that all the above countries claimed the exclusive right to represent their nation not only in order to play international football but also to be able to present themselves to the world as their nation's sole legitimate representative. Given this situation it was impossible for FIFA to solve the conflicts to the satisfaction of all those concerned.

Looking back, the best solution was provided in the case of German football. Despite a few skirmishes, both German football associations were able to co-exist without serious disruption until the country was reunited in 1989. There was even a match between the two teams in the 1974 World Cup in the West Germany, which East Germany won! By contrast, relationships between the football associations of South and North Korea, which had been accepted by FIFA in 1948 and 1958 respectively, were never good. North Korea withdrew from the Olympic football tournament in 1964 because South Korea was playing and were met with sanctions from

FIFA for unsporting behaviour. Moreover, they took part in the 1966 World Cup in England after most other Asian countries withdrew. Since then, North Korea has been largely isolated, although its association still continues to be a member of FIFA. The People's Republic of China, on the other hand, resigned from FIFA in 1958 because of Taiwan's parallel membership, claiming that FIFA was 'controlled by imperialistic elements'. It was not until 1979 that the People's Republic of China could once again be accepted as a member and then only after the Taiwan association, which had acted faultlessly over many years, had been renamed Chinese Taibei football assocation.

Due to the Soviet struggle for superiority in the Cold War FIFA found itself after 1945 in situations like those Norway faced during the German occupation, where its bureaucratic system was exploited to sanction attacks against individual member associations. This can be traced back to 1946 when the Soviets joined FIFA and were readily offered one of the vice-presidencies. The upshot was that it became practically impossible to take any disciplinary action against them. This meant that during the Hungarian uprising in 1956 FIFA had to officially ignore the complaints of Hungarian clubs and the Hungarian football association that their football grounds had been destroyed by Soviet tanks. When the Soviets marched into Czechoslovakia with the support of East Germany, Bulgaria, Poland and Hungary in August 1968, FIFA preferred to reason at arm's length. After Sir Stanley Rous received a letter from the Czechoslovakian football section begging him, in moving tones, to impose a sporting boycott on the aggressors, the general-secretary Helmut Käser reacted with the standard question: 'What is the current situation concerning football in your country...?'

The global perspective

The desire to stay clear of any disputes with the Soviet Union can also be explained by the fact that FIFA was taking its claim to represent the whole world more and more seriously during the 1950s and 1960s. The organisation wanted to exploit its membership potential to the full and was willing to pay almost any price to keep the Eastern bloc states on side. This policy should be seen against the background of a second fundamental change in world politics which FIFA was forced to face up to in the post-war period: the general acceptance of the principle of the nation state. During the post-war years more than one hundred former colonies, break-away territories and a wide variety of other political communities became independent nation states. All were founded on a similar pattern. The countries involved claimed their own sovereignty and the right to make their own laws within their own borders. They issued their own currency, organised postal services, set up their own police force and army to ensure law and

23

order at home and in their dealings with outside states. In short, the newly-founded countries set themselves up as equals in the world community of states. This principle was sanctioned by the United Nations, which had been set up in 1945 and which, despite its name, was not a league of nations but of states.

At first this global, egalitarian re-structuring simply confirmed FIFA in the adequacy of its own organisational principles. Equality between the states had been one of world football's fundamental priorities from the start. It had an additional positive spin-off in that there was now considerably more potential for enlisting new members. FIFA exploited this all the more comprehensively when nation states discovered that it was easier to become a member of FIFA than of the UN. While the latter waited until 1960 until ratifying its 'Declaration on the Granting of Independence to Colonial Countries and Peoples', FIFA persisted with its tradition of liberal door policies. In exceptional cases it also accepted football associations from independent political communities on condition that the national membership organisation of the state containing this community voted in favour of admission and put in a corresponding application. Among the countries which joined FIFA earlier than they joined the UN on this basis were Kenya, Lesotho, Mauritius, Nigeria, Sudan, Uganda, Cyprus, Malaysia, Singapore and Syria. Taken as a whole, in the twenty years following the end of the war, FIFA's membership grew by more than one hundred per cent – twice as quickly as in the first forty years of its existence. But there were also disadvantages to this successful expansion. One of these was the huge increase in the number of delegates at FIFA general assemblies. This had important effects. Within a few years there were few delegates who still knew each other personally, the more so because mortality rates among prominent representatives of the 'old guard' began to rise around the mid-1950s.

24 a 24 b

Increased anonymity combined with a huge variety of languages exacerbated the growing mutual mistrust which had been fuelled by the Cold War. This grew so bad that for a time the Soviets even brought along their own translator to the Congress and committee meetings. Moreover, there were continual outbreaks of petty jealousy, especially from the South Americans who felt disadvantaged by the special privileges that had been granted to the British and the Soviets.

Another negative effect of FIFA's successful global expansion was the increase in the number of members from politically dubious states. True, in the decades after the Second World War, Portugal, Spain, Greece, Brazil, Argentina, Uruguay, the Philippines and South Korea threw aside their authoritarian regimes in favour of democratic government. Outside the OECD states, however, very few states enjoyed a constitution. A study published in 1979 showed that, of the 119 states which were examined, only thirty-five fulfilled the criteria of 'democracy' and 'constitutional state'. The majority of world states were under a centrally-organised one-man rule. Given this fact, FIFA's global mission was tantamount to a deliberate renunciation of any policy to examine the political quality of mem-

25

ber associations. FIFA took no action against corrupt politicians who viewed football as an aid to power, as did the dictatorships in Brazil, Argentina and Uruguay. It turned a blind eye to the links between clubs and drug cartels, as in Colombia, and did nothing to prevent association presidents being appointed from above, as in the Eastern block countries. It even failed to criticise them in public. Against this background, the Federation's original policy of 'no politics' had gradually developed into a statement of political bankruptcy.

During the 1960s and 70s a new global movement committed to human rights formed and FIFA could no longer afford to ignore such questions, particularly because an increasing number of representatives from member associations were also in favour of new political and moral standards. One of the first conflicts to illustrate this development and arouse widespread public interest occurred in the autumn of 1973. It arose from the question of whether to go ahead with a World Cup qualifying match in Santiago de Chile between Chile and the Soviet Union which had been set for 21 November of that year. Two months before, there had been a military coup against the elected socialist government of Salvador Allende in Chile and since then several thousand Allende supporters had been held prisoner in the national stadium. Some of them had even been subjected to torture. When the Soviets refused to play in the so-called 'stadium of death' FIFA dispatched General Secretary Helmut Käser and Vice-President Abilio d'Almeida to Chile in order to inspect the situation at first hand.

Their joint report issued on 26 October 1973 confirmed that the national stadium was indeed still being used as an internment camp. Nonetheless, they recommended that the match be played as planned. They explained that a journalist who happened to be present at the time

26

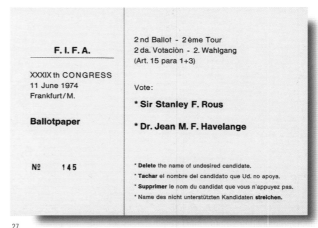

27

had been able to supply them with a first-hand account refuting any rumours of mass shootings in the stadium, and that General Pinochet's new defence minister had assured them that the stadium would be available once again for its original use at the appointed date. Not only was it difficult to persuade the international press to accept this decision, but the Soviets too remained unmoved and stood by their refusal to travel to Chile. The fact that they were then disqualified for not showing up and excluded from the 1974 World Cup was interpreted by them as evidence of an anti-communist plot within FIFA.

A further problem that illustrated the new political sensibilities was the question of how to treat the Football Association of South Africa (FASA), which organised football along racial lines. True, FASA's members did not consist solely of whites. It was however exclusively led by whites and teams were separated according to skin colour. The Confédération Africaine de Football (CAF) had annulled the association's membership as early as 1958 because it had refused to field a mixed-raced team for the African Nations Cup. Since then, representatives of the CAF and a few individual African member associations

had also been trying to have the South Africans suspended from FIFA. Their efforts finally proved successful in 1961. Nonetheless, FIFA granted the South African association one year in which to refute the charges of racism. During this time Sir Stanley Rous, the British president of FIFA, declared he would deal with the matter personally. In doing so, he made no attempt to conceal his own position. According to him, the FASA statutes in no way contravened FIFA's current ban on racial discrimination; it was rather the case that FASA based its organisation on the laws and customs of South Africa and that had to be accepted. In his report following a tour of South Africa in January 1963 he wrote: 'FIFA must not interfere with the internal affairs of any country. FIFA cannot be used as a weapon to force a government to change its internal sports' policy'. He refused to accept the alternative point of view that the grounds for discrimination were irrelevant when deciding whether any association had contravened the ban or not.

Rous's stance did not make him many friends, either among the Africans in FIFA or the representatives of the anti-apartheid movement, particularly since he was per-

26 While the military Junta turned stadiums into prisons, in Europe stadiums became the scenes of anti-Pinochet demonstrations. GFR v. Chile in West Berlin during the 1974 World Cup.

27 Rous or Havelange, British tradition or Developing Countries revivalism? Ballot for the second round of the FIFA presidential election. Frankfurt Congress 1974.

28 A handshake to mark the handing over of an important post. The Brazilian Havelange (right) replaces the Englishman Rous as the President of FIFA in 1974.

29 The victory was sought after and used by the Argentine Junta. Team captain Passarella offers the football used in the World Cup final to General Videla.

30 A disputed World Cup – a call to boycott the 1978 World Cup in Argentina.

28

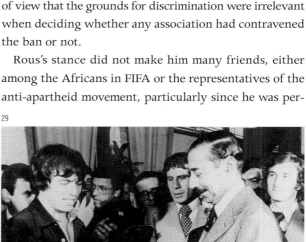

29

LIBER/AD

Argentina WM '78

30

fectly open in his personal assessment that South Africa's coloured footballers 'are happy with the relations which have been established.' In 1964 FASA was once again suspended from FIFA, this time for an indeterminate period. Ten years later, Rous was to pay the penalty for his views. Following an attempt to drum up support behind the scenes for his interpretation of the Statutes, in 1974, he was voted out of office at the FIFA congress in Frankfurt. The victorious new president was the Brazilian, João Havelange, who had been observing developments and had skilfully built the theme of apartheid into his election campaign. Havelange was helped to victory by a combination of votes from South America and Africa. Following a recommendation of the executive committee the South African association was finally excluded from FIFA at the 1976 congress in Montreal.

South Africa's case had brought national constitutions of football states irrevocably onto FIFA agenda's and strengthened the proponents of an enlightened pro-active

policy. But FIFA's internal arguments on such matters were far from settled. Just two years later they were re-ignited during the 1978 World Cup. When Argentina was awarded the tournament at the start of the 1970s the country was ruled by the elected president, Isabel Peron. In 1976 she was ousted by a coup which brought General Videla to power and his military dictatorship inherited the task of hosting the competition. Ultimately, Videla failed to realise his intention of winning over the world with the aid of football. Furthermore, the event not only did considerable damage to FIFA's image but also to that of its new president Havelange, who had agreed to appear with Videla before the eyes of the world. Although there were no boycotts of the final matches, in the majority of European countries there were vehement protests from left-wingers against the presentation of the World Cup in a land ruled by a military dictatorship. Television viewers all over the world were witness to the Dutch team declining to accept the General's congratulations as losing finalists.

31

FIFA as a global player

Since the 1980s there have been no more public scandals on such a scale. Under the presidency of João Havelange an anti-racist policy towards member organisations was integrated into the association's programme. Beyond that, under his successor Joseph S. Blatter, FIFA has instituted a policy to deal with racially motivated disturbances among spectators. Last but not least, close co-operation between the UN, UNESCO and the IOC has resulted in a consensus among the responsible bodies that the World Cup and other major tournaments will only be awarded to acceptable states in the future and that FIFA reserves the right, even at short notice, to withdraw its official consent if there are any unforeseen and serious changes in the political situation. This right was exercised in 1993 with Croatia on the occasion of the 41st international youth tournament and again in 1995 with Nigeria on the occasion of the Junior World Championship. In addition, FIFA

now scrupulously examines all membership applications and where necessary takes diplomatic action. It is now laid down as one of the firm criteria for acceptance, alongside the relevant association's political independence, that the state in question must be previously recognised by the United Nations. This practice came into being following the collapse of the Soviet Union and Yugoslavia.

Finally, in 1999, a National Associations Committee was set up to work for the interests of new candidates and current members. The specific reason for its formation was the question of how to distribute to member associations the massive income derived from the sale of broadcasting rights (see Chapter 12) and the concomitant need to control how the income was used. Since then the committee has extended its area of responsibilities. It now provides advice to member associations on how to use the money awarded to them to build up a modern, efficient system of administration, and also observes their elections. Furthermore, it intervenes in any attempt by governments to meddle in their affairs or when a member association falls into difficulties for any other reason. Like the United Nations, FIFA finances inspectors and inspections, the considerable costs being met from the recent massive source of income mentioned above.

FIFA's inspectors enable the organisation to gain a close and immediate impression of any developments in sporting politics, to try to influence matters in a pragmatic fashion and, where necessary, to threaten any association with sanctions or even suspension. Since most governments nowadays regard football as a matter of prestige such threats have proved extremely effective. All in all, during the period between 1999 and 2002 the National Associations Committee dealt with matters concerning the member associations of fifty-two countries. Most, but not by any means all, of these countries were smaller states from the developing nations and Eastern Europe. One of the inherent problems of any democratic umbrella organisation is its inability to exert influence on the political constitution of individual member associations. Here FIFA can now claim to be one of the few organisations today,

32

perhaps the only world organisation, which appears to be getting this under control.

By contrast, FIFA remains a long way from solving another of its inherent problems, the tendency of its members to form coalitions and factions. Such tensions arise from the relationships between FIFA's headquarters in Zurich and the confederations in each of the football continents. The confederations have mainly come into existence since the end of the Second World War and are modelled on the Confederación Sudamericana de Fútbol (CONMEBOL), which was set up in 1916. They are the Union des Associations Européennes de Football (UEFA, founded in 1954), the Asian Football Confederation (AFC, 1954), the Confédération Africaine de Football (CAF, 1957), the Confederation of North, Central American and Caribbean Association Football (CONCACAF, 1961) and the Oceania Football Confederation (OFC, 1966). All these bodies are indispensable in mobilising resources to regulate conflicts in world football. On the negative side they act on behalf of their own regional interests and attempt to push through their own particular agendas by using block voting and building inter-confederation coalitions. As early as the 1950s leading FIFA officials expressed fears that regionalising tendencies in world football, a 'natural' corollary to thriving global expansion, might also promote centrifugal forces and internal factions. By the end of the Havelange era it was clear that there was some substance to these fears. As FIFA's proactive development policies had encouraged African and Asian members in particular to articulate their own interests the Zurich headquarters found it increasingly difficult to enforce its viewpoint in conflicts with individual con-

FIFA AND POLITICAL PROBLEMS

federations. This shift in the balance of power was first felt to the full in a problem which arose in connection with the Israeli football association.

The state of Israel had been set up in 1948 and in the mid-1950s the Israel Football Association (IFA) applied to be taken into the European confederation. However, the Executive Committee responded that it would be more appropriate to allocate Israel to the Asian continent. At the start the Israelis were one of the best teams in the Asian Football Confederation. But from the 1960s onwards they were continually thwarted in their efforts to take part in international tournaments as a result of pressure from Islamic and communist states in Asia. This came to a head on 14 September 1974 when the Asian Football Confederation expelled Israel from its ranks on the grounds that member associations from more than fifteen states had refused to play against them, and that they therefore had no alternative. The Israel Football Association protested to FIFA and in May 1976 the Executive Committee stated that Israel's exclusion was not only a clear contravention of the ban on discrimination laid down in the FIFA Statutes but also that it contravened the statutes of the Asian Football Confederation. The Asian confederation was presented with an ultimatum to rescind the decision within thirty days or face suspension.

The AFC failed to revise its decision within the period of the ultimatum and FIFA failed to take any action, preferring not to carry out its threat. President João Havelange suggested to the Israel FA that it should voluntarily resign from the Asian confederation. If the Israelis were simply a direct member of FIFA this would make it easier in the long term for them to be accepted into the European confederation. The Israelis then learned from a newspaper report that Havelange thought they should consider joining the Oceania Football Confederation until this could be achieved. This implied that he expected them to fly half way round the world for an indefinite period of time in order to take part in World Cup qualifying rounds. Matters became all the more demoralising for the Israelis when, despite repeated pleas from the FIFA President and General Secretary, UEFA waited until 1986 before it slowly began to open itself up to the Israel Football Association. Membership was confined at first to the youth teams. Only after the collapse of the Soviet Union and the Eastern block states was UEFA able to accept the Israeli FA as a whole. The final decision was made in 1993, almost two decades after Israel's expulsion from the Asian Football Confederation.

To date, the Israel conflict remains unique, not least because geography is only one of many factors when deciding which confederation is the most appropriate for new members. However, the main cause of the conflict between FIFA and the confederations remains unsolved. It is in part fuelled by a subconscious antagonism on the part of the confederations towards the growing power the Zurich headquarters wields, but its heart can be found in the divergence of interests between UEFA, whose influence within world football has been systematically eroded by FIFA's deliberate

33

34

globalisation policies, and the growing predominance of the non-European confederations. Although European countries still make up sixty-three per cent of all registered football players and sixty-eight per cent of all the teams in the world and finance the organisation disproportionally, the egalitarian FIFA constitution means that they have no more voting power than the countless 'paupers' from the developing countries who can together make up a majority. Voting procedures are laid down according to countries and European members amount to no more than twenty-five per cent of the total. Unless it can come to a previous arrangement with the FIFA headquarters, the European federation is forced to co-operate with precisely those confederations whose influence they would prefer to curb, and this can only lead to unsatisfactory results.

In the run-up to the Presidential elections in 1998, when it put up its own president, Lennart Johansson, as a candidate, UEFA arranged an electoral alliance with CAF, the African confederation. But this proved ineffective because of the conflict of interests between the anglophone and francophone countries. Johansson lost the election and the new President Joseph S. Blatter, who had served as General Secretary under Havelange, continued with the policies set in motion by his predecessor. At the following presidential election in 2002 UEFA followed another strategy principally because Johansson refused to stand as a candidate again.

In the hope of being able to exercise some indirect influence many European football associations now supported the candidature of Issa Hayatou from Cameroon, the ruling president of CAF. But Hayatou also failed to get enough votes and Blatter won once more. This development has grown into a problem for FIFA insofar as all the presidential elections since 1974 had been overshadowed by rumours of corruption and vote-buying, rumours which have been eagerly taken up and exaggerated by the European media. Despite the fact that all the accusations have always eventually been withdrawn. FIFA's image has been considerably tarnished because, instead of making the headlines, news of the withdrawals is tucked away on the inside pages.

It is not possible to forsee how this power struggle will resolve itself – there are simply too many unpredicatble variables. However, if the Europeans cannot voluntarily accept FIFA's global development policy, conflict will only cease when the developing countries are able to match European standards in both sporting and financial terms. This itself depends on whether the contested development policies continue to have an effect.

One hundred years after its foundation FIFA has successfully developed strategies for dealing with global political problems. Precisely for this reason the World Football Federation will itself continue to be subjected to political scrutiny and debate in the future.

THE FUTURE OF FOOTBALL

The story of FIFA's one hundred years

follows the history of the century itself.

1 French supporters welcome the world. Opening match of the 1998 World Cup.

2 Poster to advertise the German bid to organise the 2006 World Cup.

3 Amongst bombs and reprisals. Palestinians children play football…

4 … with Israeli soldiers in Ramallah, 2002.

Conclusion

Born out of the enthusiasm of a group of volunteers, today FIFA is present in every country around the globe. It survived two World Wars and the Cold War, emerging even stronger than before. It adapted to changes in world politics following decolonisation, was able to understand the impact that television would have on the spread of football and took advantage of the development in air travel. The development of an international football competition was a founding aim of FIFA and, although it took twenty-five years to achieve it, the World Cup is now recognized as the premier global media event.

Countries will do everything possible to win the privilege of hosting the World Cup.

The history of the Federation is primarily that of the global passion for a game that established itself due to its simplicity and universality. Although modern football was born in England, it was the European players who developed the idea of creating an international federation to develop both the numbers of participants and relations between national football associations. The globalisation of FIFA was not without problems. From the very early days FIFA responded to queries from members about the interpretation of the rules and disagreements between associations about player transfers. The success of the

5 The Fair-Play flag displayed during the 1996 Futsal World Cup.

6 Buddhist monks watch the Cambodian league final in 1999.

World Cup also brought an increase in the interaction between international football, politics and diplomacy. FIFA's history can be divided into four distinct periods. The first phase lasted twenty-five years during which the organisation was established. FIFA consisted of a few voluntary directors who sought to assert themselves and govern football's international relations. Undermined by internal conflict and a difficult relationship with the British FA, FIFA had no headquarters or permanent staff and at this point was not in charge of any competition. Establishing the headquarters in Zurich, recognising professionalism, holding the first World Cup in 1930, and employing a full-time General Secretary all signalled the start of the second phase of FIFA's development, which was one of consolidation. FIFA sought to bring together associations from all over the world and to make the new World Cup centre stage in the sporting calendar. Despite the exit of the British and the refusal of the Russians to join, both of which limited FIFA's influence, the Federation was recognised in South America and continental Europe as the governing authority over the popular game of football.

In the years following the Second World War, FIFA entered a new phase, one of expansion. The return of the British and membership of Russia consolidated FIFA's international standing. De-colonisation in Africa and Asia brought many new members to the Federation which became a sort of United Nations, with the

Europeans at its heart, but increasingly in a minority. The creation of continental Confederations and the politics between these entities made the running of FIFA even more complicated. At this time, training for referees was launched in an attempt to harmonise interpretation of the rules. Football's global presence was consolidated by the television coverage of the World Cup, which at this time was still FIFA's only tournament.

The return of the People's Republic of China in 1980 was the pinnacle of this period of geographic expansion. From this point onwards FIFA would clearly govern world football and had more members than the United Nations. This also saw the start of an era of diversification and further globalisation. The quadrennial World Cup, which remains the jewel in the Federation's crown, is now only one of FIFA's competitions. In 1977, FIFA launched the World Youth Championships for under-20-year-olds, and would later create the under-17-years-old, women's and indoor football championships. With help from commercial partners, FIFA ran large development programmes, became involved in the training of the people who worked for national football associations and set up numerous humanitarian projects. The beginning of an open market for television rights and FIFA's use of marketing and merchandising increased revenues considerably. It also meant increased influence over the member associations.

5

6

7 Official reception in Frankfurt in honour of the German 2003 Women's World Cup winning team.

8 Swedish supporters celebrate the return of their players who were losing finalists in the 2003 Women's World Cup (Stockholm 2003).

9 Students in Peking watching the 1999 Women's World Cup Final between China and United States.

10 The use of art in football. 'The football-globe 2006 FIFA World Cup' in Frankfurt.

11 The return of football to Afghanistan. A match between Kabul United and an International Forces team, February 2002.

The Future

It is difficult for historians to look forward to the future, so FIFA's President was asked what general direction the policies of FIFA were likely to take.

First of all, FIFA must continue to foster that passion for the game that exists all over the globe. Football mainly attracts children, and it is there that the organization should concentrate its attention. Via the member associations and its development projects, FIFA should seek to offer every child the chance to play football. Before it became big business, football was a game, and when sponsorship and television rights are discussed this basic principle should not be forgotten. FIFA should seek to become more involved in providing children all over the world with pitches, equipment, qualified coaches and specialist medical advice. The Federation should also help national football associations participate in all competitions for young people which serve to strengthen understanding and communication. FIFA also needs to pay special attention to stop the international transfer of minors from Africa to European countries which is often little more than a trade in children. As in recent years, FIFA will continue to be involved with child aid programmes concerning such things as vaccination and medical care. It will also work with UNICEF against the exploitation of child workers.

The development of women's football is another priority for FIFA. For the most of its one hundred years FIFA has considered football an exclusively male sport. Twenty years ago women's football officially became part of FIFA and today there are many tens of millions of players, with a Women's World Cup attracting great support. The matches are high quality and the crowd, often sceptical at the kick off, are soon impressed. Television companies and sponsors should become more involved in the promotion of women's football, which is still not widely publicised. There is much work to be done to offer girls the same playing opportunities that boys have. Each association should have a department dedicated to women's football. At the heart of the governing authorities, too, women merit a more important role. Recently, FIFA created a Committee for Women's Football to manage the FIFA women's competitions. It is hoped that women can soon progress to governing positions within the Executive Committee and elsewhere within the Federation.

Following the success of the World Cup jointly hosted by Japan and Korea, the first in Asia, it is hoped that

7

8

9

10

11

12 Despite the war, a football match was played in Monrovia, the capital of Liberia in May 2002.

13 *Football the King,* oil on canvas by Hannes H. Wagner, 1974.

14 The footballer for the third millennium. Japanese robot developed by Sony in 1998.

15 Coca Cola advertisement in 2003. A merging of the drink and football.

16 Action from the match between Sweden and Australia, 1999 Women's World Cup.

in turn, Africa will be given the opportunity to organise a World Cup. The practice of only granting the World Cup to countries within the continents of Europe and South America should be replaced by a rotation system that includes all FIFA confederations. The last two Olympic football tournaments were won by Nigeria and Cameroon and show the progress that has been made in Africa since many of the countries gained independence. Development projects, some of which were the responsibility of Joseph Blatter in the 1970s, training of players, technical guidance, refereeing and infrastructure have all improved in leaps and bounds. During the last Confederation Cup in France, the Cameroon team showed the quality and vivacity of African football in the Final when France eventually beat them only after extra time.

Football also needs managers; the management of an association or a club has become very complicated and the era of volunteers fulfilling the role has passed. On the one hand, this is a shame, but it is important that trained managerial, legal, financial and economic personnel are employed within national football associations. FIFA has long funded training for referees, coaches and specialists in sports' medicine around the world. If the organisation is going to continue this work, then it must also seek to train management executives who are able to draw up a balance sheet, manage budgets and run competitions, while at the same time taking account of various factors regarding public safety and media management. FIFA will work towards the training of these specialists.

Finally, FIFA is the product of national associations, which means that the Federation should be ready to listen to its members and promote a policy of fair distribution of profits which will allow each association to develop according to need. To achieve this, FIFA must guarantee the autonomy of the associations but insist on openness about the use of the grants and participation in the development projects. The first Article in the Statutes of 1904 hoped to achieve the promotion and development of football around the world and now more than ever this objective is FIFA's primary goal for the century to come.

12

13

14

15

THE AUTHORS

Pierre Lanfranchi studied history at the University of Montpellier, Institut fuer Europaeische Geschichte (Mainz) and the European University Institute (Florence). As Research Fellow, he led the multi-disciplinary project on Sports Culture in Europe the EUI. Since 1993 he has been Professor at the International Centre for Sport History and Culture at De Montfort University Leicester. He is the author of several books and articles on football including *Les footballeurs professionnels des années trente à nos jours* (with Alfred Wahl) 1995, *Moving with the Ball* (with Matthew Taylor) 2001 and edited various collections on sport including *Sport Storia Ideologia* (1989), *Il Calcio e il suo Pubblico* (1992), *European Heroes* (with R. Holt and JA Mangan).

Christiane Eisenberg studied history and sociology at the University of Bielefeld (Germany) and taught at the University of Hamburg. Since 1998 she has been professor of British History at the Humboldt University in Berlin. She has worked extensively on the cultural history of Sport in Germany and on the comparative aspects of leisure in Britain and Germany. She is the author of numerous works on German Football History and edited a volume on the development of the game worldwide, *Fussball, Soccer, calcio* (1997) and an important monograph on the introduction of sports in Germany, *English Sports and deutsche Buerger: Eine Gesellschaftsgeschichte* (1999).

Tony Mason studied History at the University of Hull and taught at Edinburgh and Warwick. He has been since 1998 Professor at the International Centre for Sport History and Culture at De Montfort University Leicester. His pioneering work in the social history of football in Britain, *Association Football and English Society* (1980) has been followed by numerous works on modern sports including an edited volume *Sport in Britain: A social history* (1989), *Passion of the People? Football in South America* (1995) and a recent co-written monograph *Sport in Britain 1945-2000* with Richard Holt (2000).

Alfred Wahl studied History at the University of Strasbourg and directed the Centre for Contemporary History at the University of Metz. A recognised specialist of German history and the history of football in France, he is the author of several articles and three monographs, *Les archives du football* (1988), *Les footballeurs professionnels* (with Pierre Lanfranchi) (1995) and his *La Balle au pied histoire du football* (1990) has been translated in various languages and reprinted in 2000.

SOURCES

CHAPTER 1

• Collins, Tony *Rugby's Great Split: Class, Culture and the Origins of Rugby League Football*, London 1998.
• Goulstone, John, *Football's Secret History*, London 2001.
• Harvey, Adrian, An Epoch in the Annals of National Sport: Football in Sheffield and the Creation of Modern Soccer and Rugby, *International Journal of the History of Sport*, Vol. 18 (4), December 2001, pp. 53-87.
• Mason, Tony, *Association Football and English Society 1863-1915*, Brighton, 1980.
• Russell, David, "Sporadic and Curious": The Emergence of Rugby and Soccer Zones in Yorkshire and Lancashire c.1860-1914, *International Journal of the History of Sport*, Vol. 5 (2), September 1988.
• Williams, Graham, *The Code War : English Football Under the Historical Spotlight*, London 1994.

CHAPTER 2

• Andersson, Torbjorn, *Kung Fotboll. Den Svenska fotbollens Kulturhistoria fran 1800-talets slut till 1950*, Stockholm Symposion, 2002.
• Brüggemeier, Franz Josef (e.a) *Der Ball ist rund. Die Fussballaustellung*, Essen Klartext, 2000.
• Cocchi, Juan Carlos, *Cuatro cetros del fútbol mundial*, Buenos Aires: Master Fer, 1963.
• Delaunay, Pierre (e.a.), *Cent ans de football en* France, Paris, Atlas, 1986.
• Deutscher Fussball Bund, *Hundert Jahre DFB*, Berlin, Sportverlag, 1999.
• Eisenberg, Christiane (Ed.), *Fussball, Soccer, Calcio. Ein Englischer Sport auf seinem Weg um die* Welt, Munchen, DTV, 1997.
• Escobar Bavio, Ernesto, *El Futbol en el Rio de la Plata,* Buenos Aires, Frigerio, 1923.
• Federacion Peruana de Futbol, *75 anniversario*, FPF, Lima, 1997.

• NVB, *Het NVB Boek. Gdenkboek bijhed 40 jahrig Bestaan van den den Niedrlandschen Voetbalbond*, NVB, 1929.
• Papa, Antonio, Panico, Guido, *Storia sociale del calcio italiano*, Bologna, Il Mulino, 1993.
• Serra, Luciano, *Storia del calcio 1863-1963*, Bologna, Palmaverde, 1964.
• Wahl, Alfred, Les archives du football, sport et société en France (1880-1980), Paris, Gallimard, 1989.
• Wahl, Alfred, *La balle au pied. Histoire du football*, Paris, Gallimard, 1990.

CHAPTER 3

FIFA Archive
• *Bulletin Officiel de la FIFA*, 1904-1906.
• *World's Football*, 1, 16.4.1929, Historical notes.
• *World's Football*, 2, 15.5.1929, Notes sur la fondation de la FIFA.
• *World's Football*, 4, 23.7.1929, Historical notes: season 1905-1906.
• *World's Football*, 7, 15.10.1929, Disputes Committee, 1920.
• *FIFA Handbook*, 1927-1939.
• *Minutes*, 1922.
• *Official Communications of Commitee* 1911-1915.
• *Voetbal Almanach 1904*.
• *FIFA, 25ᶜ anniversaire 1904-1929*, FIFA, 1929.

Media
• *L'Auto*, Paris, 1904.
• *La Vie Sportive*, Bruxelles, 1904-1922.
• *Kicker*, Munich, 1920-1922.
• *Football Association*, Paris, 1919-1920.

CHAPTER 4

FIFA Archive
• Players : Kubala, Laszlo.
• Confederations : Conmebol 1949.
• Correspondence Rimet – Schricker 1950.
• Emergency Committee, Bruxelles 12 juin 1951.
• Executive Committee, Zurich 21 December 1950; Madrid 31 March 1951; Basel 16 August 1951; Zurich 21 June 1957.
• National Associations, Algérie (1962-83), Argentina 1949, 1950, Austria 1962, Bolivia 1950, Colombia1949, Costa Rica (1932-1973) 1951, Finland 1953, Italy 1951-1958, Mexico (1931-1967) 1949, 1954, 1955, Norway 1966, Peru 1949-1950, Thailand (1932-1983) 1956, USA (1965-1969) (1980-86).
• Suspension of players in Australia.
• Suspension of players in Hungary1957.

• Baumgartner, Leo, *The Little Professor of Soccer*, Sydney: New South Wales Marketing Productions, 1968.
• Castillo, Juan José, *Kubala: El futbol es mi vida*, Barcelona: Mundo Deportivo, 1993.
• Fernandez Santander, Carlos, *El futbol durante la guerra civil y el franquismo*, Madrid : San Martin, 1990.
• Garcia Candau, Julian, *Madrid-Barça: Historia de un desamor*, Madrid : Aguilar, 1996.

• Lanfranchi, Pierre, "Le football Sarrois de 1947 à 1952", *Vingtième siècle*, 26, 1990, 99 59-65.
• Mason, Tony, "The Bogota Affair", in J. Bale, J. Maguire (eds.), Glob*al Sports Arena*, London : Cass, 1994, pp. 39-48.
• Pelaez Restrepo, Hernan, *Nuestro futbol 1948-1976*, Bogota : Renteria 1976.
• Wahl, Alfred, Lanfranchi Pierre, *Les footballeurs professionnels des années trente à nos jours*, Paris: Hachette, 1995.

CHAPTER 5

FIFA Archive
Congress
• Amsterdam, 1928.
• Barcelone, 1929.
• Budapest 1930.

• *Commission d'Étude* 1928-1929.
• *Executive Commitee*, 1927-1930.

• *World's Football*, 23, 27.2.1931, Historical Notes on the institution of a World's Championship.

• Buero, R, *La organización de la Coupe du Monde. Negociaciones internationales*, Bruxelles, 1932.

THE CONSTRUCTION OF LARGE STADIUMS:
FIFA Archive
• National Associations, Grenada 1974-1976, Kazakhstan 1990, Kenya 1965-1969, Madagascar 1962, Malaysia 1957, Mauritius 1960, Singapore, 1976.

• Barassi, Ottorino, *Coppa del Mondo*, Rome : FIGC, 1934.
• Cocchi, Carlos Alberto, *Cuatros cetros de futbol mundial*, Buenos Aires : Master Fer, 1963.
• Dietschy, Paul, *Football et société à Turin 1900-1960*, Doctored thesis, Lyon II, 1997.
• FIFA, *Technical recommendations and Requirements for the Construction or Modernisation of Football Stadia*, Zurich : FIFA, 2000.
• Hill, Jeffrey, Varrasi, Francesco, « Creating Wembley : The construction of a National Monument », *The Sports Historian*, 17, 1997, 2, pp 28-43.
• Lanfranchi, Pierre, "Bologna : The team that shook the world", *International Journal of Sport History*, 8,1991, 3, pp 336-346.

• Leite Lopes, Sergio, "Le Maracana, cœur du Brésil", *Sociétés et représentations*, December 1998, pp. 129-140.
• Onofri, Nazario Sauro, Ottani Vera, *Dal Littoriale allo stadio. Storia per immaginidell'impianto sportivo bolognese*, Bologne: CCC, 1990.
• Randl, Christoph, « Das Fussballstadion : Ein Typus der moderner Architectur », in M. Herzog (ed.), *Fussball als Kultur phaenomenon*, Stuttgart, 2002, pp 179-196.
• Ray, Dutta, *Indian Football Association West Bengal Official Souvenir*, sl : IFA, 1953.
• Sheard, Rod, *Sports Architecture*, London : Spon, 2001.
• Tummers, Tijs, *Architectuur aan de zijlijn. Stadions en tribunes en Nederland*, Amsterdam: D'Arts, 1993.
• Varrasi, Franceso, *Economia politica e sport in Italia*, Florence: Fondazione Franchi, 1999.

CHAPTER 6

FIFA Archive
• Executive Committee, June 1957.
• Referees' Committee May, June 1929; November 1934, 1939; March 1949; October 1952; June 1965.
• Technical Development Committee, January 1966 Congress, May, June 1913 ; May 1923.
• Official Communications, July 1925.

Confederation Files
• African Football Confederation, October 1968.
• Asian Football Confederation, February 1970; August 1980.

National Association Files
• All India, March 1954.
• Burma, September 1954.
• Denmark, February, March 1938.
• Ghana, October 1960- March 1961.
• Hong Kong, 1956.
• Ivory Coast, 1970.
• Mali, July-August 1977.
• Netherlands, October 1979 ; December 1982; January 1983.
• Nigeria, October 1960-March 1961.
• Norway, December 1985.
• Turkey, July-August 1935.
• USA, August 1956; February 1969 ; 1970-1983.

FIFA Publications
• FIFA, *Football History, Laws of the Game, Referees*, FIFA, Zurich, 1986.

SOURCES

- FIFA, *Official Bulletin*, 10 June 1955 ;
24 December 1958, June 1960.
- *Football World*, December 1938,
January 1939, March 1939.
- *Laws of the Game,* 1999 e.d.
- *World's Football*, October 1929.

Secondary sources
- *FA News*, June 1957.
- Bellos, Alex, *Futebol : The Brazilian Way
of Life,* London 2002.
- Hay, Roy, 'Black (Yellow and Green)
Bastards: Soccer Refereeing in Australia ...',
Sporting Traditions, Vol. 5 (2), May 1999.
- Mason, Tony, *Passion of the People ?
Football in South America*, London, 1995.

CHAPTER 7

FIFA Archive
- Executive Committee, December 1990.
- Technical Development Committee, World.
- Cup Reports, 1966-2002.
- *Football World*, December 1938 ;
January, April 1939.

Secondary sources
- Archetti, Eduardo, *Masculinities, Football,
Polo and the Tango in Argentina,* Oxford
1999.
- Bellos, Alex, *Futebol: The Brazilian Way
of Life,* London 2002.
- Hobsbawm, Eric, *Nations and Nationalism
since 1780*, Cambridge 1990.
- Joy, Bernard, *Soccer Tactics,* London, 1956.
- Kuper, Simon, *Ajax, The Dutch, The War :
Football in Europe During the Second World
War,* London 2003.
- Lanfranchi, Pierre, Taylor, Matthew,
*Moving with the Ball: The Migration of
Professional Footballers*, Oxford, 2001.
- Mason, Tony, « Grandeur et déclin du
"Kick and Rush" anglais ou la révolte d'un
style », Helal, H., Mignon, P., (eds.)
Football, jeu et société, Paris 1999, pp. 47-64.
- Meisl, Willy, *Soccer Revolution,* London,
1955.
- Winner, David, *Brilliant Orange :
The Neurotic Genius of Dutch Football,*
London 2003.

CHAPTER 8

FIFA Archive
- Bulletin officiel de la FIFA, 1905.
- Comité consultatif des règles du jeu et
de l'arbitrage 1929.
- Comité exécutif, Londres, 26 juillet 1948.

Congress
- Congrès d'Amsterdam, 19-20 mai 1907.
- Congrès de Vienne, 7-8 juin 1908.
- Congrès de Paris, 24-28 mai 1924.
- Congrès d'Amsterdam, 25-26 mai 1928.
- National Associations Committee,
URSS 1951-55.
- Referee's Committee, Madrid
24 January 1958.
- Secrétariat général, 1952.
- Claremont, Henry, *Le Livre des sports
athlétiques et des jeux de plein air*, Paris :
Pierre Roger, 1909.
- Deutscher Fussball-Bund,
Deutsches Fussball-Jahrbuch 1920, Kiel :
DFB, 1920.
- Di Salvio, Alfredo Luis, *Antonio Ubaldo
Rattin, El Caudillo*, Buenos Aires :
ESBA, 2002.
- Ducret, Jacques, *Le Livre d'or du football
suisse*, Lausanne : L'Âge d'homme, 1994.
- Eisenberg, Christiane (ed.), *Fussball,
Soccer, Calcio. Ein Englischer Sport auf
seinem Weg um die Welt,* Munich : DTV,
1997.
- FIFA, *Football History Laws of the Game
Referees*, Zurich: FIFA, 1986.
- Gondouin, Charles, Jordan,
Le Football rugby – américain – association,
Paris : Lafitte, 1910.
- Lanfranchi, Pierre, Taylor, Matthew,
Moving with the Ball, Oxford :Berg, 2001.
- Lecocq, Jacques, *Football, ses conquêtes,
ses problèmes, sa technique*, Marcinelle
Charleroi, Dupuis, sd.
- Papa, Antonio, Panico Guido,
Storia sociale del calcio in Italia (1887-1945),
Bologne: il mulino, 1993.
- Schweickard, Wolfgang, *Die "Cronaca
calcistica". Zur Sprache der Fussballberich-
terstattung in italienischen* Sporttages-
zeitungen, Tuebingen : Niemeyer, 1987.
- Veisz, Arpad, Molinari, Aldo, *Il giuoco
del calcio*, Varese: Corticelli, 1930.
- Verdu, Vicente, *El futbol. Mitos,
ritos y simbolos*, Madrid :Allianza, 1980.
- Wagg, Stephen (ed.), *Giving the Game away.
Football, Politics & Culture on Five Continents,*
London: Leicester University Press, 1995.
- Wahl, Alfred, *Les Archives du football*,
Paris : Gallimard, 1989.

CHAPTER 9

Archives FA
- Executive Committee, March 1952 ;
November 1954; September 1955 ;
June 1956 ; December 1983 ; March 1988 ;
December 1990.
- Secretary's Report, 1952-53; 1954-55.
- Technical Development Committee,
January, May 1969, April 1970, August
1972.
- Congress, June 1954, July 1988.

Confederation Files
- African (CAF), July 1966,
January 1968.
- Asian (AFC), October 1975; October 1977 ;
September, October 1981; November 1983.

National Association Files
- Finland, September 1973.
- Netherlands, October 1972.
- Nicaragua, 1951-52.
- Norway, April 1972 ; November 1990.
- USA, October 1972.

FIFA Publications
- Activities Report, April 1986-March 1988.
- FIFA Official Survey, *The Big Count of
Football 2000 Worldwide* (Zurich, 2001).
- Women's World Cup Reports, 1991,
1995, 1999.

Secondary sources
- Brandle, Fabian, Koller, Christian,
*Goooal!!! Kultur und Sozialgeschichte des
modernen fussballs*, Zurich, 2002.
- *Special Magazine*, Addis-Ababa 2002.
- Williams, Jean, '*A Game for Rough Girls?'
A History of Women's Football in England*
London, 2004.

CHAPTER 10

FIFA Archive
- Executive Committee, June 1957 ;
February 1958 ; April 1959.

Secondary sources
- *Guardian*, 22 May, 14 June 2003.
- Amis, Martin *London Fields*, London, 1989.
- Barnes, Julian, *A History of the World*,
London, 1989.
- Bellos, Alex, *Futebol, The Brazilian
Way of Life*, London, 2002.
- Carr, J.L., *How Steeple Sinderby Wanderers
Won the FA Cup*, London, 1999.
- Chazaud, Pierre, *Art et football, Football*

and Art 1860-1960, Toulaud (France), 1998.
• Glanville, Brian, (ed.), *The Footballers'
Companion,* London, 1962.
• Hornby, Nick, *Sight and Sound,* Vol. 3 (5),
May 1993, p. 40
• Jenkins, Robin, *The Thistle and the Grail*
1954 ; 1983 edn. with introduction by
Cairns Craig.
• Preston, Tom, 'Art', Richard Cox,
Dave Russell and Wray Vamplew (eds.),
Encyclopedia of British Football
London 2002.
• Rogers, Byron, *The Last Englishman :
The Life of J.L. Carr,* London 2003.
• Russell, Dave, 'Literature,' Cox, Russell
and Vamplew above.
• Sillitoe, Alan, *The Loneliness of the Long
Distance Runner,* London 1959.
• Sylvester, David, 'Football and the Fine
Arts', *The Listener,* 29 October 1953, p. 736.
• Taylor, D.J., "Rally around your havens!"
Soccer and the Literary Imagination', *Perfect
Pitch,* Vol. 1 (1), 1997, pp. 77-99.
• Welsh, Irvine, *Trainspotting,* London 1993.
• Williams, Gordon M., *From Scenes Like
These* 1968.

CHAPTER 11

FIFA Archive
• Correspondence with National
Associations: Cameroun.
• Correspondence of Confederations:
Oceania Football Association.
• National Associations Committee, Protocol
22 March 2000; 26 October 2000.
• National Associations Committee: Bhutan
Football Association.
• Technical Committee, Montreal, 11 July
1976, Protocol.
• Technical Development Committee,
Session Nr. 18 of 27.8.1975, Agenda.
• Treffen du Technical Committee, London,
25 May 1965; Munich, 4. June 1966;
Londres, 9 July 1966; 5 July 1972.
• Futuro 1991-1993, The FIFA / Coca-Cola
World Football Development Programme:
Introduction.
• Futuro stage at Macão, 21-26 août 1991;
Népal, 18-23. September 1991;
Benin, 28 March-2 April 1992;
Togo, 8-13 April 1992;
Dominican Republic, 14. bis 19. September
1992;
Mozambique, 15-20 October 1992;
Guam, 22-27 September 1998.

Books and articles
• Anheier, Helmut /Nuno Themudo,
Führung und Management von
Internationalen Mitgliederorganisationen,
Christiane Franz/Annette Zimmer (Ed.*),
Zivilgesellschaft international. Alte und neue
NGOs,* Opladen (Leske & Budrich) 2002,
p. 303-325.
• Boli, John /George M. Thomas (Ed.),
*Constructing World Culture. International
Nongovernmental Organizations since 1875,*
Stanford (Stanford UP) 1999.
• Clark, Marie, Non-Governmental
Organizations and their Influence on
International Society, *Journal of
International Affairs,* 48/2, 1995, p. 507-524.
• Edwards, Michael /Alan Fowler, Introduc-
tion: Changing Challenges for NGO Mana-
gement, Edwards/Fowler (Ed.), *The Earthscan
Reader on NGO Management,* London
(Earthscan Publications) 2002, p. 1-12.
• Gareis, Sven Bernhard /Johannes Varwick,
*Die Vereinten Nationen. Aufgaben,
Instrumente und Reformen,* Opladen
(Leske & Budrich) 2002 (2ᵉ ed).
Gordenker, Leon /Thomas G. Weiss (Ed.),
NGOs, the UN, and Global Governance,
London (Lynne Rienner Publishers) 1996.
• Kistner, Thomas Geld und Medien,
Frankfurt (Fischer) 1998.
• Kuhn, Berthold /Jens Weinreich, Das
Milliardenspiel. Fußball, Zivilgesellschaften
aus der Perspektive der
Entwicklungsländer, Arnd Bauerkämper
(Ed.), *Die Praxis der Zivilgesellschaft.
Akteure, Handeln und Strukturen im
internationalen Vergleich,* Frankfurt/M.
(Campus) 2003, p. 391-413.
• Lindenberg, Marc /Coralie Bryant, *Going
Global. Transforming Relief and Development
NGOs,* Bloomfield/CT (Kumarian Press)
2001, p. 8-12.
• Monnington, T., Crisis Management in
Black African Sport, J.C. Binfield/John
Stevenson (Ed*),* Sport, Culture and Politics,
Sheffield (Sheffield Academic Press) 1993,
p. 113-128.
• Riordan, James, *Sport in Soviet Society.
Development of Sport and Physical Education
in Russia and the USSR,* Cambridge
(Cambridge UP) 1977.
• Salamon, Lester M., The Rise of the
Nonprofit, *Foreign Affairs* 73/4, 1994,
p. 109-122.
• Stirrat, R.L. /Heiko Henkel, The
Development Gift: The Problem of
Reciprocity in the NGO World, *The Annals
of the American Academy of Political and
Social Science* 554/1997 (Special Issue: The

Role of NGOs: Charity and Empowerment,
éd. V. Jude L. Fernando/Alan W. Heston),
London/New Delhi 1997, p. 66-80.
• Streeten, Paul, Nongovernmental
Organizations and Development,
*The Annals of the American Academy of
Political and Social Science 554/1997*
(Special Issue: The Role of NGOs :
Charity and Empowerment, éd. V. Jude
L. Fernando/Alan W. Heston), London/New
Delhi 1997, p. 193-210.
• Sugden, John /Alan Tomlinson, *FIFA and
the Contest for World Football. Who rules the
peoples' game?,* Cambridge (Blackwell) 1998.
• Sugden, John /Alan Tomlinson, *Great
Balls of Fire. How Big Money is Hijacking
World Football,* Edinburgh/London
(Mainstream Publishing) 1999.
• Take, Ingo, Neue Allianzpartner, *Politische
Ökologie 72/2001 (Sonderheft NGOs im
Wandel),* p. 34-36.
• Willetts, Peter, What is a Non-Governmental
Organization?, *UNESCO Encyclopedia of Life
Support Systems, Section 1: Institutional and
Infrastructure Resource Issues,* Article
1.44.3.7: Non-Governmental Organizations.
*http://www.staff.city.ac.uk/p.willetts/CS-
NTWKS/NGO-ART.HTM,* consulted
(14.11.02).

CHAPTER 12

FIFA Archive
• Auditor's Report 1955.
• Coca-Cola, 1980-1986.
• Executive committee, Paris, 17 November
1934 ; Madrid 31 March 1951.
• Emergency commitee,
Zurich, 5 December 1951.

Congress
• Amsterdam Congress, 25-26 May 1928,
Treasurers' report 1927-1928.
• Congrès de Séoul, 28 May 2002, Financial
Report.
• Correspondance Rous – Courte / Käser.
• Correspondance with Confederations,
UEFA 1955-1976.
• Finance Committee, 40.
• General Secretary's Report 1954 1955,
1958-59.
• Message of Sir Stanley Rous, April 1974.
• Referees' Committee, Madrid
24 January 1958.
• General Secretary, 1952.

• Andreff, Wladimir *Économie politique du
sport,* Paris: Dalloz, 1989.

SOURCES

• Bourg, Jean-François, *L'Argent fou du sport*, Paris : Table ronde, 1994.
• Cornu, Jean « un nouveau président », *Football Magazine*, July 1974, pp. 17-20.
• Problèmes économiques, 15 January 1997, Numéro monographique « Économie du sport »?
• Sloane, P.J:, "The Economics of Professional Football: The Football Club as a Utility Maximizer", *Scottish Journal of Political Economy*, 1971, pp. 121-146.
• Solberg, Gratton, C. "The Economics of TV Sports Rights: the Case of European Football", *European Journal of Sport Management*, 2000, 7, pp 68-98.
• Szymanski, Stefan, Kuypers, T., *Winners and Losers: The Business Strategy of Football*, London: Viking, 1999.
• Ziebs, Alexander, *Ist Erfolg kaeuflich? Analysen und Ueberlegungen zur sozialoekonimischen Realitaet des Berufsfussballs*, Muenchen: Utz, 2002.

FIFA Archive
• Marketing and Television Advisory Board – Agenda and Minutes (1984-2000/01).
• Media Committee – Agenda and Minutes (1968-2002).
• 45th FIFA Congress 1986, Report by the General Secretary for the period from May 1984 to March 1986.
• FIFA Media Office, 41.100 hours of 2002 FIFA World Cup™ TV coverage in 213 countries, in :

BBC Written Archives Centre
• R9/10/21; T14/3272; T14/3264/1.
• Baimbridge, Marc, Satellite Television and the Demand for Football: A Whole New Ball Game?, Andrew Zimbalist (Ed.), *The Economics of Sport*, t. 2, Cheltenham (Elgar) 2000, p. 237-253.
• Cairncross, Frances, *The Death of Distance. How the Communications Revolution will Change our Lives*, Boston/Mass. (Harvard Business School) 1997.
• Castells, Manuel, *Das Informationszeitalter I: Die Netzwerkgesellschaft,* Opladen (Leske & Budrich) 2001.
• Chisari, Fabio, *«Bringing the World Cup to You». Televising the 1966 Jules Rimet Cup*, M.A. Thesis Sports History and Culture, De Montfort University, Leicester 2001.
• Cowie, Eleanor /Vivien Marles, The Public and Sport, *BBC Broadcasting Research Findings* 7, 1980, p. 91-99.
• Diesbach, Martin, *Pay oder Free*-TV ? Zur Zulässigkeit der v *verschlüsselten Exklusivübertragung sportilicher Grosse-*

reignisse, Baden-Baden (Nomos), 1998.
• Drescher, Willibald, *Der Sport im Deutschen Rundfunk*, Diss. Berlin 1941.
• Fiske, John, *Television Culture*, London/New York (Routledge) 1987.
• Garhammer, Manfred, *Wie Europäer ihre Zeit nutzen. Zeitstrukturen und Zeitkulturen im Zeichen der Globalisierung*, Berlin (Edition Sigma) 1999.
• Guttmann, Allen, *Sports Spectators*, New York (Columbia UP) 1986.
• Hackforth, Josef, *Sport im Fernsehen. Ein Beitrag zur Sportpublizistik unter besonderer Berücksichtigung des Deutschen Fernsehens (ARD) und des Zweiten Deutschen Fernsehens (ZDF) in der Zeit von 1952-1972*, Münster (Regensberg) 1975.
• Hartmann-Tews, Ilse /Bettina Rulofs, Die Bedeutung von Geschlechterkonstruktionen in der Sportberichterstattung, in: Jürgen Schwier (ed.), *Mediensport. Ein einführendes Handbuch*, Hohengehren (Schneider) 2002, p. 125-150.
• Haynes, Richard, A Pageant of Sound and Vision: Football's Relationship with Television, 1936-1960, *The International Journal of the History of Sport* 15/1, 1998, p. 211-226.
• Heinemann, Klaus /Manfred Schubert, *Der Sportverein. Ergebnisse einer repräsentativen Untersuchung*, Schorndorf (Hofmann) 1994.
• Herman, Edward S. /Robert W. McChesney, *The global media. The new missionaries of global capitalism*, London/Washington (Cassell) 1997.
• Holt, Richard, *Sport and the British. A Modern History*, Oxford (Oxford UP) 1989.
• Horak, Roman /Matthias Marschik, *Vom Erlebnis zur Wahrnehmung. Der Wiener Fußball und seine Zuschauer 1945-1990*, Wien (Turia und Kant) 1995.
• Katz, Elihu /George Wedell, *Broadcasting in the Third World. Promise and Performance*, Cambridge/Mass. (Harvard UP) 1977.
• Kunczik, Michael /Astrid Zipfel, Mediengiganten in Lateinamerika: Globo und Televista, Nord-Süd aktuell. *Vierteljahreszeitschrift für Nord-Süd und Süd-Süd-Entwicklungen* 10/4, 1996, p. 768-779.
• Lanfranchi, Pierre /Stephen Wagg, Cathedrals in Concrete: Football in Southern Europe, Stephen Wagg (Ed.), *Giving the Game Away: Football, Politics and Culture on Five Continents,* Leicester (Leicester UP) 1995, p. 125-138.
• Laudisio Correa, Fabio /Guilherme Furst/Gustavo Oliveiro Vieira, *Crisis in*

Brazilian Football. Project Work for International Master in Management, Law and Humanities of Sport, DeMontfort University Leicester/SDA Università Bocconi Milano/Université de Neuchatel 2000/2001.
• Marschik, Matthias /Doris Sottopietra, *Erbfeinde und Haßlieben. Konzept und Realität Mitteleuropas im Sport*, Münster (Lit-Verlag) 2000.
• Mason, Tony, *Passion of the People? Football in South America,* London (Verso) 1995.
• Mason,Tony, *Sport in Britain*, Cambridge (Cambridge UP) 1988.
• Mellor, Gavin, The Genesis of Manchester United as a National and International 'Super Club' 1958-1968, *Soccer and Society* 1/2, 2000, p. 151-166.
• Miller, Toby /Geoffrey Lawrence/Jim McKay/David Rowe, *Globalization and Sport. Playing the World*, London (Sage) 2001.
• Reinboth, Gerhard, Italiener und der Rundfunk, *Welt-Rundfunk* 2/2, 1938, S. 147-151.
• Schildt, Axel, *Moderne Zeiten. Freizeit, Massenmedien und « Zeitgeist » in der Bundesrepublik der 50er Jahre*, Hamburg (Christians) 1995.
• Seifart, Horst, Sport im Fernsehen, *Die Gründerjahre des Deutschen Sportbundes. Wege aus der Not zur Einheit,* Schorndorf (Hofmann) 1990, p. 209-215.
• Shadwell, Arthur, England, *Deutschland und Amerika. Eine vergleichende Studie ihrer industriellen Leistungsfähigkeit (Industrial efficiency)*, Berlin (C. Heymann) 1908.
• Steinitz, Kurt v., Rundfunksender in Südamerika, *Welt-Rundfunk* 2, 1938, cahier 6. p. 408-499.
• Szymanski, Stefan, Sport and Broadcasting. Paper presented at the IEA on 18 October 2000, London 2000 *(*www.ms.ic.ac.uk/Stefan/IEA.pdf - consulted 23.10.2002).
• Tunstall, Jeremy, *The media in Britain*, New York (Columbia UP) 1983.
• Wagenführ, Kurt, Zum englisch-italienischen Rundfunkkrieg, *Welt-Rundfunk* 2, 1938, p. 151-155.
• Wagner, Bernd, Kulturelle Globalisierung. Von Goethes « Weltliteratur » zu den weltweiten Teletubbies, *Aus Politik und Zeitgeschichte* B 12, 2002, p. 10-18.
• Whalen, David, Communications Satellites: Making the Global Village Possible, *http://www.hq.nasa.gov/office/ pao/History/ satcomhistory.html* consulted le 22.9.2002).

• Whannel, Garry, The unholy alliance: notes on television and the remaking of British sport 1965-85, *Leisure Studies* 5, 1986, p. 129-145.
• Wheen, F., *Television,* London (Century Publishing) 1985.
• Zerlang, Martin, Artikel «Entertainment», *International Encyclopaedia of the Social and Behavioral Sciences,* Edit.: v. Neil J. Smelser/Paul Baltes, vol.. 7, Amsterdam (Elsevier) 2001, p. 4540-4545.

CHAPTER 13

FIFA Archive
• Marketing and Television Advisory Board – Agenda and Minutes (1984-2000/01).
• Media Committee – Agenda and Minutes (1968-2002).
• 45th FIFA Congress 1986, Report by the General Secretary for the period from May 1984 to March 1986.
• FIFA Media Office, 41.100 hours of 2002 FIFA World Cup[TM] TV coverage in 213 countries,

BBC Written Archives Centre
• R9/10/21; T14/3272; T14/3264/1.
• Baimbridge, Marc, Satellite Television and the Demand for Football: A Whole New Ball Game ?, Andrew Zimbalist (Ed.), *The Economics of Sport*, t. 2, Cheltenham (Elgar) 2000, p. 237-253.
• Cairncross, Frances, *The Death of Distance. How the Communications Revolution will Change our Lives*, Boston/Mass. (Harvard Business School) 1997.
• Castells, Manuel, *Das Informationszeitalter I: Die Netzwerkgesellschaft,* Opladen (Leske & Budrich) 2001.
• Chisari, Fabio, *«Bringing the World Cup to You». Televising the 1966 Jules Rimet Cup,* M.A. Thesis Sports History and Culture, De Montfort University, Leicester 2001. -TV oder Free-TV? Zur Zulässigkeit
• Cowie, Eleanor /Vivien Marles, The Public and Sport, *BBC Broadcasting Research Findings* 7, 1980, p. 91-99.
• Diesbach, Martin, *Pay oder Free-TV ? Zur Zulässigkeit der v verschlüsselten Exklusivübertragung sportilicher Grossereignisse,* Baden-Baden (Nomos), 1998.
• Drescher, Willibald, *Der Sport im Deutschen Rundfunk*, Diss. Berlin 1941.
• Fiske, John, *Television Culture,* London/New York (Routledge) 1987.
• Garhammer, Manfred, *Wie Europäer ihre Zeit nutzen. Zeitstrukturen und Zeitkulturen im Zeichen der Globalisierung*, Berlin (Edition Sigma) 1999.
• Guttmann, Allen, *Sports Spectators*, New York (Columbia UP) 1986.
• Hackforth, Josef, *Sport im Fernsehen. Ein Beitrag zur Sportpublizistik unter besonderer Berücksichtigung des Deutschen Fernsehens (ARD) und des Zweiten Deutschen Fernsehens (ZDF) in der Zeit von 1952-1972*, Münster (Regensberg) 1975.
• Hartmann-Tews, Ilse /Bettina Rulofs, Die Bedeutung von Geschlechterkonstruktionen in der Sportberichterstattung, in: Jürgen Schwier (ed.), *Mediensport. Ein einführendes Handbuch*, Hohengehren (Schneider) 2002, p. 125-150.
• Haynes, Richard, A Pageant of Sound and Vision: Football's Relationship with Television, 1936-1960, *The International Journal of the History of Sport* 15/1, 1998, p. 211-226.
• Heinemann, Klaus /Manfred Schubert, *Der Sportverein. Ergebnisse einer repräsentativen Untersuchung*, Schorndorf (Hofmann) 1994.
• Herman, Edward S. /Robert W. McChes*ney, The global media. The new missionaries of global capitalism*, London/Washington (Cassell) 1997.
• Holt, Richard, *Sport and the British. A Modern History*, Oxford (Oxford UP) 1989. Horak, Roman /Matthias Marschik, *Vom Erlebnis zur Wahrnehmung. Der Wiener Fußball und seine Zuschauer 1945-1990*, Wien (Turia und Kant) 1995.
• Katz, Elihu /George Wedell, *Broadcasting in the Third World. Promise and Performance*, Cambridge/Mass. (Harvard UP) 1977.
• Kunczik, Michael /Astrid Zipfel, Mediengiganten in Lateinamerika : Globo und Televista, Nord-Süd aktuell. *Vierteljahreszeitschrift für Nord-Süd und Süd-Süd-Entwicklungen* 10/4, 1996, p. 768-779.
• Lanfranchi, Pierre /Stephen Wagg, Cathedrals in Concrete: Football in Southern Europe, Stephen Wagg (Ed.), *Giving the Game Away: Football, Politics and Culture on Five Continents,* Leicester (Leicester UP) 1995, p. 125-138.
• Laudisio Correa, Fabio /Guilherme Furst/Gustavo Oliveiro Vieira, *Crisis in Brazilian Football. Project Work dans le cadre de l'International Master in Management, Law and Humanities of Sport,* DeMontfort University Leicester/SDA Università Bocconi Milano/Université de Neuchatel 2000/2001.
• Marschik, Matthias /Doris Sottopietra, *Erbfeinde und Haßlieben. Konzept und Realität Mitteleuropas im Sport*, Münster (Lit-Verlag) 2000.
• Mason, Tony, *Passion of the People ? Football in South America,* London (Verso) 1995.
• Mason,Tony, *Sport in Britain*, Cambridge (Cambridge UP) 1988.
• Mellor, Gavin, The Genesis of Manchester United as a National and International 'Super Club' 1958-1968, *Soccer and Society* 1/2, 2000, p. 151-166.
• Miller, Toby /Geoffrey Lawrence/Jim McKay/David Rowe, *Globalization and Sport. Playing the World*, London (Sage) 2001.
• Reinboth, Gerhard, Italiener und der Rundfunk, *Welt-Rundfunk* 2/2, 1938, S. 147-151.
• Schildt, Axel, *Moderne Zeiten. Freizeit, Massenmedien und «Zeitgeist» in der Bundesrepublik der 50er Jahre*, Hamburg (Christians) 1995.
• Seifart, Horst, Sport im Fernsehen, *Die Gründerjahre des Deutschen Sportbundes. Wege aus der Not zur Einheit,* Schorndorf (Hofmann) 1990, p. 209-215.
• Shadwell, Arthur, England, *Deutschland und Amerika. Eine vergleichende Studie ihrer industriellen Leistungsfähigkeit (Industrial efficiency)*, Berlin (C. Heymann) 1908.
• Steinitz, Kurt v., Rundfunksender in Südamerika, *Welt-Rundfunk* 2, 1938, cahier 6. p. 408-499.
• Szymanski, Stefan, Sport and Broadcasting. Paper presented at the IEA on 18th October 2000, London 2000 *(*www.ms.ic.ac.uk/Stefan/IEA.pdf– consulté le 23.10.2002).
• Tunstall, Jeremy, *The media in Britain,* New York (Columbia UP) 1983.
• Wagenführ, Kurt, Zum englisch-italienischen Rundfunkkrieg, *Welt-Rundfunk* 2, 1938, p. 151-155.
• Wagner, Bernd, Kulturelle Globalisierung. Von Goethes «Weltliteratur» zu den weltweiten Teletubbies, *Aus Politik und Zeitgeschichte* B 12, 2002, p. 10-18.
• Whalen, David, Communications Satellites : Making the Global Village Possible, *www.hq.nasa.gov/ office/pao/History/satcomhistory.html* consulté le 22.9.2002).
• Whannel, Garry, The unholy alliance: notes on television and the remaking of British sport 1965-85, *Leisure Studies* 5, 1986, p. 129-145.
• Wheen, F., *Television, London* (Century Publishing) 1985.

SOURCES

• Zerlang, Martin, Artikel «Entertainment», *International Encyclopaedia of the Social and Behavioral Sciences*, Edit.: v. Neil J. Smelser/Paul Baltes, vol.. 7, Amsterdam (Elsevier) 2001, p. 4540-4545.

CHAPTER 14

FIFA Archive
Congress : 1904-1939
• Correspondence Schricker – Rimet.
• Correspondence Schricker – Seeldrayers.
• Correspondence Schricker – Andrejevic.
• *FIFA Handbook, 1937.*
• *Official Communications* (1924-1929).
• *World's Football*, 1-16 (1929-1938).

• Deutscher Fussball Bund, *Hundert Jahre DFB*, Berlin, Sportverlag, 1999.
• Devoto, Beto, *Cien Anos con el futbol*, Buenos Aires, Manrique Zago, 1993.
• Ducret, Jacques, *Le livre d'or du football suisse*, Lausanne, L'Age d'homme, 1994.
• Goksøyr, Matty, Olstad, Finn, *Fotball!* Oslo, Norges Fotballforbund, 2002.
• Heinrich, A. "Ruecksichtslos deutsch,. Peco Bauwens, das Fachamt Fußball und die FIFA, *Sport Zeiten*, 2, 2002, p. 39-52
• Mason, Tony, *Passion of the People? Football in South America*, London, Verso, 1995.
• Horak, Roman, Maderthaner, Wolfgang, *Mehr als ein Spiel. Fussball und populare Kultur in Wien der Moderne*, Wien, Locker, 1997.
• Meisl, Willy, *Soccer Revolution*, London Panther, 1957.
• Murray, Bill, *Football. A History of the World Game*, Aldershot, Scholar Press, 1994.
• Riordan, James, *Sport in Soviet Society. Development of Sport and Physical Education in Russia and the USSR*, Cambridge, Cambridge UP, 1977.
• National Associations Committee, Agenda - Minutes, 1999-2002.
• Correspondence with National Associations – Israel 1973-1996; Hungary, Box 1: 1937-1965; Germany: Box GER (FRG) 1955-61; China Popular Republic 1952-1986; Denmark; Norway; Popular Republic of Korea 1955 ff.; Russia/USSR 1923-1983; Sweden 1939-2001; Czechoslovakia, Box 1 : 1939-1988; South Africa 1951-1994
• Correspondence with Confederations - AFC 1971-1976, 1977-1980.
• Correspondence Schricker-Rimet 1946 (box Members of the Executive Committee – Persoanl Dossier, M. Jules Rimet).
• Country files – FIFA General Secretary – Palestine Football Association (1923-1973).
• ExCo – Report of the meeting in Moscow, 21./22.6.1957; Report of the meeting in Rome, 6.11.1974.
• FIFA/UEFA General Correspondence (1987-1991).
• 25th General Congress 1946, Minutes; 41st FIFA Congress in Buenos Aires, Minutes, 20.5.1978; 48th Congress 1992, Zurich. Activity Report [of the General Secretary] April 1990-March 1992.
• Minutes of the Extraordinary Congress held on 14th and 15th November 1953, pp. 6-7.
• 55.5 Affaires des Joueurs.
• Box Individual ExCo members, folder Sir Stanley Rous.
• Rapports de visite du Président et autres : 1963-1969.
• World Cup 1974 Germany: Chile-USSR.
• FIFA-Conference on Racism, Buenos Aires 6 July 2001, Zürich (FIFA) 2001.
• 'The big count' in: 52nd FIFA Congress, 4./5. Aug. 2000, Zürich, Rapport d'activité Avril 1998-avril 2000.

Secondary sources
• Arbena, Joseph L., Generals and *Goals. Assessing the Connection between the Military and Soccer in Argentina*, The *International Journal of the History of Sport* 7, 1990, No. 1, p. 120-130.
• Archetti, Eduardo, Argentinien, Christiane Eisenberg (Ed.), *Fußball, Soccer, Calcio*, op. cit. p. 149-171.
• Chiu, Hungdah, Taiwan and the United Nations, Martin Ira Glassner (Ed.), *The United Nations at Work*, Westport/CT (Praeger) 1998, p. 161-170.
• Darby, Paul, Africa, The FIFA Presidency and the Governance of World Football 1974, 1998 and 2002, in: *Moving Bodies* 1, 2003, p. 47-62.
• Darby, Paul, *Africa, Football and FIFA. Politics, Colonialism and Resistance*, London (Cass) 2002.
• Goksøyr, Matty /Finn Olstad, *Fotball!* Oslo (Norges Fotballforbund) 2002, p. 309-311.
• Linz, Juan J., *Totalitäre und autoritäre Regime*, Berlin (Berliner Debatte Wissenschaftsverlag) 2000.
• Meyer, John W. /John Boli/George M. Thomas/Francisco O. Ramirez, World Society and the Nation State, *American Journal of Sociology* 103, 1997, S. 144-181.
• Murray, Bill, *Football. A History of the World Game*, Aldershot (Scholar Press) 1994.
• Pfetsch, Frank R., *Internationale Politik*, Stuttgart (Kohlhammer) 1994 (2ᵉ édit.).
• Strang, David, From dependency to sovereignty: an event history of decolonization 1870-1987, *American Sociological Review* 55, 1999, p. 846-860.
• Sugden, John /Alan Tomlinson, *FIFA and the Contest for World Football. Who rules the peoples' game?*, Cambridge (Blackwell) 1998.
• Sugden, John /Alan Tomlinson, Football, *Ressentiment and Resistance in the Break-up of the Former Soviet Union*, Culture, Sport, Society 3/2, 2000, p. 89-108.

PICTURE CREDITS

Foreword FIFA
Introduction ullstein bild

CHAPTER 1
1 H. P. Egede, Beschryving van Oud-Groenland , Delft 1746,
Courtesy UB Basel
2 Milwaukee Public Museum MPM 54238/20186
3 National Archaelogical Museum, Athens object inv. n° 873
4 The Trustees of The British Museum
5 Germanisches Nationalmuseum Nürnberg, Inv.-Nr. HS 22474
6 Giovani de' Bardi, Memorie del Calcio Fiorentino. Tratte da diverse scritture
(1st ed. 1580), 4th ed., Florence, 1688. Reproduced from the original held by
the Department of Special Collections of the University Libraries of Notre
Dame, IN, USA
7 FIFA Museum Collection/National Football Museum of Preston (NFMP)
8 & 9 Sportmuseum Schweiz, Basel
10 Breiz-Izel ou Vie des Bretons de l'Armorique. Texte d'Alexandre Bouët,
dessins d'Olivier Perrin (1835)
11 Breiz-Izel ou Vie des Bretons de l'Armorique. Texte d'Alexandre Bouët,
dessins d'Olivier Perrin (1835)
12 & 13 FIFA Museum Collection/NFMP
14 Bodleian Library, University of Oxford, Douce Prints E.2.1. Item 191
15 FIFA Museum Collection/NFMP
16 The Graphic (8 Jan 1870) Courtesy Zentralbibliothek Zurich
17 FIFA Museum Collection/NFMP
18 > 20 FIFA Library
21 The Illustrated Sporting and Dramatic News (1883),
Mary Evans Picture Library
22 The Book of Football (1900), Mary Evans Picture Library
23 FIFA Museum Collection/NFMP
24 The Book of Football (1901), Mary Evans Picture Library
25 FIFA Museum Collection/NFMP
26 Hulton Archive
27 The Graphic (24 Feb. 1872), Courtesy UB Basel
28 FIFA Museum Collection/NFMP
29 FIFA Museum Collection/NFMP
30 FIFA Museum Collection/NFMP
31 Illustrated London News (5 May 1923), Courtesy UB Basel
32 Illustrated London News (27 Apr 1901), Courtesy UB Basel
33 & 34 Hulton Archive
35 Courtesy F. Brändle / C. Koller
36 FIFA Museum Collection/NFMP

CHAPTER 2
1 DHM Berlin
2 Fédération Française de Football (FFF)
3 Union Royale Belge des Sociétés de Football Association (URBSFA/KBVB)
4 Pan Savidis, Leukoma ton en Athenais B' Diethnon Olympiakon Agonon
1906, Athens 1907. Courtesy: bibliothèque du Musée Olympique de Lausanne.
5 Österreichischer Fussball-Bund (OFB)
6 Leipziger Illustrirte Zeitung, May 1892, Courtesy Zentralbibliothek Zurich
7 Archivo general de la Nacion, Buenos Aires
8 FIFA Library
9 Private Collection Richard Pitcairn-Knowles Gallery, Sevenoaks, Kent UK
10 Hulton Archive
11 Sporting and Dramatic News 1903. Courtesy UB Basel
12 Mary Evans Picture Library
13 FFF
14 Copyright CIO/Musée Olympique
15 & 16 A. A. Artis, Cincuenta Anos del C. de F. Barcelona 1899-1949,
Barcelona 1949, FIFA Library
17 FFF
18 DHM Berlin
19 J. Elias y Juncosa, Les Sports. Football Associacion,
Barcelona, n.d., FIFA Library
20 Collection privée.
21 Der Kicker March 1931. Courtesy UB Leipzig Sportwissenschaft.
22 T. Mazzoni, Historia do Futebol no Brasil, Sao Paulo 1950, FIFA Library
23 Collection Sir Hamilton Bruce Lockhart, with the permission
of the Trustees of the National Library of Scotland.
24 T. Mazzoni, Historia do Futebol no Brasil, Sao Paulo 1950, FIFA Library
25 The Fifth Olympiad. The Official Report of the Olympic Games
of Stockholm 1912, Stockholm 1913, FIFA Library
26 Courtesy Library BASPO Bundesamt für Sport Magglingen CH
27 Das Fussballspiel, Zürich 1910, FIFA Library
28 Courtesy: Canadian Soccer Hall of Fame
29 FIFA Archive
30 The Fifth Olympiad. The Official Report of the Olympic Games
of Stockholm 1912, Stockholm 1913, FIFA Library
31 La Vie au Grand Air, 1905. Courtesy Library BASPO
32 The Fifth Olympiad. The Official Report of the Olympic Games of Stockholm

1912, Stockholm 1913, FIFA Library
33 J. Wagner/A. Eichenberger, Olympische Spiele Stockholm, Zürich 1912,
Courtesy Zentralbibliothek Zürich

CHAPTER 3
La Vie au Grand Air, 1914. Courtesy Library BASPO
1 > 9 FIFA Archive
10 FIFA Museum Collection/NFMP
11 E. Seybold, Olympische Spiele 1912 Stockholm, München (n.d.).
Courtesy Library Olympic Museum
12 Courtesy BASPO
13 FIFA Museum Collection/NFMP
14 FFF
15 Copyright CIO/Musée Olympique
16 Luxemburger Erziehungs- und Sportministerium,
Abteilung Freizeitsport und Sportarchiv (Archiv)
17 FIFA Archive
18 Museo del calcio, Firenze.
19 > 23 FIFA Archive
24 FFF
25 Courtesy UB Leipzig Sportwissenschaft
26 > 30 FIFA Archive
31 AFP
32 Courtesy FFF / UB Leipzig Sportwissenschaft
33 FIFA Archive
34 Schweizerischer Fussballverband (SFV)
/ Association Suisse de Football (ASF)

CHAPTER 4
1 & 2 FIFA Archive
3 & 4 Archivo General de la Nacion, Buenos Aires
4 & 5 FIFA Archive
6 & 7 Archivo General de la Nacion, Buenos Aires
8 Millonarios. 50 años de gloriosa historia, Bogota 1996
9 & 10 FIFA Archive
11 Millonarios. 50 años de gloriosa historia, Bogota 1996
12 Museo del calcio, Firenze
13 Hulton Archive
14 FIFA Archive
15 © Manel Manoral
16 AFP/MARCA
17 AFP
18 FIFA Library
19 AFP/MARCAMEDIA
20 Carl und Liselott Diem-Archiv Köln (CuLDA)
21 a & b FIFA Library
22 FIFA Archive
23 FIFA Magazine 1993
24 > 27 FIFA/Intercarto

CHAPTER 5
1 Hulton Archive
2 Fussball. Illustrierte Sportzeitung 1924, Courtesy DB Leipzig
3 Uruguay. Campeon del Mondo, 1931, FIFA Library
4 Der Sportbericht 1928, Courtesy UB Leipzig Sportwissenschaft
5 Copyright CIO/Musée Olympique
6 AFP
7 FIFA Library
8 FFF
9 Fussball. Illustrierte Sportzeitung 1924, Courtesy DB Leipzig
10 Uruguay. Campeon del Mondo, 1931, FIFA Library
11 FIFA Handbook 1931/ FIFA Library
12 FFF
13 Presse Sports
14 FIFA Library
15 & 16 Coppa del Mondo. Cronistoria del campionato di calcio,
1936, FIFA Library
17 FIFA Archive
18 FIFA Library
19 All Sport/Stanley Chou/FIFA Archive
20 DHM Berlin
21 AFP
22 AFP
23 J. Wagner/A. Eichenberger, Olympische Spiele Stockholm,
Zürich 1912, Courtesy Zentralbibliothek Zürich
24 FIFA Handbook 1928-29, FIFA Library
25 Hulton Archive
26 FIFA Archive
27 & 28 Coppa del Mondo. Cronistoria del campionato di calcio,
1936, FIFA Library
29 Programma ufficiale Campionato del Mondo 1934, FIFA Archive

30 Coppa del Mondo. Cronistoria del campionato di calcio, 1936, FIFA Library
31 FIFA Archive
32 IVe Campeonato Mundial de Futbol 1950, FIFA Archive
33 DHM Berlin
34 Hulton Archive
35 SFV/ASF
36 picture-alliance/dpa
37 Onze Mondial/A. Gadoffre/FIFA Archive
38 D. Hoffmann/FIFA Archive
39 DFB
40 FIFA Archive
41 Congopress/H. Goldstein/FIFA Archive
42 Agence TempSport/Christian Liewig/FIFA Archive

CHAPTER 6
1 FIFA Museum Collection/NFMP
2 DHM Berlin
3 > 6 FIFA Archive
7 Leemage, Paris
8 > 10 FIFA Archive
11 ullstein bild
12 A. Paul Weber-Museum Ratzeburg, © ProLitteris, 2004 8033 Zürich
13 AFP
14 Popperfoto/David Joiner/FIFA Archive
15 ullstein bild
16 > 19 FIFA Archive
20 AFP
6 > 21 Copyright CIO/Musée Olympique
22 DHM Berlin
23 > 25 FIFA Archive
26 Hulton Archive
27 UPI/FIFA Archive
28 > 30 ullstein bild
31 Keystone/Kim Jae-Hwan
32 picture-alliance/dpa/Matthew Ashton

CHAPTER 7
1 FIFA Library
2 Popperfoto/FIFA Archive
3 Popperfoto/Fresco/FIFA Archive
4 Chung Sung-Jun/Getty Images
5 The Illustrated Sporting and Dramatic News (Jan. 1898). Courtesy UB Basel
6 Archivo General de la Nacion, Buenos Aires
7 UB Leipzig Sportwissenschaft
8 AFP
9 Pressefoto VOTAVA
10 Der Kicker (25 March 1930). Courtesy UB Leipzig Sportwissenschaft
11 SFV/ASF
12 AFP
13 Fussball. Illustrierte Sportzeitung (30 Oct. 1924).
Courtesy UB Leipzig Sportwissenschaft
14 FIFA Library
15 Archivo general de la Nacion, Buenos Aires
16 CuLDA
17 F. Alonso de Caso, Fútbol, Madrid 1924/FIFA Library
18 FIFA Archive
19 & 20 CuLDA
21 BIPPA/FIFA Archive
22 AFP
23 picture-alliance/dpa/Heidtmann
24 & 25 FIFA Archive
26 ullstein bild/Horstmüller
27 FIFA Archive
28 picture-alliance/dpa/Schnörrer
29 FIFA Archive
30 WEREK /FIFA Archive
31 ullstein bild/Klaus Schlage
32 Thomas Sports/Thomas/FIFA Archive
33 Action Image/FIFA Archive
34 FIFA Archive
35 picture-alliance/dpa/Roberto Schmidt

CHAPTER 8
1 & 2 FIFA Library
3 Indian Football Association West Bengal,
Official Souvenir Book 1953/FIFA Library
4 > 11 FIFA Library
12 > 16 FIFA Archive
17 FIFA Library
18 > 22 FIFA Archive
23 W. Meisl, Soccer Revolution (1955)/FIFA Library

CHAPTER 9

1 Bildbyran/Bjoern Tilly/FIFA Archive
2 Bundesarchiv Koblenz/Zentralbild/Berg 24 142/2 N.
3 Ruskii Sport (7 Aug. 1911). Collection Sir H. B. Lockhart,
with the permission of the Trustees of the National Library of Scotland
4 FIFA Museum Collection/NFMP
5 Courtesy Zentralbibliothek Zurich
6 & 7 FIFA Museum Collection/NFMP
8 a & b Fussball. Illustrierte Sportzeitung (Aug. 1924).
Courtesy UB Leipzig Sportwissenschaft
9 FA News (Nov. 1970)/Football Association
10 AFP/Baum
11 Bildbyran
12 SCANPIX/Inge Gjellesvik
13 SCANPIX/Born Sigurdson
14 FFF
15 > 17 FIFA Archive
18 Motzsports/FIFA Archive
19 > 20 Popperfoto/Bob Thomas/FIFA Archive
21 FIFA Archive
22 Mary Evans Picture Library
23 FIFA Library
24 FIFA Archive
25 Kishimoto/FIFA Archive
26 > 28 FIFA Archive
29 Bongarts/FIFA Archive
30 Sports Illustrated/George Tiedemann/FIFA Archive
31 Action Images

CHAPTER 10

1 C. Richard Wynne Nevinson , Any Wintry Afternoon in England,
Manchester Art Gallery. Courtesy of the Artist's Estate/Bridgeman Art Library
2 La Vie au Grand Air (7 Oct. 1900). Courtesy BASPO
3 Rumanian Football Federation
4 Umberto Boccioni, Dinamismo di un footballer
© Photo SCALA Florence/ Museum of Modern Art (MoMA) New York
© 2003/The Sidney and Harriet Janis Collection
5 Pablo Picasso, Joueurs de ballon sur la plage, Paris,
musée Picasso © Photo RMN - R. G. Ojeda
6 Robert Delaunay, Football, Musée d'Art Moderne de Troyes,
France - Donation Pierre et Denise Lévy, photographe: Daniel Le Nevé
7 A. Rodschenko, Politischer Fussball (1930)
© ProLitteris, 2004 8033 Zürich
8 J. Heartfield, Fussball (1929) © 2004,
The Heartfield Community of Heirs / ProLitteris, Zürich
9 W. Baumeister, Fussballspieler (1929) aus der Mappe Sport
und Maschine - 20 Originallichtdrucke, Berlin 1929 Staatsgalerie Stuttgart.
Graphische Sammlungen © ProLitteris, 2004 8033 Zürich
10 J. Jacoby, Football (1924) (c) CIO/Musée Olympique
11 La Vie au Grand Air (20 Feb.1921). Courtesy Baspo
12 Archivo general de la Nacion, Buenos Aires
13 P. Howson, Just Another Bloody Saturday,
Scottish National Gallery of Modern Art
14 L. S. Lowry, Going to the match (1953), © The Lowry Estate Office.
Courtesy Ms Carol Lowry. Photo © Ben Blackall
15 Sybil Andrews & Cyril Power, Football (1933)
© TfL Reproduced Courtesy of London's Transport Museum
16 > 19 FIFA Archive
20 A. Garcia Schlee (1997)/Mercado Aberto
21 N. Hornby (1992)/Victor Gollancz
22 N. Bhattacharya (1992)/Martin Secker & Warburg.
Courtesy Random House
23 FIFA Library
24 Rumanian Football Federation
25 Peter Terson (1970)/Penguin Books
26 Khyentse Norbu (1999)
27 © Eran Riklis and Moshe Igvi (1991)
28 FFF
29 Courtesy Filmmuseum Frankfurt am Main.
30 Courtesy Filmmuseum Frankfurt am Main © Bundesarchiv-Filmarchiv
31 Ozias, Tumulto no campo (2000)
© Museu Internacional de Arte Naïf do Brasil, Rio de Janeiro
32 Hannes H. Wagner, Fans (1979) © ProLitteris, 2003 8033 Zürich

CHAPTER 11

1 & 2 FIFA Archive
3 FIFA Library
4 FIFA Archive
5 & 6 ullstein bild
7 AFP
8 Courtesy Filmmuseum Frankfurt am Main.
9 > 19 FIFA Archive
20 Kishimoto/FIFA Archive
21 & 22 FIFA Archive
23 H. Szwarc/FIFA Archive
24 AFP
25 Sven Simon/FIFA Archive
26 Bongarts/Mark Sandten/FIFA Archive
27 WEREK/FIFA Archive
28 FIFA Archive
29 H. Szwarc/FIFA Archive
30 Keystone/Franck Fife
31 > 33 FIFA Archive

CHAPTER 12

1 > 3 FIFA Archive
4 & 5 H. G. L. Schimmelpenning/Netherlands FA
6 AFP
7 > 13 FIFA Archive
12 14 Hulton Archive
15 > 22 FIFA Archive
23 H. Szwarc/FIFA Archive
24 > 27 FIFA Archive
28 Keystone/STR
29 FIFA Magazine 2001

CHAPTER 13

1 Der Kicker (7 May 1929). Courtesy UB Leipzig Sportwissenschaft
2 Berliner Illustrirte Zeitung (13 Oct 1929). Courtesy Staatsbibliothek Berlin
3 FIFA Archive
4 Keystone/Walter Bieri
5 FIFA Archive
6 El Grafico, Buenos Aires
7 Hulton Archive
8 Museo del calcio, Firenze
9 & 10 Courtesy B. Glaring/P. McNeill, Seventy Years of BBC Sport, London 1999
11 Courtesy DFB
12 UPI/FIFA Archive
13 > 15 Courtesy DFB
16 FIFA Archive
17 FFF
18 & 19 FA World Cup Report 1966/FIFA Library
20 FA World Cup Report 1966/FIFA Library
21 FFF
22 Hulton Archive
23 CuLDA
24 Panos/ Morris Carpenter

CHAPTER 14

1 Bundesarchiv Koblenz/IV Chile G IXc 1973/ADN/ZB
17-10-1973/B/M 1017/ 24N (A)
2 ullstein bild/Horstmüller
3 L'Illustration (29 Jul. 1916). Collection privée
4 FFF
5 FIFA Archive
6 SLUB Dresden/Deutsche Fotothek/Erich Höhne/Erich Pohl
7 SLUB Dresden/Deutsche Fotothek/Willy Ehrlich
8 SFV/ASF
9 Copyright CIO/Musée Olympique
10 CuLDA
11 ullstein bild
12 & 13 AFP
14 SFV/ASF
15 > 17 FIFA Archive
18 Bundesarchiv Koblenz/Zentralbild/XIII 30 Sep 1954/S 9 b / SU Ung
19 Bundesarchiv Koblenz/Zentralbild Hsinhua News Agency 8 June 1957/S 9
b/ China / Indon
20 AFP
21 FIFA Archive
22 ullstein bild
23 FIFA Archive
24 a Bundesarchiv Koblenz/IV Chile G IXc 1973/ADN/ZB
17-10-1973/B/M 1017/ 24N (A)
24 b Bundesarchiv Koblenz IV Chile G IXc 1973 ADN-ZB/ZB
/15-10-1973/B/Chile/ M 1015 /23 N (A)
25 picture-alliance/dpa
26 Keystone
27 & 28 FIFA Archive
29 Archivo general de la Nacion, Buenos Aires
30 DHM Berlin
31 ullstein bild
32 Bongarts/Lutz Bongarts/FIFA Archive
33 FIFA Archive
34 FIFA Archive

CHAPTER 15

1 Bongarts/Henri Szwarc/FIFA Archive
2 FIFA Archive
3 Getty Images/Marco di Lauro
4 Getty Images/Marco di Lauro
5 FIFA Archive
6 Magnum/ John Vink/FIFA Library
7 picture-alliance/dpa/Boris Roessler
8 Getty Images/Sven Nackstrand
9 Getty Images/Peter Rogers
10 AP/Bernd Kammerer
11 Getty Images/Paula Bronstein
12 Keystone/Georges Gobet
13 Hannes H. Wagner, König Fussball (1974) © ProLitteris, 2004 8033 Zürich
14 Keystone/Yoshikazo Tsuno
15 FIFA Archive
16 Keystone/ Doug Mills

INTERVIEWS

Fold from top to bottom, then left to right.

Presse Sports/L'Equipe
Empics/Tony Marshall/FIFA Archive
Presse Sports/Landrain
Presse Sports/Fevre
Presse Sports/Fevre
Presse Sports/Popperfoto
Presse Sports
Presse Sports
Presse Sports
Presse Sports
Presse Sports/Boutroux Legros Pichon
FIFA Archive
Presse Sports/Boutroux
Presse Sports/Popperfoto
The FIFA 100
The FIFA 100/Patrick Lichfield
Hulton Archive
Chuck Korr
J.Y Guillain, La Coupe du Monde de football. L'oeuvre de Jules Rimet,
1998/FIFA Archive
Presse Sports
picture-alliance/dpa/Arne Dedert
Presse Sports
Presse Sports/Popperfoto

We would like to thank Wolfgang Bartosch,
of Fotohaus Römerhof (Zurich), for his outstanding
digitalisation work.